T0354434

"DEATH" BY THE POTTER'S WHEEL

A TRUE STORY
OF SPIRITUAL INSPIRATION, TRANSFORMATION, AND PROGRESSION...

CONRAD M. FOLLMER

BALBOA.
PRESS

A DIVISION OF HAY HOUSE

Balboa Press books may be ordered through booksellers or by contacting:

Balboa Press
A Division of Hay House
1663 Liberty Drive
Bloomington, IN 47403
www.balboapress.com
1 (877) 407-4847

COVER DESIGN: Stephanie O'Neill Dubeck, the author's niece, is the creative design artist for the front and back covers. Her design expanded upon an image from SermonView, from whom we have secured permission for its usage.

Print information available on the last page.

ISBN: 978-1-5043-5796-8 (sc)
ISBN: 978-1-5043-5798-2 (hc)
ISBN: 978-1-5043-5797-5 (e)

Library of Congress Control Number: 2016908739

Balboa Press rev. date: 08/03/2016

Isaiah 64:8

"... Yahweh,
you are our Father;
we the clay, you the potter, we are all
the work of your hand."

DEDICATION

This book is dedicated to the living spirit of Jennie, who in this lifetime was my aunt, godmother, spiritual counselor, soulmate, friend and the inspiration for this book about her remarkable life.

This labor of love is also dedicated to our truly magnificent angel, "W," without whom this book, as well as our Sacred Journeys, would have been impossible. "W," thank you most graciously for being the Guiding Light in our lives.

Image #1: This photo of Aunt Jen (at age 90) and me was taken on Christmas Eve, 2012. This is one of the last photographs taken of Jen, before her passing on August 3, 2013.

CONTENTS

PREFACE

You are a "Seeker" like me. That assumption binds us together and allows us to share the remarkable story contained within the pages of this book. It is my hope that in reading this true story, your Sacred Journey will be as enriched as mine has been over the past fifty years.

At various points in our lives, we Seekers feel a restless dissatisfaction, sensing a need to seek the Truth concerning who we really are, and what we really need and want in order to feel more fulfilled and whole. We find ourselves seeking more sensible answers about the meaning and purpose of life and creation. We ache to better understand the inner workings of our lives, and how we fit into this awesome schema called Life. Jungian psychology refers to this as the "second life," when one's emphasis shifts from a focus on maintaining the *external* life to a deeper *internal* searching. Those Seekers who cross this threshold to pursue Individuation or personal Awakening can testify that following this wondrous path changes their lives, inevitably shifting the focus from the "without" to the "within"!

Part and parcel of this shift is a magnetic-like force that draws Seekers one to another. Through the power of this force, Seekers gravitate toward relationships, experiences, challenges, books, articles, websites and lectures that potentially foster greater growth, the discovery of new realities, and a lessening interest in life's distractions and material possessions. It takes on a life of its own! Unannounced, strangers suddenly enter our circle. Unanticipated windfalls and barriers alter our path. Books we are "meant" to read, come to us in various ways, possibly even tumbling from their shelves into our hands (Yes, that has really happened). We may wake in the morning, humming a familiar song only to realize that the title or lyrics relate directly to an issue about which we have been pondering or praying. The seeming "coincidences" of life add a new vibrancy and alertness to the moments of our days, transforming life into something more magical, helpful, and less irrelevant.

As the bestseller, *Celestine Prophecy* by James Redfield (Warner Books, 1993), asserts, "...through an apparent series of 'coincidences,' we are becoming conscious of what we are really looking for, of what this other, more fulfilling experience really is..." (page 6). This suggests that there are no "coincidences!" With a dawning awareness, we begin to trust the hints and odd events that the Universe sends our way, propelling us in new directions and to new realizations. Things we had earlier taken for granted, or ignored as trivial, suddenly carry deeper meaning.

As Jesus said, "He who has ears to hear, let him hear!"

As Seekers, we are destined to travel an increasingly solitary and demanding path toward a light that cannot be seen, toward a peace that cannot be defined, and toward a destination that is unknown to the conscious mind. Yet, we feel a "pull" to march on anyway. There is a point reached by every pilgrim – some would say, after many lifetimes of searching and evolving – when he/she emerges into the Light of a personal Awakening. This new dawn, this new baptism, leads us through an "Involution" that promises to reveal a vista of who we truly are and the true nature of our Sacred Journey.

As a Seeker, you certainly know that life has now taken on a new joy, a new depth of meaning, a new seriousness and sense of personal responsibility. There is as well, a growing consciousness of the awesome Spirit that fills that void of restlessness unlike any earthly prize or pleasure. If you have reached this juncture in your personal progression, then you are *The Seeker* I have assumed you to be. *Somehow*, but surely *not* by "coincidence," you have come upon this book. If nothing else, by reading this story, you may derive at least some comfort in knowing that you are *not* alone; that many others are traveling the same general path, sharing similar yearnings and uncommon experiences of heightened awareness. Like you, other Seekers are discovering a parallel world reality that did not appear to exist before entering the doorway to their personal progression.

"A new path comes into existence, from where, that is not known..." ("The First Message," November 12, 1966)

If you are actively searching for the enlightenment and guidance that is vital during this period of unfolding, then it *will* appear to you. If you are faithfully seeking the comfort and assurance that comes from knowing that you are not alone, then that comfort *will* come to you. If you are trusting that you are being led, then you *will* begin to see and feel the hands of The Great Potter, molding and reshaping your life as if you were made of clay, an image that conveys the intention behind the title of this book.

Whether or not you personally accept the notion that we are truly "...**spiritual beings on a human journey, rather than human beings on a spiritual journey...**" (paraphrased from Teilhard de Chardin, the French Jesuit priest and philosopher), consider the concept that we, on the mortal plane, are *not* the *true* representation of our actual being, that we are never alone, that we are part of a Grand Plan, and that when we die, we simply shed our cumbersome mortal trappings, and *continue* on our Sacred Journey. Though our hungry mortal ego would have us believe otherwise, we are *not* our limited ego-selves or are we defined by the roles to which we have been assigned in this lifetime. We are all Souls of eternal Spirit, and are the Beloved creations of The Infinite, Limitless and Energizing Force that brought the universes into existence. That Force continues to exist, monitor, guide, and care deeply about each of our Sacred Journeys. We are all Loved equally to a degree that is immeasurable and unfathomable by an Awesome God Force, Who set us upon our experiential journeys to an earthly "classroom."

The above concept, *if* accepted, completely alters nearly everything we have been programmed to believe about ourselves and about the purpose of our lives. However, permit me to add one more notion: *before* "Life," there is "Death"…

This book recounts the actual experiences of ordinary people of modest means who met their symbolic "deaths," starting on November 11, 1966, through a series of inspired and inexplicable events that have stretched out over the past fifty years.

This is the true story of Jennie, a suburban housewife, living in the Philadelphia area, who spent her lifetime as an ultimate Seeker. Her life unfolded in miraculous ways, expanding from humble beginnings into one whose life has inspired and comforted many. As her nephew and godson, I am among the tens of Seekers whose lives were immeasurably affected by her many mystical and psychical gifts and her human kindness, and ultimately reshaped by the hands of The Great Potter. These shared blessings have been supremely memorable to those of us whose lives were renewed, a gift that is likewise promised to all Seekers who are open to listening, learning, and growing in the Spirit.

I invite you to enter this story with an open mind. I anticipate that many of Jen's unique experiences may *sound* fabricated to amaze or entertain the reader, but let me assure you that *all* of the events related in this story are true. Understandably, her unique dreams, visions, gifts, and psychic and mystical experiences may well *sound* exaggerated or embellished. Please accept my word that they are not changed in the least from the way in which they unfolded in her life. She was as uplifted and inspired when they happened to her as the readers are likely to be when they read about these true accounts. A critical point to make here is what happened *to* Jen and *through* Jen is lovingly available to all ascending souls when that Guidance is sought and sanctioned.

As a major participant in this true-life story, I serve as Jennie's chief witness. As the humble recipient of hundreds of "Messages" that came through Aunt Jen for nearly a half-century, I am a better person for knowing and loving this special woman who was groomed to become an uncommon channel for Wisdom and Guidance from the Sublime Realm. Know that, though this book is largely about how the lives of Jen and her close circle of fellow Seekers were clearly shaped by The Great Potter, it is *more* about how the Universe sees, loves, and guides *all* of us as aspiring Souls. Based upon that awareness, I can state that this story is as much about *you* as it is about Aunt Jen and me.

In today's world, when proof based upon the five physical senses and the application of the scientific method are seemingly required as the *only* acceptable means of validating events, I ask you to remind yourself that the best things in life -- like Love, intuition, and faith -- are *not* subject to the limits imposed by testing and empirical evidence. Yet, they *do* exist, as the Unseen Reality exists all around us! As is suggested in that famous quote from Shakespeare's Hamlet, "There are more things in heaven and earth, Horatio, than are dreamt of in your philosophy."

Although I cannot produce scientific "proofs" regarding the events you will read about in this book, I ask for your trust. It is an accounting of a soul's search for the Truth, and what she and many others in her circle found along that journey. If you are The Seeker whom I assumed at the start of this Preface, then you already suspect that everyone of us is entitled to the same rich blessings and mystical guidance that were bestowed upon Jen, our main character.

Regarding the evolution of this book, I want to say that out of pure inspiration and gratefulness, I have been "moved" to write about the deeply significant events that altered my life and the lives of a small core group of fellow Seekers, beginning in 1966. In the mid-1970's, at the age of thirty, less than a decade after I received my "Letter from God," I started to tell this story. In preparation, I read a number of books about similar experiences of channeling, metaphysics and spiritual searching. I extensively interviewed the key participants in the events about which you will soon read, to record their direct quotes and honest reactions. Without the modern assistance of a computer or word processing software, I laboriously typed the first drafts of Chapters One and Two. I laugh now when I look back on that earliest work-in-progress to see faded paper evidences of *real* cut-and-paste technology, the type involving scissors and Scotch tape.

Back then, for some *inexplicable reason*, the writing suddenly stopped, not to be picked up again until the late 1990's; however, even then, after a brief flurry of activity, the writing once again *was stopped*, and in fact, all evidence of this book was mysteriously *lost*. A computer crash wiped out all traces of the second attempt. Was this an act of "coincidence"?

It was not until August of 2015, when hard copies from both previous authoring attempts that had been *lost* back in the 1990's, were surprisingly uncovered in an old dusty box in our basement.

With that discovery, a renewed surge of inspiration overtook me as I wiped away tears from re-reading about those life-shaking and life-shaping spiritual events that began in 1966.

Now, at my current age of seventy-one, it finally feels "right" to create this book. Since 1966, I have learned to trust that each occurrence of unique events, opportunities, tragedies, relationships, beginnings and endings has a "right" time and place in our lives to "shape" our maximum growth potential. Therefore, even with an earlier computer crash that wiped away weeks of hard work, I have accepted the fact that neither in the 1970's nor in the 1990's was it the "right" time to work on this project. It *does* feel "right" today, given many more years of life-perspective and learning.

I believe that this is an important and a potentially beneficial story, and that there is no one else who could tell it as authentically as I can, given my first-hand experiences during the decades when these brilliant, inspiring and humbling Gifts were bestowed. I feel "charged" and inspired with the heart-felt mission to provide historically accurate testimony to the awesome events that began almost fifty years ago. Given that I do not believe in "coincidences," I must accept the fact that this *is* the "right" time to create that accurate narrative for those who are seeking "proof" that the Age of Miracles did not precipitously end 2000 years ago, that we are each Loved and Guided by the Sublime, and that our angels and our guides are simply an invitational thought away.

As a final note, I want to add that Aunt Jen passed away in August of 2013, two months short of her 91st birthday. Though she is gone from this mortal dimension, her goodness and inspiration live on in the many persons whose lives she helped to change forever while she was among us. Scores of people called her "Aunt Jen," though only a few of us were relationally entitled to use that personal address. This familial tribute of love and respect was engendered in most people she met, especially after November 11,

1966. I suspect that you will feel that same warmth and respect for Jennie as you read about her life story.

I greatly miss Aunt Jen, my soulmate, though I fully suspect that she continues to provide inspiration, but from a higher vantage point!

Please accept my warmest wishes that you may find the inspiration you are seeking within these pages...

Conrad

ACKNOWLEDGEMENTS

Given the uniquely inspired content contained within the pages of this story, I must begin by offering my prayers of thanksgiving to the Sublime Realm. The awesome gifts of Wisdom, Love, and personalized communications from "W," our special angel, the ascended souls of the "Great White Brotherhood," and the many other masterful Teachers from the Sublime Realm, *ARE* the Heart and Soul of this story. To Them, I acknowledge my gracious and humble thanks for "shaping" my life, and for guiding the development of this book.

I will forever be indebted to Aunt Jen, who was my soulmate and the inspiration for this deeply touching story about her mystical and psychical gifts, channeled Messages, and an inspired life of unconditional Love. Her quoted words of testimony create the convincing authenticity in this book, just as she contributed to the greater authenticity of my life.

To Rosie, my dear wife, I extend my deepest gratitude for your encouragement, patience, and love, not only during the months of writing this book, but for our thirty-eight years together. Your outstanding editorial suggestions are clearly reflected in the flow of this book. You mean more to me than you could ever know.

To the current members of our Spiritual Group (Suzanne, Jeannie, Anita, George, and Ed), and to past members, I extend my sincere appreciation for your inspiration, advice about and contributions to this story, and for touching my soul. To Sandra-Lee, my cousin, I extend my special thanks for your heart-felt encouragement and love. Your shared memories and unshakable faith have been invaluable to me.

To my creative niece, Stephanie O'Neill Dubeck, I extend my deep gratitude for your inspired cover design work. I will always be grateful!

To my dear friend, Brad, I offer my warm thanks for your technological expertise in creating the two drawings in this book, and for restoring my entire manuscript when it appeared to have been destroyed by malware. Thanks also for your genuine friendship.

To Dorothy Herrmann, my talented editor, I extend my deep gratitude for helping this first-time author to present my story in a more accurate and polished style than otherwise would have been the case.

Finally, my thanks go out to the team at Balboa Press, for helping me to self-publish this book.

CHAPTER ONE

THE EVENTS LEADING UP TO THE NIGHT OF NOVEMBER 11TH...

Achieving a sound sleep was highly unlikely on that fateful night of November 11, 1966, as Jennie fitfully reviewed the parade of *seemingly* bizarre events that underscored the strangeness of the preceding weeks. Life had become both exhilarating and confusing -- exhilarating because of its spiritual promise and confusing because of the unsettling and inexplicable developments that had invaded her life without warning or expectation.

As she lay sleepless in her darkened bedroom next to Mike, her husband, Jen vividly recalled the night of October 31st – but then who wouldn't remember a night like that one?

Reflecting on that strange night, eleven days earlier, Jen recounted, "I had an extremely intense headache. Any sudden movement or sound sent a throb through my body. Mike was a dear, suggesting that I forget making dinner, but simply go up to bed to find relief. He helped me into my nightgown, adjusted the window blinds to dim the late evening glow, and then he quietly closed the bedroom door to muffle the sounds from the downstairs TV. I was especially grateful for his genuine concern."

An hour or so after Jen had fallen asleep, she was suddenly awakened from her slumber. "I heard a series of loud metallic pinging sounds. I painfully opened my eyes and looked around the darkening room, but seeing nothing, I concluded that the noise must have come from the downstairs TV. I tried to block out the pounding in my brain and thankfully recaptured a sound sleep."

The second interruption to Jen's rest on that Halloween night, came after the room had completely darkened. "I was once again startled awake by a series of pinging noises. This time I slowly sat up, trying not to further aggravate the pain still pounding in my head. I realized that the strange rapping appeared to be coming from the metal lamp shield on the night-light resting on the bed's headboard. It sounded like flicking a finger against thin metal."

Suddenly, Jennie's attention was arrested by a pinpoint of light in the far-left corner of the bedroom, between the window and the closet door. With the near total darkness in the room, the point of light in contrast was totally absorbing. "As I looked, transfixed, this became two pinpoints of light."

Riveted, Jen saw the two dots of rotating white energy, like eyes reflecting moonlight, begin to move toward her. "The speed of their approach increased as they turned into larger glowing circles, irradiating waves of white light, almost as if they were on fire." Sensing their approach, Jen was utterly frightened.

"When they were only inches from my face, the glowing orbs became the cavernous eyes of a skeletal mask. Now irradiating white light from the eye sockets and the perimeter of the mask, it hesitated, pulsing immediately before my face. Strangely, I did not feel that I was in danger, yet I wanted to scream!" Jennie tried without success to close her eyes and pressed more tightly against the unyielding headboard in an attempt to escape a collision with the fiery mask. Then, before she collapsed, laser-like beams of light suddenly bored into her eyes.

Jen later recalled, "The last thing I remember, was sliding down into my bed. I don't know if I actually fainted, but I was out cold until morning. Each time I think back on that frightening experience, it seems even more hair-raising."

In the morning, she remembered the entire chilling episode but kept it to herself for fear that her family would think she was losing her grip on sanity. No one would have believed that the bizarre experience was anything more than a scary nightmare since Jennie was well known for her vivid and frequently portentous dreams.

Much to her surprise and relief, a week or so later Mike heard the pinging sounds from the bed lamp for the first time. "The instant I heard the pinging," Jennie explained, "the entire event of the previous week flooded back into my mind. I grew tense and looked at Mike for his reaction. But dear, practical, skeptical Mike simply explained it away by saying that it was noise made by the contracting of the metal lampshade, as it was being heated or cooled. He then turned over and went to sleep, leaving me with the crawling feeling that the experience of the 31st was going to happen all over again."

It was not until several years later that Jen received a compelling explanation for the events of that unsettling October night. As she learned, they were certainly *not* the interventions of a lowly spirit, as she initially feared; rather, they were an empowering initiation into an awesome mystical process that changed the course of her life.

Jennie, born Genoeffa, the Italian equivalent of Genevieve, was enjoying her role as a suburban housewife to Mike, a skilled carpenter, and as the mother of two children, Michael Jr., who was in the US Air Force in Colorado, and Anna Maria, who was a high school junior.

For a number of years, Jen had worked as an administrative assistant to help the family through hard financial times. Now she was doing what she most cherished: cooking, baking, caring full-time for her family, and enjoying the company of her two closest sisters, Virge and Jo. Domesticity seemed the norm for second-generation Sicilian women, especially to those like Jen and her seven siblings, who had been reared on a poor Bucks County, Pennsylvania farm. Farm life meant hard work, but even more than her siblings, Jen embraced it.

Her friends and family members have described Jen as being friendly and cheerful (even if a bit aloof), a skilled conversationalist, athletic, attractive, a loyal defender of friends and family, and someone who could always be trusted. She had an attractive face and a full head of soft, naturally curly, fine-textured brunette hair. She was above-average height for a girl, with long legs. Jen was always serious in nature, but was also known for her contagious laugh, which betrayed her *joie de vivre*.

A warm, honest, strong-willed person, Jennie never viewed herself as being particularly unique. Though the youngest in a loving family of eight children, as a child, she always preferred her solitude. After her many farm chores were done, Jen remembers that among her favorite pastimes were climbing the hills and exploring the forested portion of their farm, accompanied only by Rojo, her protective German shepherd. In those moments of sitting on the hilltop, keeping an eye on the small herd of lowing cows, smelling the grasses, and sensing the beauty of nature, she was happy in spite of the hard work. Especially in these solitary and contemplative moments, Jen remembers a restless yearning to learn more about the truth of life, a quality that was to lead her forward, especially in later years. However, even as a very young child, she distinctly remembers repeating to herself, "I have much to learn."

The solitude and expanse of natural beauty of the farm was not to be found in a tight development in Philadelphia's western suburbs, to which she, her husband and two young children moved in the 1950's. However, knowing how important natural tranquility was to Jen, Mike, her husband, created a handsome screened-in porch addition onto their modest two-story brick colonial home in Havertown. Screened from nearby neighbors in the development by a bed of roses, aucuba and euonymus shrubs, and a curtain of azaleas and evergreens, Jen frequently sought out this favorite spot to be alone with her thoughts, accompanied by Vicki, her Scottish terrier. Especially during the fall of 1966, this tranquil retreat, with a view of scampering squirrels and chirping birds, was what Jennie most needed to sort out the inexplicable events that were redefining her life.

For three nights prior to November 11th, another curious but not frightening experience had occurred, repeating itself for just those three nights. Vicki, the bright and highly independent family dog, had historically claimed the bottom of Jen and Mike's bed as her own. At night, when she was ready for sleep, she jumped onto the bottom of bed, where she remained throughout the night. In the morning, she was ready to be taken downstairs to start her busy day of barking at the squirrels and birds. This was Vicki's pattern, both prior to and after the three nights in question.

Jen remembered, "On November 9th, Mike and I had settled ourselves under the covers, and were chatting about the meeting I had attended that evening with Anna's homeroom teacher. Suddenly, in the middle of our conversation, Vicki nervously stood up, jumped off the bed, jumped back on again, and came over to lie between my legs. She strangely stared at me expectantly, looking like she was about to speak. Mike and I watched this behavioral departure from the norm, and as we were about to comment on it, Vicki got up again and moved off to the right side of the bed to lie beside Mike. We had no idea what to make of this."

"Now this certainly wasn't so dramatic an experience but the simple fact that Vicki performed the same behavioral change for *only* those three consecutive nights, including on the eleventh, really captured my attention. Vicki never did it before and she never did it again for the rest of her life."

This bit of canine behavior by itself is neither startling nor especially noteworthy; however, the symbolic meaning for this temporary change in Vicki's sleeping routine became clear on the morning of November 12th in a rather unforgettable manner.

With the intense October headache, the encounter with the "fiery mask," and the unusual change in Vicky's behavior, this period of time was unsettling for Jen. However, her emotional state at this time was strained for other reasons. Jen recalled, "I was on a roller coaster of emotions during that period, principally over concerns for the well being of Michael, my son, and Conrad, my nephew (the author). My son was stationed at a Colorado Air Force base, and Conrad had started his first semester of a two-year Master's Program at Bucknell University, in Lewisburg, Pennsylvania. I am embarrassed to say that much of my concern on behalf of my son, was due to an irrational encounter with a Ouija Board. An especially stressful episode happened at my birthday party, on October 11th."

It was tradition for the closest members of the Italian clan to gather in celebration of one another's birthdays. Without the family and the laughter, a birthday was merely another cup of coffee and slice of cake. To celebrate Jennie's special day, her two closest sisters, Josephine (Jo) and Virginia (Virge), along with their husbands, John and Henry, drove to Havertown from their homes in South Philadelphia. Gus, Jo's older son, also joined the little circle, bringing his pregnant wife, Florence, and their little boy. Within minutes of the arrivals, the "Three Musketeers," as the inseparable sisters were nicknamed, were sipping black coffee and chattering away as usual. It seemed that whenever Jen, Jo, and Virge got together, it was one of two eventualities: non-stop talking and laughing, or non-stop cooking and baking.

On the afternoon of Jen's birthday, Anna, her daughter, had enjoyed spending a few hours with a neighborhood friend, experimenting with the girl's new purchase of a Ouija Board. Anna had had such an amusing time that she begged her friend to allow her to borrow it for the evening's gathering. Anna always appointed herself social director; the Ouija was her selection for a night of novelty.

For the benefit of readers who have never toyed with an Ouija Board, permit me to explain. The board itself is printed with the letters of the alphabet, the numerals from zero to nine, and two corner answer boxes, labeled "Yes" and "No." The planchette is a triangular pointer resting upon three short felt-tipped legs, and has a circular plastic window at its center. It is the device through which the two operators view the letter, number, or word to which the Ouija is pointing in answer to a question from either an operator or an audience member. The directions call for two people to sit opposite each other, knees touching, with the board resting upon their laps. They lightly rest their fingertips on each side of the planchette and await a question to be asked. Once the question is posed, the planchette "magically" circles and inevitably spells out the answer, letter by letter, supposedly from the mystical beyond, or from the conscious or subconscious motivation of the people in the room.

It is appropriate to point out at this juncture that many trained psychics warn novices to avoid the Ouija Board or to minimize the time invested at any one sitting. They claim that, conditions being ripe, restless spirits can take advantage of the receptivity of the operators and subsequently take control of the board and/or the people. When this event occurs, often frightening and base messages can be spelled out to an unsuspecting audience. On the other hand, some psychologists have explained the seemingly automatic movement of the planchette is caused by the creative energy of the subconscious minds of individuals in the room, who are strongly willing specific answers to emerge from the board.

No one at Jen's birthday party knew anything about the controversy surrounding this new "psychic toy." After some experimentation, Jen and Anna seemed to be the pair best equipped to get the Ouija to "speak." At first, the answers were playful. Henry (or Hank as he was called) -- Virge's husband, and the author's father -- asked the Ouija to guess his weight. This only non-Italian in the group was the family clown and the frequent butt of jokes. In reply to his question, the planchette rapidly whirled in circles, appearing to be sizing up the hefty questioner, and finally answered, "2978." Laughing, Mike insisted that the Ouija's estimate of Hank's weight was close enough to be considered an accurate answer. Anna laughed, realizing that she had wisely selected the evening's diversion.

Then Florence, who was pregnant with their second child, discovered a way to test the Ouija. Only she and Gus, her husband, knew the names they had selected for the expected baby, one for a boy and one for a girl. Florence smugly asked the Ouija, "Is the child going to be a boy or a girl?" The planchette again whirled into action and spelled, "GIRL." Then, brimming with confidence, Florence asked, "What is the name we picked for her?" The pointer circled more erratically and rapidly than after any previous question, then it appeared to stall. Florence was beginning to enjoy her victory, until the planchette suddenly spelled, "GINA." From the look on Florence's face it was clear that the Ouija was correct. In a moment of fury, Florence turned on her husband, assuming that he had told the group, counter to their private agreement, to keep the names a secret until after the baby's birth. With a flurry of denials and a hasty farewell, Gus took his outraged wife and little boy home. Three months later,

Florence gave birth to a baby girl, whom they named Gina, as they had previously planned to do.

Though the party atmosphere was dampened by their early departure, Anna convinced the family to return to the board. This time, however, the Ouija Board did not wait to be questioned. In rapid succession, it spelled out a series of predictions, including a serious automobile accident that was to occur within the next two weekends, leaving Michael, Jen's son, permanently paralyzed.

The crowd grew quiet. The party was over! Though everyone agreed that the hastily abandoned game was a hoax, a lingering pall remained in the air. The family members silently ate their pieces of birthday cake and soon returned to their homes, leaving Jen to deal with a pile of dirty dishes and a fearful prediction.

After the post-party clean up, Jennie's anger overcame her fear. She reluctantly "forced" Anna back into the living room and re-approached the Ouija Board. Treating it as an unwelcome guest, they flung open the box and prepared to confront the Ouija, "... as crazy as that sounds", as Jen later observed. Before they could either question or curse it, the Ouija picked up where it had left off, describing bloody details, ending with, "...and you are helpless to prevent it!" A fitful night followed.

Thinking of little else the next morning, she decided to call her son at the Air Force base. After numerous attempts, she discovered that finding a single airman on a huge base was nearly impossible. However, as "coincidence" would have it, Michael called home that afternoon.

Jen remembered, "I didn't tell him about the Ouija Board because even I thought it sounded dumb. Instead, I told him that I had had a vivid warning dream, in which I saw him seriously injured in a car accident that was to occur sometime over the next two weekends. My son didn't react at first, sensing the deep emotion in my voice. Then he promised me that he would avoid the temptation to drive or ride in a car during that time period." Though Michael was as skeptical and scientific-minded as his father, he believed in his mother's warning dreams, having seen many of them come true over the years.

After the telephone call, Jen started feeling more confident. She could hardly wait until the end of the school day to share Michael's promise with Anna, who was also worried about the gruesome prediction. Immediately upon Anna's return from school, as with one mind, the two of them decided to return to the Ouija Board.

Jen reported, "When I look back on that afternoon, I realize what a terrible emotional strain I had been under. After all, confronting a mere toy with intense fury could not possibly be normal! At any rate, Anna and I sat down with the board on our knees and triumphantly announced the good news of Michael's promise. The planchette circled. When it stopped whirling, it 'spoke,' 'You think you have solved the problem, You have not. You will be called at 7 a.m. on the morning of the accident. Michael will stop on the road to help a girl drive her disabled car to a gas station. That's when it will happen. Try as you may, you cannot stop it.'"

Jen later recounted, "That's when I lost it! I viciously looked at the board and screamed, 'If your purpose is to scare me, you have succeeded! I am scared, but the power of God Almighty is supreme. Your prediction that my son will be hurt doesn't make it so. If it is the Lord's will, then I shall pray for the strength to bear my sorrow. Then, my daughter and I threw the board across the room, and sobbed, acutely aware that we obviously believed in the prediction. The next two weeks of waiting was almost more than I could handle emotionally."

Earlier that fall, because of a growing interest in psychic and mystical events, Jennie had decided to enroll in the E.S.P. class of her township's adult evening school program. The write-up in the brochure promised to cover a number of fascinating topics over the course of the ten Tuesday evenings. The one dealing with dreams and dream analysis was the real draw for Jen. At that point in her life, it was the only topic in the psychic field about which she had extensive personal experience. That, of course, was soon to change dramatically!

On the Tuesday after Jennie's stressful birthday party, a psychic was scheduled to speak to the class. Mr. Voelker seemed well informed and personable; therefore, during his talk, Jen made up her mind to tell him about her frightening experiences with the Ouija Board.

Jen remembered, "I decided that *if* Mr. Voelker would use the words, 'Ouija Board,' any time during his 90-minute presentation, I would speak with him after class. As crazy as that may seem, I believe in such signs. Near the end of his presentation, he spoke about the dangers of using a Ouija Board. I was so excited that I didn't really hear the balance of his presentation. Afterwards, I shared my emotional episode with him, choking back tears. I half expected him to say something like, 'Well, wasn't that a lovely experience,' but instead, he grew serious, placed his arms around me and invited the few remaining ladies to join us."

Jen remembered, "He said, 'This woman has actually been confronted by an entity.' He paused and then continued, 'Though this was her first experience, she naturally reacted in the proper manner by telling this low spirit that God is the greater power.' He then went on to repeat his warning about the unprotected use of the Ouija Board."

"Mr. Voelker walked me to my car, and then asked if I would shake his hand. At the time, his request seemed strange to me; however, I later learned that he was trying to sense my vibrations. He held my hand tightly and said, 'I know that I am in the presence of a good person.' Well, the moment he took my hand in his, I felt this good force enshroud me. It filled me with a peace that I had not felt in some time. In fact, when I arrived home later that evening, both my husband and my daughter remarked that I looked different."

"Before I left him in the parking lot, Mr. Voelker inquired about my life's ambition. I answered that I saw such misery, bigotry, hatred, and trouble in people's faces that few of them can smile with their whole being. I said that all I wanted to do was to make people happy. He smiled and replied, 'Go home and pray. Place yourself in God's service. Surrender yourself. Ask for His protection and allow Him to use you in any way that He chooses.' With this parting advice, we went our separate ways."

Jen continued, "That night, though apprehensive that God might actually take me up on my offer, I fervently prayed as Mr. Voelker had suggested. I easily drifted off to sleep, unlike the previous two nights. In the morning, I recalled having had a dream. I dreamt that I was in outer space. I was wearing a spacesuit, like the astronauts, and was floating above the earth. Just as I had put on the see-through helmet, it started to rain (which even in the dream, I knew was impossible... but this was a dream, which comes from a different kind of reality). In the dream I rejoiced and said that these drops were the Blessings of Heaven. I awoke that sunny morning, feeling strong enough to face the next two weeks, yet praying that I would not receive that 7:00 a.m. call from Colorado."

While Jennie fought the urge to lose her emotional control during the two-week vigil for her son, her control was also being taxed with a growing concern for yet another young man whom she loved, Conrad, her nephew (the author).

Throughout my young life, I had long felt that Aunt Jen and I were intricately connected. Our bond was unique and deeply special; a relationship that shortly was destined to become even *more* special in wondrous ways.

Starting that August, I had accepted a two-year, federal fellowship to Bucknell University, leading to a Master's Degree in Educational Research. Family and friends assumed that I was happily immersed in my new venture. No one knew that with each passing day, I was becoming more depressed. I felt alone. I became increasingly convinced that I was the least capable of the twelve graduate students in our group. The steady and rapid erosion of my self-confidence led me to the local Roman Catholic Church, where I sought counseling from the pastor. I was close to quitting Bucknell, as well as giving up on life itself. I desperately needed an intervention.

With a touch of synchronicity, more than a week after her October birthday, Aunt Jen later reported that she was alarmed by a disturbing dream about me. She later described, "There was another family gathering at my home. Everyone was seated around the dining room table, except for Conrad, who was seated by himself in the living room, appearing to study the pile of opened books around him. In the dream I asked him to join us in a card game of Crazy Eights, but he refused. I awakened with the distinct impression that Conrad was not studying, and that he was lost in both personal and scholastic frustrations. I knew that something was wrong with my nephew!"

"Early that next morning," Jen recalled, "I telephoned Virge to ask if Conrad had called home recently. I hesitated, not wishing to disturb my sister, especially if there were no truth to the situation. Then I explained the dream and my conclusion. Of course, Virge immediately called her son at Bucknell to learn about his feelings and state of mind. She called me right back."

Virge and Jen, the two youngest of the eight children in their family, had always been the closest siblings. Virge remembered,

"Knowing about the special bond between my son and my sister, I called Jennie to report what I had learned about the truth of her dream. Although mindful that she was still under the strain of the Ouija's 'sentence' on her own son, I pleaded with her to do anything that might comfort *my* depressed son. As always, she agreed to do whatever she could to help."

In retrospect, it seems that a unifying influence to many of Jennie's mystical experiences came from her dreams and visions. Particularly Michael, Mom and I had never questioned her dreams, because they consistently seemed different from everyone else's, and frequently came true. Her dreams seemed more believable. We all knew about her many portentous dreams, with periodic warnings from her deceased mother and her Aunt Mary (her father's sister) about upcoming illness or loss. It was uncanny, but whenever she received a warning dream from them, she knew to prepare for the worst. Uncle Mike, who never remembered his dreams, often told his wife in frustration, "Jen, why can't you just be normal? Go to bed and sleep for a change, like normal people!" But Jen was not "normal" in that regard!

Although I recognize that I am interrupting the story flow about this tense period of time, I feel that this is the place to shine a spotlight upon Aunt Jen's dreams and visions, in order to help the reader craft a deeper understanding of this special individual. Her dreams were a key element leading up to the unique events of November 11th and 12th.

Recalling earlier dreams, Jen remembers, "A number of years before the 1966 events, when my children were nine and seven, I had one of my most vivid and unusual warning dreams. I dreamt that I was ascending the stairs of a large church when I was handed a vase containing human ashes. I couldn't see who gave the urn to me, but he told me to scatter the ashes on the church steps. After asking about the ashes, I was told that they were the ashes of St. Catherine."

Jen continued, "The day after I had this dream, I visited the Monsignor of my church to explore my long history of unusual dreams. The highly respected priest – who was later to serve as a representative to the First Vatican Ecumenical Council in Rome – greeted me warmly. When I started by telling him that it was probably true that dreams were against the church teachings, he brusquely interrupted me by saying, 'Well, certainly not, Jen. Aren't you aware that much of the Bible, especially the Old Testament, is composed of dreams, visions, and voices of prophecy?' I grew restive as he cited a few common accounts from the Great Book. I had never really read the Bible, especially the Old Testament, which was the norm for Catholics. I suddenly felt quite stupid."

"I told him about the St. Catherine dream and all the times my mother and aunt come to warn me about impending problems. When I finished my story, I held my breath. I was rather surprised when Monsignor Falls told me that I had a sixth sense. I specifically remember his saying that the invisible world was there to aid us, and that in particular, I seem to get more than my share of help. I sensed that he was working up to something, as I saw him shifting his weight in the large maroon leather chair. He looked me squarely in the eyes, and with a serious tone, he warned me to look for danger caused by fire. Before I could voice the obvious question, he said, 'St. Catherine of Siena is the patron saint of fire and firemen. Perhaps she has come to you in your dream to warn you of some hazard.' With a special blessing, he walked me to the door."

Jen continued, "The following day was Saturday. Anna's new bedroom furniture was delivered early that morning before Mike and I had a chance to do our weekly food shopping. Anna had selected feminine violet drapes and bedspread, and was eager to see it all come together. However, Mike suggested that we first do our grocery shopping, leaving the kids home to watch TV, and afterwards, finish Anna's room. I remember that I suddenly felt very uneasy. Stalling for time, I quickly insisted that Mike at least hang the mirror before going to the supermarket. While he was measuring the wall above the new dresser, Michael came running up the stairs, shouting that smoke was pouring out of the TV. I never saw Mike move so quickly! Fortunately, the TV didn't burst into flames until he had successfully dragged it out onto the front lawn."

"It wasn't until later that I recalled the warning that the Monsignor had shared about the St. Catherine dream."

Jen continued, "Two other experiences over the years were preceded by a clairaudient impression -- a psychic term denoting a 'clear hearing' of words/sounds from paranormal sources -- of the name, St. Catherine. On one occasion, I was in my robe, frying bacon for breakfast. Suddenly, I heard a whispered voice say, 'St. Catherine!' Seconds later, the sleeve of my robe erupted in flames."

Visibly tensing as she remembered another dream, Jen related, "It was shortly after those two fire episodes that I had the most memorable dream of my life. I still get the chills when I think of it. The dream was so real! I dreamt that I was sitting at my kitchen table, drinking coffee with my sister, Virge. As I realized that a large pair of scissors was resting on the table before us, we both became aware that the sky was rapidly darkening. In minutes, it was like night, and as quiet as before a hurricane. Assuming that it was an approaching storm, we went onto the back screened-in porch. It was dark and eerie. Upon reaching the porch, the scene shifted and we found ourselves on a stage, looking out at the darkness. We became aware that our deceased parents were both there. The four of us looked into the black sky and noticed a rotating pinpoint of white light. This part reminds me of the night of my intense headache and the fiery mask. The light rapidly approached, then suddenly burst into the form of a white lamb. Our father knelt and said, 'It is the Lamb of God.' We reverently knelt in awe, reciting the Lord's Prayer in unison. The Lamb advanced to a point about thirty feet from us before bursting into a flood of brilliant white light, and then transmuting into the form of Jesus. He was dressed in a blue tunic with a dark red robe, trimmed in gold. As I prayed, I became aware that the four of us were kneeling on the stage that was separated by a deep rift from where the Lord stood. When Jesus crossed the rift, walking toward us, I started pleading, 'Don't leave me behind! Take me! Take me!', to which He responded, 'Many are called, but few are chosen.' Jesus walked between Virge and me. Then He paused, causing the golden hem of His garment to rest on my knee. I fondly caressed the cloak as He departed. After repeating my pleas for Jesus to take me, I turned to my sister and asked if His passing meant that we were left behind. Virge answered, 'That's just the way He speaks, in parables.' Then the scene changed, and we were on the curb in front of my home, greeting our sister Jo and telling her all about the dream."

"That next morning, I was sipping coffee, replaying the dream in my thoughts, when Virge paid a surprise visit. I started telling her about the dream. As we talked about it, Virge, with a smile, pointed to the pair of scissors resting on the table. Our nervous laughter abruptly halted when we became aware of the darkening sky. We looked at each other in silence, both thinking what we didn't dare to utter aloud. We walked to the porch, and witnessed the sky turning dark. The few minutes it remained that way, felt like an eternity. We were relieved by the return of the sunshine, and walked to the front of the house, to see if the dark clouds had drifted northward. To our shock, as in the dream, there, standing on the curb, was Jo, our sister! Her presence was totally unexpected, because she had told us both that she intended to visit our brother Tony's farm in Vineland, New Jersey. 'Something suddenly changed my mind this morning,' Jo explained."

Jen emphasized, "I shall never forget the impact of that lifelike dream, but I get goose bumps thinking about its near reenactment that morning."

With that brief glimpse into Jen's history of vibrant dreams and visions, the reader can return to the late-October timeline of our unfolding story with a growing sense of Jen's unique readiness for the mystical life that was about to dawn.

With the passing of the second weekend of the Ouija Board's prediction of doom for her son, Jennie was mercifully released from the burden of tension. "It was such an incredible weight off of my shoulders that I felt like I could fly. The entire episode strengthened my faith in prayer and offered an optimism that even the weighty problems on my nephew Conrad's shoulders would soon fall away."

With internal and external pressures building, I simply *had* to escape Bucknell for a comforting respite at home, even though the Thanksgiving holiday was close at hand. As I think back on that time in my young life, I remember how confused I was. Yes, I was depressed. On the spur of the moment, I decided to hop a Friday afternoon bus home to South Philly at the start of the weekend of November 11th. I feared that once I stepped into the loving cocoon of home, I might never want to return to Lewisburg. I arrived home in the early evening, before dinnertime. My mother was especially happy to see me. I was at home for the first time, since I had left for the University in August. It felt comforting! After dinner, Mom announced that she had invited Aunt Jennie and Uncle Mike for coffee and dessert.

My spirits lifted more easily than I had anticipated, as my parents and aunt and uncle surrounded me with their love and good company. Dad was in rare form that Friday night. He easily maintained his reputation as the family comic, telling jokes at which most of us continued to laugh, even though we had heard them many times before. He was a funny guy!

During the evening, the topic turned to the Ouija Board encounter at Aunt Jen's birthday party. Uncle Mike reminded the group of its correctly guessing Hank's weight, and the uncanny guessing of Florence and Gus' secret name, Gina, for their expectant daughter. Not having heard anything about the harrowing predictions of the Ouija from that night in October, I briefly left to borrow an Ouija Board from a neighbor friend, assuming that it would provide an evening of entertainment.

I was wrong in my assumption! The furtive glances of the four veterans of Aunt Jen's party revealed that they were not overjoyed at the prospect of interacting a second time with the cause of two emotionally draining weeks. Aunt Jen reluctantly agreed to work the board with me, later telling me that she did so *only* because she felt that she had mastered her fear, by enlisting God's protective blessings.

As Aunt Jen recalled that night, "The planchette started the same way as before, whirling around in circles, faster and faster. My nephew, who was also new to this device, looked amazed as the two of us spelled the answers to mundane questions from the folks around the kitchen breakfast nook. But it didn't take long for the board to go from funny lines to serious matters. Within ten minutes, the Ouija took over! After appearing to circle nervously for emphasis, the planchette spelled: 'CONRAD SHALL DIE.' Sensing a repeat performance in progress, Mike and Virge angrily insisted upon returning the board to its box. Mike actually stood up in an attempt to rip the thing from our grasp; however, Conrad's interest was whetted. His unemotional manner caught my attention; but the important thing for me was that I didn't sense anything malevolent, as I had a month earlier. In fact, as I look back on this experience, I felt that a kindly force was controlling the Ouija. I can't explain my feelings and how I 'knew' that, but we continued, at Conrad's pleading. Finally, Conrad unemotionally asked the Ouija how he was supposed to die. The circling accelerated before spelling out the answer, 'DEATH BY THE POTTERS WHEEL.'"

Jen continued her account of that evening. "At that point, I remember taking my fingers off of the planchette and half seriously asked the group how anyone could possibly die by a potter's wheel. My brother in law, Hank, as always, tried to lighten the mood by suggesting that he could picture his son's head buried in the glob of clay, with his legs in the air, spinning dumbly around and around. None of us laughed this time."

As I look back on that weird experience, I admit that I believed that the prediction about me would come true. In fact, I was even elated at the prospect. Perhaps influenced by my depression, I viewed this prediction as a promise of release from the dark grip in which I was held. Mom and I stayed up late that night, talking about the Ouija's words. She grew frightened that I took them as possible truth. Ultimately, before going up to bed, we agreed upon a symbolic interpretation in which we found some comfort: that if God were the Potter in question, then understandably I would be eager and ready to "die" at His hands.

Aunt Jen later told us about her unsettling departure from our home to hers that Friday night. "On that night of the 11th, when my husband and I got into our Rambler to drive back to the suburbs, I was immediately accosted by Mike's fury. He hollered at me for causing yet another night of fear and upset. When I lamely protested that all I was trying to do was to make people happy, he viciously retorted, 'The only thing you are succeeding in doing is ruining people's lives by trying to kill them off with that damn

Ouija-thing!' I knew better than to argue with Mike when he got into one of his emotionally charged moods."

"I became quiet for the balance of that uncomfortable ride home, wondering if, as Mike had suggested, I had caused more consternation than consolation, when suddenly, I heard a deep voice speak clearly to me. It said, '**You shall be shown!**' This promise of help set my mind at ease for the rest of the trip home. As I reflect upon it, I must have been in an altered state to accept so calmly that I had heard a disembodied voice."

Before finally drifting off to sleep on the night of November 11th, Jen remembered the inspiring dreams and visions, the frightening experience with the metallic pinging sound that preceded the fiery mask, the inexplicable change in behavior of Vicki, her precious Scottie, the Potter's Wheel episode, and the resonant voice in the car, promising that she would be shown. Little did she suspect that she *would* be "shown," and that this night would mark the beginning of a new life for her, her nephew, her sister, and for many others, all of whom were "shaped" to one degree or another by the spinning Potter's Wheel.

This was the night that it all formally began!

CHAPTER TWO

A NEW PATH COMES INTO EXISTENCE...

"On the morning of November twelfth, I woke up feeling as mentally exhausted as if I had been up all night, cramming for a final exam," Jennie recalled.

Jen described her unusually vivid dream that seemed to account for all of her sleeping hours. "A white bearded figure was teaching me philosophy. He was dressed in a black flowing robe, girdled with a gold band across the chest, and he wore a strange, two-tiered black hat. The philosopher led me through a series of three-dimensional circles, teaching, for what felt like hours, about the seven circles. As he finished his presentation about each one, he stepped onto the next higher circle that suddenly materialized, to continue his lecture. The circles were stacked on one another, increasing in size and height. Finally, after extensive lessons, the bearded teacher stood on top of the seventh circle that was rimmed with a reddish-orange glow. He outstretched his arms, encompassing them all, and announced that I had been taught the 'Seven Stages of Life.'"

Jennie sat up in bed, feeling awe, confusion, exhaustion, and disappointment. Though she had experienced a number of unusual dreams before, this one had been overpowering with the brilliance of both the teacher and the lesson. It seemed like far more than just a dream! For that reason, it had been awe-inspiring. Her confusion and disappointment came from not having understood *any* of his teachings. Jen was dismayed as she realized that she could not recall anything of substance about the "Seven Stages." Nor was there anything she could use from the lesson to help me, her nephew. That "voice" in the car on the preceding night had promised that she would be "shown," and Aunt Jen was convinced that her special vivid dreams would be the vehicle for these new revelations.

As Jen attempted to rise out of bed, she suddenly sensed that a presence was in the room. She turned...

"My heart skipped a beat as I turned to see a monk-like, cowled figure standing behind me, between the headboard and the wall. He was real as life! As I was trying to rationalize how anyone could fit within that four-inch space, the monk slowly raised his robed arm and pointed to Vicki, my Scottie. In a deep resonant voice, he said, 'Look unto the dog.' With that, he simply vanished.

Only momentarily did I wonder about this monk-like figure, but his words reminded me about the three nights of Vicki's changed sleeping habits. Yes, I thought, there *was* something more to her unusual behavior than sheer coincidence. I reviewed the change as I remembered it: from the bottom of the bed, she had come up to lay between my legs; she rested there, watching me intently; and then she moved off to the right side, to lay beside Mike. Not knowing what to make of it all, I put it out of my mind, donned my robe, and went downstairs to make breakfast. Even after all these years, I cannot understand my blasé reaction."

"As soon as I reached the kitchen table, I felt compelled to search for a yellow tablet and a pen. This is what I found myself writing:

From the outside looking in,
Comes into the protective fold --

Finds comfort and assurance,
Then moves away.

"It was as though I was used to doing things like that all my life. I didn't even bother reading the note, and I temporarily 'forgot' the encounter with the hooded figure in the bedroom. I prepared breakfast for my husband and me, following my usual routine. I kissed Mike as he went off to work, and set about my usual daily routine."

Jen continued, "Then, still oblivious to what had happened, I returned to the kitchen, and gazed into my back yard, wondering once again how I could possibly help Conrad. This had become an obsession with me. I just couldn't sit by, watching my nephew and godson drowning in his depression."

"Suddenly, I heard a voice in my head that *told* me to get the tablet and pen again and to prepare for dictation. My many years of secretarial work had prepared me for this task. Not questioning the command, I sat poised at the table, ready to write."

Jen remembered, "The monkish figure I had seen in my bedroom suddenly reappeared and stood beside my kitchen chair. I now remember thinking that he didn't look like a ghost. He looked completely real! I obediently wrote as he dictated, without hesitation. At the conclusion of what has since been termed, 'The First Message,' I unemotionally put down the pen and went upstairs to wash up and to prepare for my daily chores. Overtime, I realized that I had been placed into an altered state of consciousness while taking dictation, because the moment it was over, and the monkish figure had vanished, I acted as though nothing had transpired."

"While calmly dressing, my thoughts again returned to my nephew. I remembered the prediction of the Ouija Board from the previous night, 'Death By The Potter's Wheel,' and, as I tried to make sense of that strange statement, I instantly seemed restored to full consciousness, remembering that I had written something in the kitchen. With the excitement of a child about to open a wrapped present, I ran downstairs to find the writing. As I read the words, I sank into my chair, shaking my head in total disbelief."

Man emerges on the right and is led on by tether -- his way isn't clear, but strewn with thorns – a new path comes into existence, from where that is not known – only the faithful seek it. Once on this path there is no swerving – only patience – the search of the new kingdom – the keys lie within the grasp. Acknowledgement is divine – seek and ye shall find. Wisdom creates a mental vacuum and comes to those who seek. Look – don't you see the clouds of learning? Haze begets clearness – it's there! Sweetness is not all lightness – mercy holds the reins – life is to be lived. A moment of guidance and all is won. Treasures are wondrous – a multitude of wealth buried within you. How can you stay dormant? Come into my fold – there is assurance. Do you feel it? Love – love – love. Grasp life – do not be afraid – knowledge rules the roost – thus the golden eggs are hatched. Looking is for the asking – is the path too narrow? Knowledge was not meant to be so. Does the guidance strengthen you? Hold on tight – do not lose the mastery. Wisdom is truth – abide by it. A circle has no infinity – how could wisdom? Look for your blessings – they will be shown. A master knows its pupils and can easily train them because they are searching ever the way of life. Come into my kingdom – all is yours. Life is plentiful – knowledge is all around – hope lies forever in the midst – Waves of enlightenment engulf you – light radiates all around – feel the magnetism – it grips hard! Love comes from within the soul – the shroud covers it.

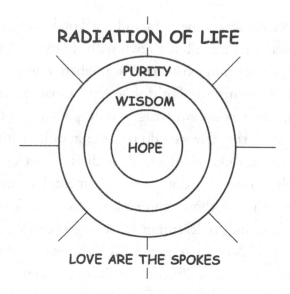

Do not abandon for I will not abandon you – life is for the asking.

Jen later reported, "The full impact of what had transpired suddenly hit me like a ton of bricks! It was as though I had been in a daze, preventing me from remembering one astounding experience to the next. Now I was well aware of all that had happened to me, especially the two appearances of the monk, the two messages, and the odd change in Vicki's behavior. One of my first reactions was to question my sanity, and then, many other unanswerable questions crossed my confused mind… all of them at once! Could I really have seen and heard a monk dictating to me? What did the message and the circle drawing mean? I knew that I didn't compose the message; how could I when I don't even know what it means? What did Vicki have to do with this? How could a monk fit behind the headboard? Why was the message written in Biblical language? Who was the philosopher with the strange hat? Why me? Why now?"

"I started to panic! Not knowing what to do, I found myself reaching for the telephone to dial my sister Virge's number. She was always my go-to person whenever I needed comfort. It seemed an eternity until Virge answered her phone. Once she did pick up, however, I was afraid to speak about these unbelievable events for fear that even my dear, kindly sister might politely confirm the fact that I *had* fallen off the deep end. Well, after a long and uncomfortable silence, I decided to tell her everything. When my story was finished, I was drained, trembling, and nervously awaiting Virge's reaction."

As Virge, my mother, later explained, "The first thing that came to my mind when she had finished speaking about the mighty things that happened to her was, 'Thanks be to God!' I told my sister that she clearly had been used by the Lord to help another human in need. I told her that I didn't understand the message or any part of it for that matter, but the message was not for me. It was for my son. I knew with certainty that he would be able to make sense of it. I felt that my dear sister needed comforting. Her voice was thin, lacking in all the usual emotion and sensitivity we commonly shared. She sounded frightened. I don't know what made me feel so certain, but I told her, 'Jen, a few weeks ago, you prayed to the Lord to place yourself in His service. Well, it seems that He heard you! Be happy. Thank Him, and place faith in His will for you.' All Jennie could say was, 'Are you sure I haven't gone crazy?'"

Virge continued, "I remember calmly reassuring her that I didn't think she was at all crazy. Then, I boldly asked her to drive to our home to hand-deliver the message to Conrad, even though she was feeling shaky. I told her that the streets were wet and covered with slippery fall leaves, and that she should drive with special care. Well, Jen listened to me like a child to her mother, promising that she would be careful."

"After hanging up the phone," Virge added, "I was filled with such joy and a humbleness that I choked up with emotion. After all, who are we to receive direct answers to our prayers, especially in such a dramatic fashion? Following the call, I went upstairs to wake my son, telling him to get ready because his Aunt Jennie was on her way to deliver a message. In a sleepy voice, Conrad asked, 'Who is the message from?' I simply said that we would both find out when she arrived."

"When Jen did arrive," Virge reported, "I was immediately aware of her altered appearance. She looked pale, emotionless, and as though she had been through a traumatic event."

"Shortly after her arrival, Conrad entered the kitchen to greet us both. Although he was always delighted to see his Aunt Jen, and his curiosity was aroused by the promise of a mysterious message, it was obvious that he still looked depressed and restless. He slid onto the bench of the breakfast nook, next to his aunt, hesitated, then asked her why she looked so strange."

Mom continued, "After about fifteen minutes, my sister began to relax somewhat, and started to tell her 'crazy-sounding' (her words) story about the dream of the 'Seven Stages of Life,' about the philosopher with the strange hat, about the monk behind her bed, who told her to 'Look unto the dog,' and finally about the dictated message for my son."

Mom added, "All three of us were fond of mystery stories, and Jen's narrative had the ingredients of a fine suspense novel. With each new disclosure, Conrad visibly became increasingly uplifted in his mood. By the time Jen pulled out the yellow legal pad from her handbag to share the promised message, my son was clearly excited. It did my heart good to see life return to his face. He took the pad from his aunt, and slowly and thoughtfully read the words aloud. It seemed to me that each new inspiring word or phrase affected him like throwing a shovel of coal into a dying furnace."

"Though I was still fearful," Jen later remembered, "I hesitantly handed the tablet to my nephew, asking him to read it aloud. We must have read through the elusive message close to a dozen times, trying repeatedly to explain possible symbolic meanings of the words and images, and to interconnect the seemingly fragmented phrases. Though neither my sister nor I could make heads or tails of any appreciable part of it, Conrad, on the other hand, with emotion choking his voice, was tearing into the symbolic aspects of the writing. As he struggled with unlocking the mystery, he said, with tears streaming down his cheeks, that he felt an intense heat emanating from the page. This heat, it was obvious to Virge and me, was rekindling a fire in him that was nearly extinguished."

"At some point in the repetitive readings, perhaps after the sixth or seventh time," Jen continued, "I recalled that in this same spot in the kitchen, on the previous night, the Ouija predicted Conrad's fate: 'Death By The Potter's Wheel.' My sister later agreed that as we watched Conrad reading, analyzing, and emoting about this mysterious message, we were seeing the 'old Conrad,' the apparently depressed Conrad, 'dying' before our eyes, being replaced by a bright-eyed, vibrant, self-assured young man of twenty-one. The Power of the dictated message, was clearly having a palpable and resuscitating effect on him, from the changed look in his eyes to the passion in his voice and his body language. Not to be overly dramatic, it was like the depressed Conrad had died away and a new Conrad was reborn. This in itself was the greatest blessing of all for me! This is what I wanted for him. The fact that I later learned that this 'Change' remained with him well into the future reaffirms my belief in the power of prayer and the Love of Our Lord."

What a special day that was for me! Looking back on that blessed day -- even from my current perspective at the age of seventy-one – I still maintain that *that* day represents the single most powerful event in my life!

It is true that depression influenced my life for the four or five years before November 11th. I never felt like a real man. I never felt special. I never felt that I could compete on any level with my peers, all of whom seemed better looking, more fit and athletic, assertive, and clearer about who they were and what they wanted. I believed that I was the least qualified of the graduate students in my Bucknell program. I had also come to realize that, generally speaking, I had out-grown the overly tight fit of Catholicism, leaving me feeling a deep emptiness. The summer before going to Bucknell, I had nine or ten sessions with a Freudian psychiatrist in Philadelphia, who sat in silence, notepad in hand, waiting for the pressure of that silence to magically work on my subconscious, forcing me to spill my guts. It didn't work! So, I carried all of my growing insecurities and deepening depression to the Lewisburg campus for the start of the first semester. Everything slipped downhill from August to November. But, on that memorable Saturday morning, my life was inexorably changed! I'll never forget that day!

As I read and reread "My Letter from God" with Mom and Aunt Jen, I distinctly recall feeling more and more positive energy and clarity. While the first read-through left us all perplexed, each new reading, brought increasing clarity and understanding to the foreground. In fact, I should add from a perspective of nearly fifty years later, every time that the "First Message" was read by me or members of our spiritual groups, greater nuance of meaning was derived. I firmly believe that this *is* the nature of inspired scripture, such as Jesus' parables, or even non-spiritual, deeply symbolic writings like mythology and fairy tales. They contain a number of layers to be peeled away, one by one, adding depth of understanding to the same words over time as the reader accrues more life experiences and wisdom to bring to those same words.

Trying to place myself back in 1966, I remember our concluding that the first part, "...his way isn't clear," and "...a new path comes into existence..." seemed to relate to a progression in which evolving mankind had spent time, groping in the dark, but finally emerged into a new light of reality. The part about being "...led on by tether..." seemed to refer to man's conscious or spiritual limitations, imposing restrictions on his free choice, and requiring greater guidance, not unlike rearing children. I remember saying to Mom and Aunt Jen that it seemed that the three of us were being invited to break out of the dark and thorny life to walk a new path, "...in search of the new kingdom."

At that time, the longer second paragraph presented more difficulty than the first one, though the beginning part was easier than the rest of it. The images of "clouds of learning," "haze begets clearness," and "wisdom creates a mental vacuum," we figured out. Namely, man begins in ignorance and grows over time and with experience to a fuller and clearer understanding; that once the clouds of ignorance are disbursed, learning can happen, clearing the clouds that initially had captured our attention. Once man sets his mind to learn, his searching creates a mental vacuum, drawing into itself the sought-after answers he is seeking. But the part about wisdom, like a circle, not having infinity, as well as other phrases, eluded our grasp that Saturday morning.

We all agreed that the parts that clearly moved us the most deeply were these: "a multitude of wealth buried within you," "come into my fold," "come into my kingdom – all is yours," and especially the most powerful last line, under the drawing, "Do not abandon for I will not abandon you…" Could this be taken as anything other than a direct and encouraging invitation from our Christ? I remember feeling a mix of emotions. I felt humbled and unworthy. Yet, I also felt elated and newly blessed with the promise of growth and new life possibilities, with His protection along the way.

The drawing was likewise inspiring. Everything starts with Hope. When man reaches the point of knowing what to hope for, the Wisdom surely comes, leading eventually to Purity. The spokes or rays of Love – the God-Energy – are ever-present in the unfolding process, which is promised to mankind.

As for the four-line message relating to Vicki's behavior change, that was easy to interpret, in contrast to the larger message. We all felt that Vicki was "used" to demonstrate the process of "being called" more consciously to the spiritual side of life. As "Seekers," before we embrace our awakening (being metaphorically at the bottom of the bed), we are on the "…outside looking in…" When ready to trust, we finally and willingly enter the "…protective fold…" (symbolized by the space within Jen's legs) where we are more consciously nourished by God's Love, warmth and Lessons, finding "…comfort and assurance…" Once we become strengthened in the Spirit, we can "…move away…" to become more independent (out of the "protective fold" off to the Father's side), resting soundly in the knowledge that we are engaged in doing His work. Without a doubt, this endearing and symbolic demonstration was a calling to us to "…come into the protective fold…" On November 12th, we answered the call!

It seemed that my depression had at least temporarily vanished, and that I was now set on a new path, beginning to sense the "comfort and assurance."

As she later explained, Aunt Jennie had other thoughts with less inspired feelings…

Jen later revealed, "Other than reminding me of the dream about the 'Seven Stages or Circles of Life,' the circle drawing at the bottom of the message meant little to me. The sentence that hit me hard was the last one, under the drawing, 'Do not abandon for I will not abandon you...' Who else but Jesus Himself could speak in first person with such authority? This, above all, increased my confusion and fear, as strange as that might seem. As inspired as my sister and nephew were becoming, I grew increasingly hesitant. The more they thanked God, the more I began to wonder if I had really gone insane, or worse, could I have subconsciously written this message, audaciously taking on a first person authorship as the Lord. Was I trying to play God, with some twisted motivation to help my nephew?"

Jen continued, "Thinking about the Tuesday night E.S.P. class in which Mr. Voelker, the psychic, had warned us about being controlled by a lesser spirit while using the Ouija Board – as seemed to be the case with that awful October prediction about my son -- I briefly wondered if a lesser spirit had given this message to me. My mind was spinning! I finally concluded that even if this message were from the highest spiritual source, as the others believed, then perhaps it meant that the Lord loved Conrad so much that he merely used me, a nobody, to help him. Conrad *was* helped, as I had prayed. There was no doubt about that! But what about me?"

Jennie spent another night of fitful sleep, caught in a tug o' war between total acceptance and complete rejection. She sorely needed some reassurance of her own.

Sunday morning, Jen and Mike were at breakfast. Mike was reading the newspaper, while Jen had barely touched her French toast. When Jen was about to push away her plate, she suddenly heard the ethereal sound of organ music, accompanied by two excellent soprano voices. As a trained operatic singer herself,

Jen knew good singing when she heard it. "The music sounded like nothing I had ever heard before, in or out of a church or a concert hall. I opened the sliding door to the screened-in porch, half expecting that the music was emanating from the Protestant church around the corner. The sheer musical beauty of the organ and the singing helped to soothe my jangled emotions."

"Being inspired, I called to Mike, and asked him if he had ever heard anything so beautiful as the organ and vocal concert. When he didn't answer, I turned around from the door to see if he was still at the table. He was there, but he was staring open-mouthed with a quizzical expression on his face. I repeated my question, pointing in the air to the beautiful voice of the woman who was now singing a solo. Yes, it finally dawned on me that my husband's expression was one of dismay and confusion. He heard nothing! It became obvious that I was the only audience to this soothing concert! This event further convinced me that my sanity was crumbling. I made some excuse to Mike, and went upstairs to dress for church. I decided that it was time to share my fears with the Great Psychiatrist."

"In church," Jen continued, "I opened my heart and mind to Our Lord and asked for assurance. Were all of these strange happenings from His Realm, from a low realm, or from my own? I *had* to have an answer, and I prayed for a sign. Suddenly, a voice, much like the one in the car on Friday night, spoke to me again. The voice said, 'Your sister's belief in you – when she and Conrad come from the Cathedral.' I was taken aback after hearing the voice, but my stubborn Libran nature questioned how that could be a sign. After all, I knew that my sister, who lived in South Philly, *never* went to the Cathedral of Saints Peter and Paul in center city. They had four Catholic churches within six blocks of their home. Why would they travel two miles to the Cathedral?

Furthermore, I knew that Conrad had to board an early bus back to Bucknell.

Not feeling satisfied, I boldly asked for another sign. After a prolonged silence, the patient voice returned, saying, 'You will see a sign in the sky when you and your nephew are alone.' I knew that this voice was definitely *not* my own. I wanted to believe the voice, but I also could not imagine when those things would happen, knowing that Conrad had to return to campus, which was three and a half hours away from home, and that it was highly unlikely that he would have the time to drive out to Havertown."

Jen continued, "I walked home from church, feeling only slightly comforted. I was assailed by too many doubts and unanswered questions."

"When I arrived home, I noticed that Mike was busy in the garage. After changing clothes, I went into the living room to read the Sunday paper. I simply had to do something to distract my swirling thoughts. Around twenty minutes later, I heard a car pull into our driveway. I dropped the paper into a messy pile on the floor, when I realized that it was Virge and Conrad. I had goose bumps."

"We moved to the kitchen where we drank coffee and dunked homemade biscotti that I had baked earlier in the week. I also decided not to tell them about the morning organ concert or about the two signs in church, unless those signs were confirmed."

Virge started the conversation, saying, "You know, Jen, I realized this morning that the three of us have something important in common. Over the past few years, we each have had many growing doubts about our religion, yet we felt that there was nothing else we were ready to move on to." Then Virge talked about specific experiences they had shared in the past about a few narrow-minded, self-righteous priests and the gnawing feeling that there was more to God and spiritual things than could be gained from simply attending Sunday church services and blindly following inflexible church dogma and routines.

After hearing Mom's point, I added that often, in my undergrad experiences, I had stayed up late on many nights, locked in religious debates with others in college dorm "bull-sessions." These discussions raised more questions than they answered, but I had to admit that my faith in religion was fading fast. Basically, I saw it as a lost cause.

Mom concluded her comments about church and religion by saying, "After the amazingly inspiring message from yesterday that we all shared, I knew that we had to do something special today, so I talked Conrad into taking me to the Cathedral on the Parkway, which I haven't visited in many years."

At this disclosure, Jen went pale, but held her counsel.

Jen later remarked, "Virge and Conrad both reaffirmed their unshakable faith in the message and declared their belief that I was clearly an instrument of God. After a pleasant, yet short, afternoon visit, they got up to leave, saying that it was getting close to the time for Conrad to get to the bus station. As their Ford backed down the driveway, I realized that I was amazed by the fact that the first 'sign' had been accurate. Unexpectedly, they *did* come from the Cathedral, as the voice had promised. However, I realized that the second sign for which I had begged, the one about seeing a 'sign in the sky,' had not been fulfilled."

"Lost in thought, I didn't see or hear their car coming back up the driveway. I turned to see my nephew get out of the driver's seat and briskly walk toward me. He said that he felt he had to return to thank me once again for delivering his 'Letter from God.' He hugged me tightly, and kissed me. Well, I swear, at the precise moment of his kiss, I saw a streak of light, like a shooting star, arc across the mid-afternoon sky! I shall never forget that moment as long as I live! Also, I had to admit that the comfort I derived from the fulfillment of those two 'signs' settled my doubting mind, filling me with renewed energy and peace, even if, by the next day, I was back to stubbornly questioning."

Years later, as I, the aspiring author of this text, was interviewing my aunt to clarify some missing pieces for Chapter Two, she reflected on how, recalling that time, she must have seemed totally ungrateful to God. She said, "Perhaps the reader will think ill of me for being such a skeptic, but I simply needed more proof before I could accept that a lowly housewife, without any fancy college degrees or training, could possibly have been chosen for such an awe-inspiring role."

The following Tuesday night's E.S.P. class featured Dr. Dallas Buzby, a psychologist engaged in psychical research at St. Joseph's University. Jen sat in the audience, surprised to learn that some frontiers of science did in fact recognize psychic abilities. The elderly speaker mentioned his work with the famous Dr. Rhine at Duke University and described the peculiarities of E.S.P. research methods.

At this point, Jennie decided to conduct some "research" of her own, as she had done with Mr. Voelker, the previous speaker in the series. She had brought "The First Message" with her to the lecture, in case there would be an opportunity to engage with the teacher about it. She decided that if the tall, slender speaker mentioned anything about his writing a book, she would approach him after class to share her writing with him and to learn his thoughts about it.

Dr. Buzby finished his talk, and then, almost as an afterthought, he wheeled around to add that he was working on a book...

"That was the second time that this type of test worked," Jen recalled. "Mr. Voelker had answered my first test by using the words 'Ouija Board,' and now this second test had worked as well. Was that coincidence, a word I found myself using a lot more lately? I once again waited until most of the class members had gone, then I unfolded the message and took it up to Dr. Buzby for his reaction. I felt like a fool, but I needed to know that I was normal, and I naively thought that this certified psychologist might be able to instantly tell me one way or the other."

"Dr. Buzby consented to read it. His expression was intense. When he finished, he said that it reminded him of Carl Jung's theory of God and the Supernatural. He seemed like a warm and trustworthy man, and I secretly had a feeling that he was marked to help me in some way. He looked down at the writing once again and suggested that I take it to my pastor. I nervously asked him if this meant that I was going crazy. He laughed wholeheartedly and said, 'My dear, we should all be that crazy! A veil of consciousness seems to have been lifted for you. This sort of thing has happened to many people, so please be comforted.' We exchanged contact information at his request, and I left the school feeling peaceful, and comforted, sensing that I would hear from him again."

Jen later reported that Dr. Buzby contacted her at least once a week over the subsequent few months, declaring that he felt his "job" was to cheer her up and to provide reassurance that her experiences, though *paranormal*, were quite sane. "In those telephone calls, he shared bits of inspirational poetry, talked with me about the theories of Carl Jung to which he had referred that Tuesday night, and extended comfort and simple human understanding in an attempt to help my state of mind. I learned that he died shortly afterwards. I must say that I have never met a more unselfish gentleman than Dr. Buzby."

Jen continued, "Meanwhile, I had decided to take Dr. Buzby's advice to see my pastor. The last time I had visited Monsignor Falls was years ago, regarding the warning dream I had about the ashes of St. Catherine of Siena, the patron saint of firemen. Talking about dreams, however, paled in comparison to what

I was about to share with him. *This* was *much* more real! I was nervous, as I waited to be shown into his office. After being seated with an exchange of pleasantries, I explained the entire complex story to him, as he studiously listened to my every word. I ended with the fact that my sister and nephew believe that the 'Letter from God,' as my nephew called it, was an answer to prayer and that I was an instrument of God. Before I handed him the message with a shaking hand, I concluded by saying, that I was dreadfully confused, doubting that the Lord would stoop to use me as an instrument even in the unlikely event that He actually sent letters down to earth."

Jen later reflected, "The wise Monsignor took his time reading the message, nodding and furrowing his forehead. When he had finished studying it, he spoke in an almost angry voice. I didn't know what to expect. Was he going to accuse me of being a daughter of the devil? Instead, much to my shock, his angry tone was directed against my skepticism. He flatly stated that this was a message from God! I was stunned! He said that I had been used by Him to help a fellow mortal in need, as Jesus had used an ass as an instrument on the evening of the Last Supper. Of course, as the reader might anticipate, I naturally saw myself as being no better than the donkey. Continuing, he warned me about getting uppity, adding that this message might be a once in a lifetime event, and would likely never happen again."

"He lectured me a little more, saying that the church fathers knew much that they could not impart to average parishioners, much that might help me to understand my present situation. He concluded by offering me what he called, a special blessing for the Divine Grace that had been bestowed upon me."

Jen continued, "I left the church rectory, thinking about what my pastor had said about not expecting a recurrence, and not getting uppity. I knew that there was little chance that I would ever feel that way. I had simply been used as an instrument, like the ass on the evening of the Last Supper. As I walked to my car, I suddenly recalled the lifelike dream from years earlier when Jesus had burst from the dark sky in my back yard. It dawned on me with some disappointment that it was likely my nephew who was being 'called,' and the one being 'chosen,' *not* me! I am almost ashamed to admit that I started feeling sorry for myself, thinking that God loved Conrad, but not me."

Jen drove home from church that day, expecting nothing else from her Lord, and feeling no more significant than the obedient ass that had also been used 2000 years earlier.

Jen was in for an inspiring surprise!

CHAPTER THREE
CLAY IN THE POTTER'S HANDS...

The title of this book, "**Death By The Potter's Wheel**," was chosen purposefully, even though these words were issued from a "psychic toy" at that South Philadelphia gathering on November 11th. Over time, Aunt Jen and I have come to believe on *that* night, the real controller of the planchette -- unlike the one on the night of the Ouija's October prediction of mayhem regarding my cousin Michael -- was one of high spiritual vibration, signifying a clarion call to "...come into the protective fold..." and to abandon a less meaningful and successful path.

For us, the idea of being "shaped" by The Potter's Hands, is synonymous with recognizing how the shaping influences of the Universe, Sublime Guidance, Grace, Fate, or God play important roles throughout the unfolding of each of our unique, individualized mortal missions, even if we are unconscious of those influences. The "Death" part of the title is indicative of a metaphorical death to one's old and perhaps less-evolved or less-productive ways of thinking and living. A caterpillar-to-butterfly type metamorphosis begins to take place. This "second life" leads to higher and deeper perspectives, and an expansion of consciousness.

In Chapter Two, the quotes from my mother and aunt describe an amazing change in my state of mind (at the age of 21), after

I had been given my "Letter from God." The permanence of that "life-shaping" intervention is the concept I had in mind when selecting the title. My re-shaping process, my "Death by the Potter's Wheel," was a near-instantaneous blessing, and an invitation to begin my "second life."

However, this book is predominantly about Aunt Jen's life. She was not a famous person. She was not wealthy, influential, highly educated, or outwardly remarkable; however, her life *is* a remarkable example of inward shaping at the hands of The Great Potter. More than most, her life was a series of opened and closed doors of opportunity carefully shaping her path. In viewing Jen's life, a pattern emerges, that leads the viewer to the conclusion that fate walked closely by her side, as it does with each of us if we are open to it. In tracking her course in the biographical glimpse that will follow later in this chapter, one is reminded of the initial lines of the "The First Message":

"Man is led on by tether – his way isn't clear, but strewn with thorns – a new path comes into existence, from where, that is not known…"

In the Preface, there was a brief discussion about the "right" timing of events in our lives (specifically with regard to the "right" time to write this book) and about the potential for the Universe to guide, support, and influence the directions we choose to take. Before beginning a close examination of Jennie's life and how it was *clearly* "shaped" in order to prepare her for her awesome new mission, let us first speak in general about this "shaping" process, and what lies behind it in the Grand Schema of Life. The next few pages are dense with some of the principles and assumptions that we learned from our Guides over the years. I made the decision to place them early in this book to introduce the readers to the foundation stones upon which our lives and the true story contained in this book are built. It is my hope that sharing these important "lenses" and their potential implications early on will provide a clearer perspective on that which is to follow.

Through the thousand or more written and oral Messages and Lessons from our "Guides" (as we refer to them, and about Whom you will learn much more in future chapters), we have come to accept a number of powerful assertions that offer a perspective about *who we really are*, and *why we are where we are* at the present point in time. Hopefully, using these assumptions as lenses, the reader will better understand how those of us who were taught these concepts were "re-shaped" in our perspectives on Life, and how considering these perspectives can help the reader do the same.

Please slowly study the list that follows, giving some depth of thought to the assumptions and more importantly, to their implications. Be aware that upon reading this list, the potential exists for some readers to discover a dissonance between what has been taught in our various religious upbringings and what is being presented here. Please understand that there is no intention to criticize anyone's beliefs, or to pressure anyone to change present tenets for new ones. We have each been granted "freedom of choice," and it is up to each of us to keep evaluating and adjusting our choices as we grow and mature through life.

So much of what is taught in our religions is surely intended to help instill an important respect for a Power much greater than our own, to provide guidelines, commandments, and sterling models from the distant past to be emulated, for living a wholesome life with our fellow travelers, and to instill a moral compass that guides our journey from childhood into adulthood. All of that is well intentioned and helpful… *as a first step.*

As adults, we have the maturity, the development, and the life experience to look more deeply into the rich stories of scriptural accounts of heroes, saints, villains, lessons, parables, and events from many thousands of years ago. There is *much* to be learned from those accounts, whether factual or allegorical in nature. As children, we are presented with the literal or surface content contained in those wonderful Biblical stories. As adults, we have the intellectual capacity to pierce the veil of allegory and symbolism, to ferret out the deeper spiritual lessons we were intended to learn from those same stories. Most scripture is written on a number of levels, inviting its readers to dig for meaning. "Seekers" (as I use the term in this book) are the "adults" who are ready to pursue those deeper meanings by questioning the literal interpretations that we were taught in our childhood. In the words from the New Testament, 1 Corinthians 13:11, "When I was a child, I spoke like a child, thought like a child, and reasoned like a child. When I became an adult, I no longer used childish ways."

These "adult" assumptions will serve as repetitive themes or lenses throughout this book and relate directly to the Journey of Progression that we are *all* traveling, consciously or unconsciously:

Assumptions About the Nature of Life, Based Upon the Teachings of Our Guides:

- **We are of Spirit,** created in God's Image, which is of the Spirit Energy of Pure Love.

- **We, being of Spirit, are eternal** and therefore, are not mortal in nature, even if mortal-appearing and feeling when in our earthly bodies and lifetimes.

- We, being creations of Love and therefore, **"children" of the One God, are all Loved equally** even though it may not appear or feel that way when we are incarnated on earth.

44

o **We *are* spiritual beings on a human journey rather than human beings on a spiritual journey.** This critical lens is different from that of fundamentalist religious teachings, in which we are viewed as sinful, struggling mortals, aspiring to reach a distant heavenly reward. What a notable distinction! Unfortunately, when on our earthly journeys, we are fooled into believing that the ego, our limited brains, and our life circumstances define who and what we really are. How untrue that perception is!

o **Life is a gift,** an opportunity to learn from and about the myriad wonders and facets of Creation and interpersonal relationships. Life on this earthy plane is a "classroom," and is certainly *not* a punishment for eating an apple offered by a serpent in a tree. We have *not* been expelled from our Sublime Home to the mortal plane as punishment for misdeeds or original sin – as a literal interpretation of the Adam and Eve story in Genesis might suggest -- but rather, we are students and ambassadors, sent on a mission to spiritualize the material (a concept to be explored later in this book). Given the vast diversity of Creation, and our mandate to run the long course of hands-on learning, it takes many incarnations or lifetimes into the "classroom" to fulfill the missions of our Sacred Journey.

o **Yes, a form of reincarnation is the vehicle through which our education and eventual transformation takes place.** When we have developed a deeper comprehension of this concept, Life suddenly takes on a much grander meaning, clarifying the understandable confusion about who we are, where we are, and why we are traveling this Journey. In a comforting and clarifying statement from one of our primary Guides, we learned what I have since used as a mantra:

We are where we are because that is where we are supposed to be, doing what we are doing, because that is what we are supposed to be doing.

That is such a powerful statement that can lead us to embrace our current life conditions and status (no matter how humble or exalted it might appear on the surface in this lifetime), in order to make the most of this learning opportunity. (Note: In Chapter Eight, I share the details given to us about reincarnation and the two-phase nature of our Sacred Journey).

○ **Everything is spiritual!** It takes an internal shift, as we "go Within," to see the glory around us and in each other. Repeated exposures to the classroom of life, learning from different vantage points, eventually lead us into a transformation. Through Progression, we can view ourselves and what in the past we have seen to be mundane, in a new Light, revealing the spiritual Truth contained in everything and everyone. We are all One in the Spirit!

○ **Sublime help abounds!** As "Seekers" everywhere have learned, the Sublime Realm has charged the Angels and Masters to support each and every one of us in this difficult, confusing, and arduous mission. Sadly, we are typically oblivious to their brilliant help and guidance, until we reach that point in our Sacred Journey, when our consciousness can expand to "see" and "hear" the ever-present Loving support. "Ask and ye shall receive!"

As I previously stated, the above assumptions and others to be uncovered in later chapters, are based entirely upon the teachings of our Guides. As a caveat, given the complexity and awesomeness of the grand metaphysical Plan, I accept full responsibility for any errors in interpretation about that which was taught to us. If we can agree that we are all searching for those Truths then, with open hearts, we can each accept the assumptions listed above that *do* make sense to us as individuals for now, and keep open minds about the rest.

Man, when in the density of the physical domain, is usually prepared to thank his lucky stars when life unfolds as he wishes; on the other hand, when his plans do not materialize, he is eager to curse his misfortune. We have grown accustomed to believing that God has heard our prayers *only* when we receive the objects of our prayerful requests. What would our lives truly be like if we got everything for which we prayed? God forbid!

In retrospect, over the course of our own lives, *can* we say with confidence that all we have gained or have become was due solely to our own ego-driven efforts and good planning? Our ego would want us to believe that as a fact. Or do we understand that, to some degree, a higher force has used certain opportunities to mold or to guide us toward or away from unsuspected ends?

Before proceeding, spend a moment in reflection. Examine your life as objectively as you can. Locate those instances when you felt that fortune dealt you a harsh blow. Find the times when the course of your life took on a new direction or a new meaning without your own direct input. In short, find how the effects of "coincidence" or "chance" or "fate" or Divine Intervention have led or shaped you.

Perhaps the early death of a parent was responsible for the course of your development. Perhaps a surprise scholarship or unexpected business opportunity took your career to new heights, or even changed your profession or direction. Maybe it took an accident, a disability, or a tragedy in your life to bring you to the position of inner strength, confidence, or wisdom that you enjoy today. The more you reflect upon your life, the more evidences you will uncover of "The Potter's shaping process."

It is sometimes easier to depict the dramatic effects of fate in other's lives than in our own. Examples of these interventions are all around us. During the TV coverage of the Montreal Olympics many years ago, I recall the announcer reporting the case of a U.S. female runner who had been stricken by polio at an early age. This great "misfortune" could have ruined her life, leaving her feeling sorry for herself. Most of us would label it as a stroke of "bad luck." Yet, the young athlete said that the handicap inspired her with the determination to rise above it. That U.S. athlete won the gold metal, probably reaching greater heights in life as a result of having had that "bad luck."

We have all heard the accounts of people who were delayed by heavy traffic or misfortune on the way to the airport, preventing them from making their flight, a flight that later crashed.

Perhaps our lives pale in comparison to such famous names as Helen Keller, F.D.R., Madame Curie, Stevie Wonder, Nelson Mandela and many other leaders, inventors, artists, musicians, and writers, each of whom had either handicaps, misfortunes, or seeming serendipity to thank for their eventual successes and breakthroughs. Great or small, the shifting sands of destiny that help to shape us, affect us all.

Destiny, Fate, Luck, or Divine Intervention... sooner or later our lives are unexpectedly molded by their hands. One soon realizes that good or bad luck are neither good nor bad until evaluated as such by the passage of time. It is frequently said that we grow best through adversity and limitation than if our lives were totally placid and positive. I believe that to be true! Also true is that it is not sufficient to wait for those interventions to shape us; it is what we bring to the table in thought, hard work, and planning that help us to make the most of our lives.

After this long but important side bar – and I thank the readers for their patience as I interrupted the story flow once again -- let's move closer to examining Jen's most recent incarnation, a lifetime in a near-final stage of her Journey of Involution. Now that I have set a number of foundation stones in place, it is time that we learn more about Jennie's life, seeing it as a clear example of "shaping" at the hands of The Potter. In truth, I know of no other person in my social circle, whose life was so evidently shaped as that of Aunt Jen.

Born in Philadelphia on October 11, 1922 to Vincenzo and Maria, poverty-stricken Italians, Jennie was the youngest of eight children. At her young age of five or six, the family relocated to a small, highly mortgaged trucking farm near Doylestown, Pennsylvania. Shortly thereafter, Jen was struck down with a childhood disease that sent her to the hospital in Doylestown, for a two to three month stay, where she was segregated in quarantine. Apparently, the nurses in her unit doted upon her, and Jen remembers that they were the ones who taught her to speak some English. During this impressionable age, and as a result of being separated for so long from her beloved family, Jen felt that she was alone in life. These feelings of being abandoned stuck with her into her adulthood. According to Jen, this negative experience was one reason she developed an inner core of strength, self-reliance, independence, as well as a certain degree of aloofness. A positive outcome from a negative-appearing event reminds us that developments in life are neither good nor bad no matter how they may appear on the surface until evaluated by the passage of time.

Later in her life, Aunt Jen confided to me, "One thing that helped me to feel less alone during those many weeks in the hospital was the comfort of having had a supportive companion, a man who visited me periodically to cheer me up. All I really remember about him is that he was nice, strong, tall, and he made me feel safe." It was to be many decades before Jen would discover the true identity of this special visitor.

Later, after Jennie returned home from the hospital, a wealthy childless couple, who lived in the vicinity of her parents' farm, was entranced by her. They made a serious offer to Jen's parents to adopt her, promising to give her all the advantages that their money and formal education could provide. Though Jen was still quite young, her father took her aside to discuss the proposal. Fighting his own resistance to losing his sweet child and being overcome with the selfless vision of what this could mean for Jen's future benefit, he tried to present this plan to her as a wonderful opportunity.

Jen later explained, "I distinctly remember that day! My father always treated me as if I were much older than my years. We respected each other. I listened to my father as he explained how much better off my life would be if I went to live with that couple. When he was finished speaking, I looked into his eyes, and pleaded with him *not* to permit this adoption to happen, saying that my place was here with the parents, sisters and brothers I loved. No matter how much better my life might be with the couple, I could never be happy apart from them. Throughout my life, I have always been a ferocious defender of my family and close friends, willing to take on anyone who would try to criticize or demean them. But on that day, seeing that I was resolute, my father relented, tearfully hugging me with a reassuring embrace. He later thanked the couple but affirmed that I would be staying with my family."

Vincenzo, Jen's father was her greatest inspiration. He was a strong and independent man, who literally inherited only the debts of his Sicilian parents. They knew that he was the only one of their children who demonstrated the strength of character to clear the family name. As a young man, he accepted a job working in a quarry in Argentina to work off those debts, and to save for his own family's future. During his time in South America, an explosion crippled him with a permanent injury to his left leg, causing him to limp for the remainder of his life. Nevertheless, he did not permit this setback to prevent him from earning and saving enough money to eventually move from Sicily to the United States, with his young wife and three daughters. After the relocation to Philadelphia, three more girls and two boys were added to the family, Jen being the youngest.

On their farm, her crippled father tended to the acres of tomatoes, beans, and squash, cared for the farm animals, and maintained the farm equipment from dawn to dusk, demonstrating his fortitude despite his physical infirmity. Ben and Tony, his muscular two sons, could barely keep up their father's tireless pace. Her father's stamina impressed Jen, influencing her own attitude about life. The major market for their tomato crop was the Campbell Soup Company, in Camden, New Jersey. The high standards set by this company encouraged the whole family to work hard together to maintain those standards. Farm life is challenging.

"The thing that always impressed me about my father," Jen later observed, "was that he, a cripple, *never* complained. He was the eternal optimist, and always offered wise counsel to his children. That alone was a rich legacy! He would rarely answer questions with a direct 'Yes' or 'No,' but frequently would present a metaphor, permitting us to draw our own conclusions and thus solve the problem for ourselves. He may have lacked formal education, but he was both smart and wise. One example I will never forget was when I was about to go out on my first date to a high school dance."

With a smile, Jen remembered, "My father called me into the kitchen. Then he instructed me to go to the drawer to get a newly washed and ironed white linen dishtowel. Next, he said, 'Now, my child, wrinkle the towel and wipe up some dirt from the floor with it.' After I complied with his strange direction, he asked me to describe the condition of this once clean and pressed towel. As I grew impatient, he added, 'Now, my daughter, when you go on your date, think of this towel, and be mindful of the kind of towel you want to be seen as by others.'" That's what I would call a unique example of wise parenting!

According to her sisters, Jen was a sensitive, stubborn, but affectionate child, who rarely got into trouble. She had enviable brunette, curly hair and a fair complexion, along with a personality that attracted people. Though she enjoyed interacting with others, she actually had few close friends. Jen preferred to be alone with her thoughts, the farm animals, and especially her playmate, Rojo, a spirited and protective German shepherd.

"The farm held a kind of magic for me, no matter how exhausting the endless work," Jen later recalled. "For instance, I always got a kick out of standing up on the hill to call the cows home from our fields and wooded acres. I would sing out, 'Cow! Cow! Cow!' and they would amble toward us from all points of the field and woods. Rojo and I would round them up. It seemed like a gift from nature, to watch thirty-two cows, swaggering over toward us from all directions, to be led back to the barn to be milked."

Jen continued, "I also loved walking through the fields, especially during storms. Kind of crazy, I guess. The strongest memories I have from my childhood on the farm are nagging thoughts that still remain with me. One afternoon, I was left desolate. A neighbor shot and killed my dearest Rojo for trespassing on his property. I remember reacting by getting angry at God for taking away my beloved companion. I made up my mind that He didn't want me to become closely attached to people or things. From that day, I guess I have been more aloof than most people. Many things have been taken away from me in life, but maybe that's no more than usual for all of us. However, I must admit that personal loss helped to make me strong."

"The two thoughts that always seemed to be a part of me for as long as I can remember were that I must always rise above adversity without complaining, and that I had *much* to learn. No one ever told me these things, that I can recall, but I would find myself, even at a very young age, repeating, 'I have much to learn.'"

In school, Jen had ample opportunity to test her ability to rise above hardships. She recalled, "Italian-Catholics were definitely not well accepted in those days (the 20's, 30's, and 40's in particular), especially poor ones, such as we were. We stood out as being different from the other students. Being poor and Italian made us targets. The other kids would constantly make fun of our names, exaggerating the Italian pronunciation and throwing little digs that irritated me no end. My birth name was Genoeffa, and my sister Virge's given name was, Vincenzina (meaning, little Vincent, after our father). Those first names, added to our Italian last name, became a one-two punch in the hands of classmates all the way through high school. We never felt welcome! In fact, I can say that neighbors and classmates made us feel like *real* aliens."

"Of course, we did feel somewhat odd, particularly during lunch times. It makes me laugh with embarrassment as I look back on those lunch periods when Virge and I would hide in dark corners. It seemed that everyone else had dainty, crust-less sandwiches, cut diagonally into neat little triangles, while Virge and I had two irregularly shaped slices from a round loaf of Italian bread. Our sandwiches always had nourishing ingredients, such as peppers, onions, eggs and smelly grated cheese. The smell of the

CONRAD M. FOLLMER

cheese, onions, and garlic was embarrassing enough, but when our mother packed sandwiches with prosciutto ham and provolone, we knew we were in trouble. We never did master the art of biting into one of those sandwiches without having a four or five inch 'tongue' of ham dangling dumbly from our mouths. We finally convinced our parents that an Americano sandwich, with white bread slices, would be more acceptable."

"As I look back on that time, I don't believe that I have magnified the close-mindedness we experienced. However, I *do* have this prejudicial attitude of our peers to thank – as strange as that may sound – for forcing me to harden myself against the obstacles of life, especially when I no longer had my tomboy sister, Virge, to fight off my attackers. One major obstacle was our poverty. My sister and I each had *one* skirt and *one* blouse that we were expected to wear every day to school. By the time Virge got to her junior year in high school, she could no longer endure the embarrassment. She had poker straight hair, and of course, unlike our peers, never visited a salon to produce those bottle-induced curls that were all the rage. Though a straight-A student, she dropped out of school, succumbing to the adolescent social pressures that come when you don't feel like you fit in. At least, I was luckier. My hair was curly, and my skin was thicker. Virge moved into Philly with Mary, an older married sister, and got a job. With the money she earned, she would occasionally buy me new clothes to spare me the same embarrassment she had felt. But, without my dear sister and with all of my other siblings gone from the farm by that time, I felt abandoned and alone again."

Jen emerged from high school, as a well-rounded, outstanding, and self-confident student, graduating at the top of her class. "I don't know how I did so well," she mused, "given that we were not permitted to do homework at home until all of the farm and house chores were finished. By that time, we were all exhausted, and it was dark. Up to that point, we couldn't afford electricity – even though Ben, our older brother, was later trained as an electrician – so for the longest while, the only source of light we had from which to study was a kerosene lamp.

Image #2: Jen, at age 16, in her high school senior photograph

At this point, the Potter's "shaping" influences became even more pronounced...

Jen remembered, "At graduation, I was awarded a five-year scholarship to the accounting school at the University of Maryland that would have led to my becoming a C.P.A. This was a marvelous opportunity for me, *but* my joy was soon extinguished. My parents insisted that I relinquish the scholarship for two reasons: one, they could not afford to pay my living and travel expenses, and two, their old-world beliefs dictated that only loose women – derisively called 'putane' in Italian -- would live in a big city on their own. For the protection of my reputation, they refused to permit me to attend the University; however, with prodding from the school principal, my parents did permit me to move in with my sister

Mary, while accepting an alternate two-year scholarship to the Taylor Business School in Philadelphia."

Jen later reflected, "Taylor proved to be a mutually satisfying experience. I became a star on their women's basketball team. I loved the sport! *But* this led to another opened and shut door. A scout from the travelling 'Y' demonstration basketball team offered me a contract to join the team. I could hardly believe my good fortune! But, once again my parents' strenuous objections forced me to turn down this career opportunity as well."

"I was highly successful at Taylor, having accelerated my two-year program into a single intense year. At graduation, I was awarded the privilege of being trained as a court or congressional stenographer. Thoughts of making it big in Washington, D.C., came as a dazzling opportunity, especially for a sheltered Italian farm girl; however, again my parents were adamantly opposed to the idea. In those days, defying one's parents was far less acceptable than it is today. I would *never* have considered defying or embarrassing my father and mother! My only remaining option was to continue to live with my older married sister, Mary, and her family and to find a job, using my skills as an administrative assistant."

"I soon discovered that breaking into the world of employment was a major trial as well," Jen reflected, "in spite of my excellent academic and commercial training credentials. After numerous attempts, it became clear that I was being openly rejected for employment because of my Italian heritage and name. Some would-be employers suggested that I should change my last name to a more American-sounding one; others simply stated company policy not to hire Italians. At the many interviews, I was praised for my amazing typing speed of 145 words per minute, but by the end of the interview I was informed that they would place my application on file. I soon realized that they meant the 'circular file' (another term for the trash can). Finally, after many weeks of frustration, I accepted a secretarial position with the Pennsylvania Prison Society, *without* salary, working solely to gain some employment history on my resume. Shortly thereafter, I was hired by the Liberty Mutual Insurance Company where I was able to put all of my commercial training to good use. Nevertheless, these years were bitter ones as well, as I continued to endure the prejudice against Italians. I secretly felt that I must endure the hardships and await better times. As I had long believed, I had much to learn."

Jen remembered, "I spent much of my spare time socializing with my sisters. By then, sister Josephine was married to John, and they had one son, Augusto/Gus, with another one on the way. John's younger brother, Mike took an interest in me, and on many Friday nights, a group of us – Jo and John, Virge and her fiancé, Henry, and Mike and I -- would go to Wagner's Ballroom in North Philadelphia, for a night of good big band music and dancing."

"When Virge and Hank got married in June of 1942," Jen continued, "I was a member of their wedding party. As Mike later told me, seeing me in a gown at a wedding was all it took to give him the courage to propose to me. Just three months later, Mike and I were happily married."

Although this special event brought a new joy into Jen's life, literally on the morning of the wedding ceremony, Mike received his summons to join Uncle Sam's World War II team. Jen explained, "We had a hurried honeymoon, and as quickly as the joy and comfort had entered my life, it was taken away. As I tearfully waved goodbye to my husband at the 30th Street Train Station, I reflected upon the familiar pattern of loss in my life, as with Rojo, my German Shepherd, and with a number of lost

Image #3: Jen, at age 20, on her wedding day in 1942. (The photographic company, All In One Studios, in Philadelphia, PA, to whom we give credit for this photo, is no longer in business).

education and career opportunities. I must admit that I secretly feared that my dear Mike might never return from the European front."

Jen reflected, "Once again, loneliness filled my life. I searched for some diversion to consume my spare hours. Given that many people had praised the quality of my soprano voice, I decided to audition for operatic voice training. I was fortunate! I don't know where all the operatic teachers came from, but they seemed to find me, instead of the other way around. Three of them didn't even charge me for the weekly lessons because of what they determined to be my exceptional vocal potential."

"The beauty of the music, especially by Puccini and Verdi, brought a different kind of fullness to my life. I could vent my loneliness by emoting the arias that I practiced over and over. My teachers insisted that my voice was still under development, so they refused to give me permission to accept paying offers to sing in church concerts or in nightclubs. I was disappointed not to be permitted to earn some extra money, but such, it seemed, was my life pattern. This vocal training continued for over ten years, even after Mike had thankfully returned home safely from France and Germany, after two *very* long years of waiting and worrying. But looking back, I guess that that made me stronger as well."

This new operatic career opportunity began to flourish with numerous offers. Jen was groomed to sing at the Robin Hood Dell, the outdoor concert hall in Philadelphia's beautiful Fairmont Park. However, shortly before that first performance, the conductor died, and the concert was cancelled.

Next, Jen was to sing the lead role in the popular operetta, "New Moon," at the Shubert Theater. Before the curtain could rise on her starring performance, Philadelphia's theaters went on strike.

Her teachers next prepared Jen to debut in a solo concert. One tenor, upon hearing her amazing voice, literally begged her on bended knee to sing with him. She purchased her gown and had the programs printed. Jen added, "Seeing the programs in print, with my name as the lead singer, was so reassuring and exciting. I couldn't wait!" However, just days before the scheduled concert, Jen was rushed into the hospital for an unexpected nasal operation.

After so many uncanny blockages to her promising operatic career, both student and teachers were dismayed that not one concert had been performed to date. However, after she totally recuperated from her operative procedure, her concert debut with the tenor was optimistically rescheduled. The tenacity of her teachers was heartwarming. Unfortunately, the discovery of a painful rectal fissure forced Jen back into the hospital days before opening night. The concert was cancelled.

During the course of her ten years of training, the sterling quality of her voice and her natural Italianate expressiveness led her to meet famous operatic singers. She received an invitation to sing a few arias at a cocktail party in New York City, to be attended by a few Met divas and tenors. Whenever she sang, there was nothing but the highest of praise for the power, control, and beauty of her exceptional lyric soprano voice. However, on the drive up to NYC with her teacher to perform for the Met stars, she "mysteriously" lost her voice. It took two days before she could even speak.

Finally, there was a breakthrough locally. Her teachers encouraged her to audition with the Philadelphia Opera Company for a role in Verdi's "La Traviata," her favorite opera. As soon as the conductor heard her voice in the audition, he offered her the lead role as Violetta. Long hours of rehearsals followed. This seemed to be the most promising of all of her previous singing opportunities. But the conductor had a heart attack, thus, once again, dropping the curtain on the entire production.

Jen mused, "I felt jinxed! Why, I wondered, did everything I touch seem to fail, before it even had a chance to get off the ground? How frustrating! Clearly, I had much to learn!"

Following this disappointment, Jen decided to take a few years off from pursuing her operatic aspirations, for the births of her two children, even though she practiced her singing daily. After Michael and Anna Maria were both out of the toddler phase, Jennie decided to try her luck at the opera scene once again, which up to that point, she had only viewed from the wings.

After an audition for a part in Mozart's, "Marriage of Figaro," she, as twice before, was offered the lead role. It was then, that the final curtain fell. Mike admitted that he would not be happy having his wife pursue an operatic career, considering the necessary travel, money, and time it would entail. Choosing to honor her husband's wishes – as she had done earlier with her parents – she decided that her dreams of a brilliant operatic career were over, leaving a great legacy of vocal artistry and a finer appreciation of good classical music.

It was not until after "The First Message," in November of 1966, that Jen even thought to look back over her life path that was littered with many disappointments and unrealized career opportunities. "It is true," Jen later explained, "that had I pursued the C.P.A. program, *or* the Y basketball offer, *or* the congressional stenographer opportunity, I likely would have never met and married Mike, and my life would have taken a totally different course. The disappointment about not being able to pursue the operatic career was yet another life barrier I had to endure." In spite of the long string of "bad luck," Jen's inner strength reached new heights, as she strove to overcome disappointment after disappointment.

The Potter had other plans for Jen…

This amazing biographical glimpse reminds me of the scene in the "Sound of Music," when Maria is forced to leave the comfort of the abbey to experience the harsh real world. In that touching scene, with the Mother Superior at her side, Maria prayed for confidence, saying, "Whenever God closes a door, He is sure to open a window."

Jennie's window opened in November of 1966. Her new starring role, which was never anticipated or sought, ironically, called for excellent secretarial skills, the stamina of an athlete, the artistry and sensitivity of a classically trained performer, and for the compassion and empathy of being a wife and mother. Jen's life, more than anyone else I have met in my seven decades, was indisputably being shaped by The Potter's Hands for a more important mission.

CHAPTER FOUR

THE MISSION BEGINS TO UNFOLD...

Much of Jennie's time after the weekend of November 11, 1966 was occupied with preparations for the upcoming holidays. Holidays meant family, food, shopping, food, gift-wrapping, and, did I mention, food? Having all three sisters' families together (Jen's, Virge's, and Josephine's) for Thanksgiving, Christmas Eve, Christmas Day, and sometimes for New Year's Eve, was both expected and eagerly anticipated by everyone involved.

Particularly for Christmas Eve and Christmas Day, the "Three Musketeers" outdid themselves, working feverishly for weeks, shopping, preparing, and freezing the many courses of the two principal meals. There was the traditional Italian seven fishes dinner on the Eve, and the non-stop feast on Christmas Day. There were trays of assorted cookies and Italian pastries to prepare, and many other delectable treats for as many as seventeen hungry mouths. In 1966, Jo's South Philadelphia row home was holiday headquarters.

The three sisters' husbands, the married children with their families, and the younger cousins started arriving at about 5:00 on Christmas Eve, each with arms full of presents to be placed under and all around the decorated tree. A "fortress" of wrapped gifts resulted when seventeen generous people each brought multiple gifts for sixteen others. It was always quite astounding and joyfully

CONRAD M. FOLLMER

excessive, the power of modest gifts made priceless with love. With each succeeding year, the tree seemed increasingly dwarfed by the mountain of boxes and bows that were built up around it.

This 1966 Christmas Eve feast was memorable as usual, with everyone leaving enough room for what they knew was coming next: Jo's incomparable cannoli. These deep-fried cylinders of flaky pastry were filled with creamed ricotta cottage cheese, and sweetened with chopped maraschino cherries, cherry juice, and shaved chocolate. Making the six-inch shells was a time-consuming task (wrapping the pastry around wooden dowels, and deep frying them to the right color and bubbly texture), but it always took far less time for them to disappear. Mike, Jen's husband, won the prize every year for being able to consume a cannoli in only two bites without dropping a crumb!

After the meal – that word somehow being inadequate – some (namely the men) would drift off for a quick nap, while others appointed themselves guardians of the tree area, keeping the curious little children and some bigger "children" a safe distance from exploring and shaking the presents. That would have to wait!

When the women had finished the cleanup (they laughed often, always enjoying being together even for cleanup duty), the guests would gather around the dining room table to play either a card game, like Crazy-Eights or 500-Rummy, or a family bingo-like game called Pokeno. Needless to say, the fun of the game was always punctuated with the serving of more cookies.

The family frequently went to midnight mass at their neighborhood church (starting about 10:30 pm), observing a strict rule (which softened over the years) that the gifts could not be opened until after their return from church. It was always a late night, made all the more special for the children, in particular, who normally had a much earlier bedtime. Following mass, it took anywhere from two and a half to four hours to open the mountain of gifts, interrupted with another serving of coffee and cookies, to revive the weary but happy gift openers.

Each year, a different "Santa" was appointed who sat closest to the tree to distribute the gifts, one at a time, making sure that everyone opened a gift every round. The many gag gifts were often the highlights of the evening; some were even accompanied by funny poems, written by my father, Hank. One such example was the time he bought a bicycle horn for my mother's collapsible shopping cart because she had run down an unsuspecting shopper at the 9th Street Italian Market the previous week. The four stanzas of dad's poem had everyone rolling on the floor. Another such gag gift – also accompanied by a hilarious poem from dad -- was the toilet seat that my mother had earlier sat upon, *too soon* after it had been freshly painted black. There is a whole *back*story to that one, but we'll move along, leaving you to your imagination.

However, the trickster to watch out for was Anna, Jen's daughter. She searched diligently before the holiday, visiting several department stores until she could find the ugliest printed boxer shorts available, as gifts for her two uncles and her father. I think that the men actually looked forward to receiving this annual gift. Beyond that tradition were her beautifully wrapped boxes of "toot-a-loos" (empty toilet paper cylinders) that she had collected throughout the year. As the weeks approached before Christmas, Mike and Jen always found wadded stashes of unused toilet paper that Anna had stripped from their cylinders so that she would have enough for her traditional "toot-a-loo" gifts.

While the dinner on the Eve was always delicious, the shared feast on the 25th was even more magnificent, including Italian wedding soup (with tiny veal meatballs and escarole in chicken broth), home-made ravioli, plump turkey with all the scrumptious trimmings, and the many desserts, that would melt in the mouth! To say that these two family nights were always greatly anticipated by everyone, as well as being deeply bonding and enjoyable, is an extreme understatement. The holiday was *all* about food and family!

But this year the only person who didn't do his usual justice to the feast was Johnny, Jo's younger married son. His panging toothache left a few more cannoli for the other holiday guests and sent him to a local dentist later that week, where he got a shot of Novocain and a filling, before his return trip with his family, to their home in Virginia, near Washington D.C.

Preparing for the holidays with her sisters all but took Jen's mind off of the inspiring and confusing experiences of October and November; however, it wasn't long after the New Year that the short respite was over.

Shortly after the holidays, Jo visited Jen. She was upset about the sudden hospitalization of her son, Johnny. After his return to the D.C. area, he was overcome with flu-like symptoms, including severely swollen glands on both sides of his neck. Following his intense tooth pain over the holiday visit to Philly, Johnny consulted his own doctor in Virginia. The prognosis was unclear, and a series of tests were inconclusive. Doctors indicated that there was the possibility that he suffered from Hodgkin's Disease, characterized by the swelling of lymph nodes. At that point in time, his situation was a medical mystery!

Understandably, Jo was concerned for her son's well-being, and pleaded for Jen's help. Jo had been cautious in her reaction to the whole story surrounding November's "First Message." Now that a personal emergency was confronting her, Jo decided to throw caution to the wind and seek *any* kind of help. Jennie was uncertain whether she could help Johnny. After all, Monsignor Falls had told her that she should not expect a repeat performance.

After Jo left her sister's Havertown home, Jen decided that the least she could do was to pray for her nephew's swift recovery.

Johnny, like Conrad, was also a godson. She *had* to help! As she prayed, she found herself growing still, and once again, heard the "voice" directing her to prepare for dictation. Though she did not see a monk-like figure this time, she heard a compelling deep voice near her right ear. He dictated the following message:

> A node arising from the onset of a virus of a profound nature causing a mound to rupture forth on the exterior. Its contents are not malignant and method of treatment is intravenous use of antibiotics. Prognosis is two to three weeks with a marked weakened condition of the reflexes. The hearing faculties are not disturbed in any way although the patient believes he cannot hear as well. In former times cold packs were used to subside the swelling, but the treatment is no longer effective. A new drug is on the market and in most cases shows remarkable recovery without loss of action. Diagnosis is made through use of medicine previously given.

As Jen reacted in awe to this second writing, she also wondered what to do with the message. Was it medically accurate, she wondered? Did this mean that her nephew would be cured? She decided to call her family doctor, whose office and home were on the corner of her street, to test the validity of the information contained in the writing.

Without mentioning the source of the "letter," as Jen described it to her physician, she asked for his assessment. After she read it to him over the phone, she gripped the receiver with a combination of fear of ridicule and eager expectation. The friendly doctor, though still curious about the authorship of the letter, said that the writing was perfectly sound, medically speaking, except for the strange last line that spoke of diagnosing via previous medication. That line, he said hardly seemed likely; otherwise, he gave the message a clean bill of health.

Having heard that the content of the medical writing was at least logical, Jen was tempted to call her sister, Jo. However, "something" held her back. She hesitated for a moment, then reached for her pen and tablet once again. The "voice" added this:

> To John my healing powers shall be extended and his eyes shall perceive the truth. His belief in me shall create the Miracle – Divine medicine shall be granted. His suffering shall not be in vain.

Overwhelmed, but feeling more confident than the weeks since "The First Message," Jen telephoned her sister, and made arrangements to drive Jo to the Virginia hospital to deliver the message to Johnny in person.

"As we approached the hospital," Jen remembered, "my feelings of assurance started to fade. Growing somewhat ego-involved in the message, I found myself expecting ridicule for a Message I did not personally compose, though one for which I felt responsibility."

"Johnny and Shirley, his wife, were talking at his bedside when Jo and I entered his hospital room. We had seen each other the previous week for the holiday gathering, but family reunions were always joyous occasions. After the niceties of the initial greetings, I grew tense as the inevitable time drew near. I don't recall how I got into the whole subject with Johnny, but I slowly unfolded the message and handed it to him. When he read the second paragraph, the one promising Divine medicine, he acted peculiarly. He began laughing hysterically, saying, 'God would heal *me*?'"

Jen continued, "We all became alarmed when his laughing showed no signs of ebbing. Shirley, a sweet and loving person who was raised in the South with a fundamentalist Christian upbringing, gave me a few sideward glances that needed no explanation. As we attempted to calm his hysteria, I felt a strange inner stillness welling up and overtaking me, as I watched John, who was still out of control. Feeling almost like a total stranger, I saw two beams of intense light emanating from my eyes like lasers. These streams of light penetrated Johnny, and he immediately stopped the hysterical laughing! Apparently, no one else saw the light, and I felt myself returning to normal, but became quite shaken, not knowing what to make of this bizarre experience."

"I remember that Johnny began asking questions about the writing, and though I still did not feel up to talking, I tried to give him the details. While I attempted to explain the strange things that recently happened to me, it became clear that Shirley was growing uncomfortable, especially as her husband became increasingly interested in what I was saying."

Jen remembered, "Johnny told us that the doctors had scheduled him for a bone marrow test for the next morning, to be followed by an operative procedure to biopsy the swollen node. At the mention of the word 'operation,' I spoke up boldly, feeling all the assurance in the world, and said that he would most definitely *not* be operated on! I must have said that with such authority, that everyone, including myself, grew curious. I don't know what made me protest so strongly, but I *knew* that it was the truth."

The next morning, Johnny was given a shot of anesthesia to his sternum prior to the planned bone marrow extraction, which is a painful procedure. It didn't take long for John to break out in a total body rash. Concerned, the doctors were forced to cancel the procedure. In continuing discussions with his doctor about his unusual situation, John showed him the message from his Aunt

Jen. Upon telling his doctor about having gone to the dentist while in Philadelphia, John and his doctor discovered the missing link that finally explained the diagnosis, "...based upon previous medication."

The doctor explained that Johnny likely had a viral load in his system when he went to the dentist's office. His body had apparently reacted to the Novocain, causing an extreme allergic response that included flu-like symptoms and the swollen nodes. The second shot of anesthesia for the bone marrow test caused a similar reaction. At any rate, the final diagnosis *was* made through knowing about his previous medication, as the last line of the message had dictated. As predicted, Johnny's treatment consisted of intravenous use of antibiotics. It did take two to three weeks for him to recover from his generally weakened condition and the mild sensation in his ears, as was also outlined in the message.

Jen sadly recalled, "The relief and joy that Jo and I felt at the resolution of Johnny's medical mystery was soon dispelled by the reaction of his wife about the nature of the message. She quoted Scripture, trying to prove that the days of miracles ended over 2000 years ago, and that obviously, the source of my writing was clearly *not* from a Godly entity. I understood and accepted the reason for her disbelief. However, even my sister, Jo, turned on me for causing dissention. We were forced to leave Virginia for home sooner than planned."

"A few days after my return home, I received a letter from Shirley with another fundamentalist response, accusing me of dealing with the dark side. Just as I was about to run to the phone to respond to her letter, I was *told* by the now-familiar voice to get the tablet and pen. This short message emerged:

My word is law and whosoever believeth shall attain my Kingdom. My Kingdom is for the one who seeks

and believes. My Love opens the door. Whosoever
shall question thee, shall answer to me."

"I felt overwhelming discomfort, when I reread this Message,
especially upon seeing the last line. That line either indicated that
the source of the message was indeed Jesus, or that my subconscious
was rebelling against Shirley's fundamentalist attack, assuming an
identity well beyond my scope. This short message threw me into
another whirlwind of confusion and uncertainty about everything
that had transpired since November. It was impossible for me
to accept that such an exalted Source was operating through
lowly me."

Jen continued her recollection, "Apparently, I was not to be
permitted time to vacillate. Starting the next morning, the Messages
[from this point on in the book, the 'M' in Messages, the 'W' in
Writings, and the 'L' in Lessons will be capitalized in deference to
our respect for them and their Sources], became a regular part of
my daily routine. In fact, for the next year (1967), there were only
a few days when I didn't receive a dictated Message."

"Every morning, after Mike went off to work, I would clean
up the breakfast dishes, then sit at the kitchen table for a moment
of prayer. I never progressed far into my prayers before the 'voice'
directed me to reach for the yellow legal tablet and pencil or pen.
I was always conscious and concentrated as the dictation unfolded
and dutifully recorded every word and punctuation mark. The
'voice' would direct when common words should be capitalized for
emphasis, or when dashes or other marks were required, or gently
correct an error I had recorded on the tablet."

"Frequently," she continued, "a person's name would 'pop' into
my head, alerting me that the Message of the day would be for
that person. Sometimes it was for total strangers. At those times,
I was told which of my friends or relatives knew the person for

whom the Message was intended. The majority of the Messages, however, were spiritual Lessons that my Teachers offered to help us to better understand man's true nature and role in Life."

Jen added, "As the days passed, and the miracle unfolded before my eyes, my reverence for the Sources of the Writings and my appreciation for the depth of content continued to grow."

"Another vital part of my new daily routine was telephoning Virge to share the newest Writing. We spent literally hours on the telephone, oblivious to the passage of time as we jointly tried to make meaning of the deep spiritual Messages and unique occurrences. My sister became so eagerly involved in this routine that she memorized many of the lines from the early Writings. No matter the situation in which we found ourselves, Virge could call to mind an appropriate line from one of the Messages that seemed to fit the event at hand. Life had indeed changed for us both, and my dear sister had become *more* than a sister to me."

"On the morning of January 29th, after we had shared an especially uplifting Message and had settled back to more earthly topics, Virge started reading the newspaper obituary of Ann Sheridan, the American film and TV actress. As she read to me, I felt increasingly tired. I closed my eyes, relaxing my head on the hand that was holding the receiver. Suddenly, I felt myself being lifted over a reddish mountain. I was carried above it, and as I looked at the scene far below, I could see church spires, peeking through the tops of clouds. I still kept rising higher and was finally deposited somewhere. A very beautiful hand, whose coloring was different from human hands, appeared to my left. It was holding what I thought resembled stones. On my right appeared what at first seemed like billowing clouds, soft and puffy. This cloud-like formation began to glow like crystal. I interrupted Virge's reading and began relaying to her what I was being shown in this life-like, waking vision."

"Virge asked me about the nature of the crystal substance, and, in reply, a voice told me, 'It is the City.' I looked back to the hand on the left and mentally questioned what the stones were. The voice immediately answered my silent question, 'These are the pebbles of healing.' The 'City' grew and grew, and there seemed to be no end to it. It was too beautiful to describe in words. I really couldn't imagine why it was called a city, however, because there were no buildings of any kind, or any people. It was all lighted up, but glowing from within with its own source of illumination. I looked again at the hand, and the pebbles began throwing off rays of different colors of light and seemed to be emanating a life force. I was saddened to see the hand withdraw at that point and then finally disappear."

Jen continued, "As the hand exited stage left, a magnificent throne appeared and moved across my view, from the left to the right. The throne was huge, all golden, and a more than appropriate seat for the King who was seated upon it. He was magnificently dressed in a red velvet robe, trimmed with a wide golden band across the chest and at the hem of the cloak. His hair was long, brown, and wavy, and he wore a tall crown, studded with every imaginable jewel. Finally, everything moved from view and disappeared."

"In a choking voice and with a childishly shallow concept of this experience, I declared to my sister that I had seen God upon His throne. As Virge and I reviewed the details of the vision, the notion entered my thoughts that it must be my time to die. When I shared this observation with her, Virge bravely volunteered that at least I knew in advance that I was going to Heaven. That was not just small comfort for a Catholic girl! She added that if she were told to drop everything and to take His hand to leave this earthly life, she wouldn't hesitate for a second. Such was my sister's faith, upon which I heavily leaned for years to come."

Jen later reflected, "Sharing the daily Messages with my sister was both uplifting and educational for the two of us. It seemed that she had complete faith in the Writings and utter trust that *anything* that came through me was of the highest level of inspiration, whether or not we understood any of it. Her unshakable belief and Gospel-preaching attitude earned her the loving nickname, 'John the Baptist.'"

Image #4: The closest of sisters: Virge (left) and Jen (right) in their 60's

"Around this time," Jen recalled, "in one of the many long phone conversations I routinely had with Conrad, he shared that he was facing a major exam in a difficult graduate course, dealing with educational research. He confessed that it made little sense to him, no matter how hard he studied, and he feared that he would fail. Though his 'Letter from God,' as he called 'The First

Message,' had given him greater inner strength, he asked for some additional support from the Beyond."

Jen continued, "After I hung up, I did what I normally do when a loved one asks for help: I prayed. As I started to pray, I felt a great reassurance on my nephew's behalf, and I heard the Voice, asking me to take dictation. What emerged was a short special prayer that Conrad was being directed to say fervently before his test. It was entitled, 'The Student's Prayer.'"

The Student's Prayer

> Oh, Lord of infinite wisdom,
> Sustain my faith at this hour.
> Shed thy light of knowledge before me,
> The right words, for the right answers.

Within minutes of receiving the Message, Jen placed a return call. "I told Conrad to copy the prayer that had been given to him and to know that I felt assured that all would be well. I advised him to try to clear his mind right before the test, to say this prayer fervently, and to trust with all of his being that he would be helped."

Three days later, I called my aunt. I told her that I did as she had directed. I had unfolded the small paper and recited the prayer with as much of a sense of belief as I could muster before the test. Though I was no more confident that I would pass than I had been a day earlier, I tried hard to feel that reassurance. Two days after the exam, when the professor handed back the graded papers, he publically commented, when handing me my test, that I truly deserved my "A+" grade because of the clear depth of understanding I had demonstrated. I was stunned! I held back tears of relief and thanksgiving that were so ready to roll down my cheeks, Only later, when I returned to my room, did I sob privately, extending my fervent thanks for this second miracle.

As an aside for the reader, I must emphasize that the power of this prayer has proven itself to me literally hundreds of times during the many years of my professional career. I recited it before almost every presentation I gave as a teacher, as an administrator, and later as a consultant, even enlisting its effects before entering into personal confrontations with individuals. Over the years, I have shared this special prayer with many friends and colleagues, along with the manner in which I recite it, later hearing feedback that the prayer had worked for them as well. During the recitation of the first two lines, I visualize a golden triangle of supplication, rising up to the heavens. During the last two lines, I envision a descending golden triangle of response, linking itself with the other triangle. Together, they form a glowing Star of David. When I can "see" that golden star, I feel assurance that the power of the prayer will be unleashed.

Aunt Jen observed, "When I learned about the wondrous news from Conrad, I felt humbled, and once again thanked our Lord for His amazing presence in my life, reaffirming that I would obey His will."

Two weeks later, Jen had a dramatic vision while engaged in her morning meditation: "I had the strong feeling that I should light a candle as I sat praying. After lighting it, I sat down again and began gazing into the flame. Suddenly, I was stunned to see the Lord's face emerge from the fire. Then I saw a series of other ancient-looking faces. I mentally asked who they were, and when I heard the Voice say that they were the faces of the Apostles, I grew frightened, feeling that I should not be privy to this vision. As I bent down to blow out the candle, the face of the Blessed Mother Mary appeared to me. I hastened to extinguish the candle and closed my eyes to compose myself. Within a few moments, I saw a bright, oblong light, surrounded by a red glow, emerging from the darkness. It rotated rapidly and suddenly sped toward me, rising out of sight as it neared my body. Another appeared out of the blackness and repeated that same pattern. Then, everything brightened into an orange-reddish color, and from the top of my view appeared a green oblong shape that very slowly descended above me. As it descended, it fell as a drop of viscous darkening liquid. By the time it reached my position, the huge drop was black, and spattered all over me. Two more of these drops appeared and repeated the same descent and color change before covering me."

"Then, before the vision was finished, I saw several rocket-like forms shooting upward. I stood up, wondering what all of this was about, when I heard the Voice say, 'The knowledge of the world shall be shown to you.' I felt compelled to pick up the pencil. I was told to write by a voice that seemed to be echoing from a series of caverns with a roaring sound in the background."

> The cascading rains of the heavens shall descend upon the non-believing world. Troubles shall be meted out accordingly. The thundering winds shall proclaim in loud voices, all the evil that shall befall. Listen and wait for the reckoning of time. In all haste make preparations of glory. Abandon all things in the way. Trouble your heart not for the weary. Awaken to the trumpet's sound. Glory shall be to those who called.

"Shaken, I closed my eyes once again and saw the figure of Our Lord in flowing white robes with a golden cord around the waist. Rays of light emanated from Him."

She continued, "I don't mind admitting that I was petrified! I naively concluded from the vision and the Message that the world was about to come to a screeching halt. I wanted to run outdoors and shout, 'Repent! Pray! Save yourselves any way you can!' Of course, I called my sister, Virge."

"I could hardly speak as I gasped for air, but once again, my dear sister was a calming influence. She insisted that the true meaning of those awesome experiences would some day be made clear to me, and that I should wipe it from my mind for the moment, and go lay down."

"I took my sister's advice, but before laying on the couch in the living room, I fervently prayed to Jesus, asking Him to release me from whatever He had planned for me. I told Him that I was not strong enough, or clever enough to comprehend the meaning of His Messages, the dreams, and especially these latest visions. I pleaded with Him to make me a 'normal' person again."

"At that moment, a soothing inner voice said, 'No harm will come to thee.'"

Jen vividly remembered, "My attention was then immediately drawn to Vicki, my Scottie, who lay curled up on the rug, a few feet from the sofa. Suddenly, she jumped up, as though she had been kicked. She ran towards me, jumped up onto the sofa, and repeatedly kissed me, nuzzling her chin against my neck. I chuckled in spite of my anxiety level. Vicki then gamboled into the next room to her box of toys and dragged the whole box into the living room, near my feet. She began tossing toys into the air and bouncing about so amazingly that I was soon beside myself with laughter. Before I drifted off to sleep, I was simply tired; no longer was I feeling fearful, agitated or concerned, regardless of what might befall the world. That was the second time that my precious Scottie was used as an instrument for my benefit."

In the few months since that historic day in November, Jennie's world had been revolutionized. As The Potter's Wheel turned, Jen was introduced to a new and unimaginable reality, even if she did not fully grasp the symbolic significance of all that was happening to her. She felt like a child in the company of giants, but she was growing up fast!

CHAPTER FIVE

EXPANDING AN AWARENESS OF PSYCHICAL AND MYSTICAL REALITIES...

G iven that this mystical "window" had been opened to Jen only months earlier, with the Messages and visions coming at an increasingly accelerated pace, it was natural for her to want to expand her search for answers. Her fervent hope was that she might some day be well enough informed that she could explain what was happening to her, why it was happening, and what it all meant. She knew she needed to expand her education in psychical, spiritual and metaphysical knowledge, and in that search, she found an expanding circle of friends, and trusted fellow Seekers with whom she could share what was happening to her.

Signs of the Spirit's presence in her life became increasingly evident. Jen found herself walking through bookstores, wondering which books she should read, when a number of times, she reported that books would spontaneously drop off their shelves into her hands, volumes that she invariably found to be informative. As unlikely as that sounds to the reader and author alike, does it really sound any more fantastic than some of Jen's other paranormal experiences that you have read about so far?

To help the reader navigate the flow of this developing story (with periodic sidebars that interrupt that flow to explore related content), let me state that the intention of this chapter is to provide a broad look at the resources, groups, and individuals that Jen discovered and learned from, and to introduce some of the Seekers who were "led" into her circle at this time. Throughout this period, her own mystical experiences continued, creating a context in which she could apply her new learning.

Jen enjoyed attending the illuminating E.S.P. classes at the evening adult school that she had joined in the fall and rejoined for the spring semester. Before she started this lecture series, she had known little about the intriguing world of parapsychology. However, her horizons were rapidly expanding through knowledge imparted by the visiting speakers. During this period, Jen found herself reading numerous books on various psychical and mystical topics, many inspired by the E.S.P. class sessions. A bonus from attending these classes was the opportunity to develop relationships with like-minded people.

There was one older woman in this Tuesday evening class to whom Jen found herself drawn. Over a number of class sessions, Jen saw in her an aura of wisdom, kindness, and motherly understanding. As Jennie soon learned, Georgette, or Georgie, as she preferred to be called, immediately took to Jen as well. Georgie was an avid horticulturist and a long-time student of parapsychology. A second new acquaintance from this class, Ruth Ann, a slender, serious, but endearing individual, also joined Georgie and Jen, forming a compatible trio as they sat together for the balance of the speaker series. After each class, from that point on, they would stay behind to compare notes about their thoughts on the lecture and on the comments from the other participants.

One Tuesday evening in February, the subject of the lecture was about automatic writing and other forms of spirit control. Jen's pulse quickened as she listened to the explanations to see if they might account for the strange phenomenon of her own Writings.

Prior to this lecture, Jen had confided in Georgie and Ruth Ann about her Messages, so they, too, were purposefully listening to the speaker.

Reverend Oliver, the lecturer, was a precise woman, both in appearance and in speech. Her tightly combed and braided silver hair betrayed her European heritage, as did the slightest hint of a British accent. She spoke with authority and easily held her audience. Though she founded her own New Age Church in center city Philadelphia (that Aunt Jen and I later visited), this evening she was speaking on behalf of Parastudy (a "local non-profit organization, founded to critically examine and share psychic phenomena and metaphysical theories"), a group with which Jen would soon become well acquainted.

Rev. Oliver launched into the main topic, explaining that automatic writing and automatic speaking were terms used by psychical researchers and that the people who have this psychic ability are under the influence or control of a discarnate or spirit force.

"In automatic writing," the speaker explained, "the spirit agent controls the hand and the pencil of the subject to write his or her own communication, frequently in a handwriting style that is characteristically different from that of the subject. At the time of the control, an altered state of consciousness is sometimes evident; however, the person is typically a silent witness to being controlled by the discarnate source. At times, an exalted state or a heightening of intellectual faculties occurs, but at other times, the person can even be watching TV or reading a book as the hand automatically writes or draws."

Reverend Oliver's summary caught Jen's attention. The lecturer concluded, "Though the matter and the style of automatic phenomena may on occasion transcend the capabilities of the subject in his/her normal state, the published body of automatic productions does not indicate any excellence beyond the scope of the resources of the subject."

Before finishing, she added a shocker: "Many great writers, inventors, and artists have reported experiencing a control from the spirit world, among them Goethe, Victor Hugo, Brahms, and Victorien-Sardou."

After the lecture, the trio all agreed that Jen's Writings did *not* seem to match the clear definition of automatic writing that was discussed in class; however, they knew they needed more information.

A few weeks later, the three ladies learned that Parastudy was sponsoring a lecture in Philadelphia that Jen, Georgie and Ruth Ann knew they *had* to attend. In fact, Aunt Jen informed me about the upcoming lecture, and I took the bus down from Bucknell to join them. Ruth Montgomery was to be the guest speaker. She was the nationally syndicated columnist on politics and world affairs as well as the author of the New York Times best seller, *A Gift of Prophecy: The Phenomenal Jean Dixon*. Jean Dixon was the seer whose predictions included the death of F.D.R., the assassination of John F. Kennedy, the suicide of Marilyn Monroe, and the car accident of Teddy Kennedy, among many others.

Ruth Montgomery was not slated to speak about Jean Dixon that night, but rather was on a publicity tour to promote *A Search For Truth,* her newest book dealing with the psychic world. In this new book, the author revealed her own psychic experiences with automatic writing as she pursued her own search for truth.

Since "The First Message," Aunt Jen had kept in frequent communication with me. Though we didn't chat as often as she did with my mother, I had been kept up to speed with all of the latest developments in Aunt Jen's exciting and expanding world. Both of us had large telephone bills to show as proof! The invitation to see Ruth Montgomery was as good an excuse as any to return home.

Ruth Montgomery opened her lecture, mentioning a talk she had had with Arthur Ford, one of America's best-known, living trance mediums. She explained that Mr. Ford had suggested that at least once daily, she attempt to tune out the newspaper business world by spending ten minutes in meditation to renew her energies and sharpen her psychic abilities. Ruth Montgomery, a charming and convincing speaker, described her attempts at automatic writing while meditating.

She explained, "I held the pencil loosely in my hand while I attempted to clear my mind. Almost immediately, the pencil began to race around the page, drawing circles and figure eights with wild abandon. I could scarcely have stopped the nonsensical motions even if I tried." She went on to add, "With more practice, words began to form, and soon the page was filling with messages from allegedly deceased relatives. I held the pencil, yet it seemed to write without me."

In her lecture that night as well as in her best selling book, Montgomery continued to talk about the automatic writing that she claimed gave her profitable suggestions for real estate investments and several comforting notes for family and friends, presumably from loved ones on the other side. Ultimately, Aunt Jen's new friends and I agreed that Ruth Montgomery's experiences seemed vastly different from those of Aunt Jen, and I should add, vastly inferior in vibration or level. Both in the presentation and in Mrs. Montgomery's book, the nature of the content that was channeled seemed mundane, addressing down-to-earth, everyday topics, while the channeled Messages through Aunt Jen were consistently of a high spiritual nature. The search continued to explain Aunt Jen's channeling.

For the next few days, Jen tried to evaluate the Writings that were now coming through her almost daily, against the descriptions from the E.S.P. class and the Montgomery lecture. As Jennie compared them, she finally came to the conclusion that her experiences with the Messages could *not* be characterized as the psychic gift of automatic writing. She always had control of her pencil/pen. The handwriting was clearly her own. While she was mentally a spectator to the dictating figures or an active ear to the invisible voices, she was almost always consciously listening and aware. At any time, if she questioned capitalization or punctuation while the dictation was in progress, her Teachers would stop to answer those questions. Finally, the highly symbolic and allegorical content of the Writings was definitely well beyond her personal abilities to either compose or comprehend. With all of these arguments, Jen, as well as her new circle of confidants, agreed that her experiences were something different, even if they couldn't yet give that unique process a name.

Over the years, Jen continued her search to explain the source and nature of the Writings while reading about well-known psychics, mystics, and saints. Jennie rightly viewed her gifts as being in the "mystical" camp, rather than in the "psychical" camp, but this discrepancy did not stop her from learning more about both realms.

As she garnered from what she read and heard, the *psychic* is a person who possesses a natural gift of perception, beyond the normal three-dimensional human limits. With psychic phenomena, those gifts seem to be anchored within the worldly domain of the person (e.g. giving readings, telling the future, reading minds, seeing spirits, moving objects with the mind...). Though there may only be a fine line separating them, the *mystic* in contrast, seems to be more anchored in the spiritual and metaphysical domain, granting the person access to interact with what we might call the

Sublime Realm. Both categories appear able to tap the Universal Unconscious. Neither *psychical* nor *mystical* gifts are intellectual or transferrable by instruction; a person has it or doesn't! As was later validated, Aunt Jen was granted *both* types of gifts.

This was a time in her life for breaking down rigid walls and fears and a time to open up her mind to possibilities that she might surely have rejected out of hand at an earlier period. She studied extensively and thought deeply about both psychical and mystical phenomena, as well as the fascinating people who had those special gifts. Needless to say, her true underlying motivation for this intense study was to solve the mystery of what was happening to and through her.

Most people searching in the rich field of E.S.P. quickly come across the name Edgar Cayce, *the* most famous of America's trance mediums. The long list of books that have been published by the Association for Research and Enlightenment (ARE), located in Virginia Beach, Virginia, attest to the incredible phenomena of the "Sleeping Prophet," as Cayce was dubbed.

Born in 1877, Cayce was by all accounts neither well-educated nor extremely intelligent. Yet, when he lay on his couch and placed himself in a sleep-like state, he spoke with the greatest of wisdom and proprietary knowledge of the spheres. Each day, he placed himself in this somnambulistic state to answer questions put to him by trusted assistants, patients with curable and incurable diseases alike, parapsychologists and spiritualists seeking occult knowledge, and by a close group of friends and relatives who sought answers to questions raised by anyone, near or far, including Cayce himself. As a result of his amazing paranormal gift, Edgar Cayce gave roughly 15,000 readings during his lifetime. Thousands of medical diagnoses and treatment suggestions were issued to total strangers who asked for help, though they may have been hundreds or even thousands of miles away. The patients and their baffled doctors later validated the uncanny high level of accuracy of Casey's readings and the healings that resulted from them.

Many of the books that have been published by ARE, all based directly upon Cayce's thousands of readings, cover the topics of life after death, the metaphysics of the Universe, the life of Jesus, reincarnation and life readings, the lost civilizations of Atlantis and Mu, and prophecies about the future. The explanation given for his rare talents was that Cayce had the ability to leave his body while under questioning to "probe the Universal Mind for answers." The conscious Cayce was totally unaware of what the sleeping Cayce was able to do, and, furthermore, was unable to comprehend either the process or the content of most readings!

The first of the Cayce books that Aunt Jen and I read in our thirst for answers was, *There Is A River*, by Thomas Sugrue (Dell, 1945). Though Aunt Jen quickly realized that the case of Cayce was clearly unlike her own, she saw some overlap in that many of her current Messages dealt with similar subjects.

In her searching through resources about psychical and mystical phenomena, Aunt Jen came upon one case that we both found to be fascinating, even if nothing like Aunt Jen's gifts. It was about Arigo, the impressive Brazilian peasant.

In his 1974 best seller, John G. Fuller wrote about Arigo, the incredible Brazilian peasant who, when allegedly controlled by the spirit of a German doctor, both diagnosed and bloodlessly operated upon thousands of cases. The fascinating book, *Arigo: Surgeon of the Rusty Knife* (Thomas Y. Crowell Co., 1974), shares the observations of the American medical research team that investigated the phenomena. Led by Dr. Henry Puharich, a medical researcher, the team witnessed many bloodless operations performed upon non-anesthetized patients who simply stood in line against the rough-hewn walls of Arigo's modest dwelling. Arigo was allegedly placed in an altered state while being overshadowed by the spirit of a German doctor. He would glance at his patient, and within seconds he dictated the entire diagnosis as well as prescriptions and treatments to a waiting member of the medical research team. Whenever surgery was indicated, Arigo allegedly pulled out his penknife, made a bloodless incision, and in a matter of seconds completed the operation. The open wound was mysteriously sealed, and no evidence of infection ever surfaced. The patients, too, must have been in a trance because they never reported feeling any pain. The American research team reportedly witnessed everything from delicate eye operations to complex cancer operations. Among the many cures performed at Arigo's clinic include the miraculous treatment of the Brazilian President's young son, and even the removal of a lymphoma from Dr. Puharich.

As with Edgar Cayce, the "uncontrolled" Arigo was completely unaware of what transpired when being overshadowed by the discarnate source. Arigo, a peasant with a third grade education, attributed his incredible abilities to God and accepted no payment for the medical treatments.

Another fascinating phenomena that Aunt Jen read about involved such notable musical greats as Beethoven, Strauss, Brahms, Puccini, Humperdinck, Bruch, and Grieg. In a book by Arthur M. Abell, *Talks With Great Composers* (G. E. Schroeder-Verlag, 1964), the author shared his personal interviews with the above geniuses (except for Beethoven, who did not live at the same time period but who left similar evidences). Abell's goal was to discuss the topic of "inspiration" with each of the great men to determine whether or not some force from beyond themselves influenced their works. This part was especially interesting to Jennie, given her newly inspired life events. All of the musicians allegedly disclosed unique intellectual, spiritual and psychic experiences while composing their masterpieces.

The interview with Brahms is especially revealing and accurate because of the services of a bi-lingual stenographer who transcribed the verbatim record of the three-hour interview between Abell and Brahms. Brahms told his interviewer that prior to sitting down to compose, he, as Beethoven before him, spent time meditating upon the premise, "I and my Father are one" (John 10:30). The following paragraphs describe part of what ensued in that interview with Brahms:

> I immediately feel vibrations that thrill my whole being. These are the Spirit illuminating the soul power within, and in this exalted state, I see clearly what is obscure in my ordinary moods; then I feel capable of drawing inspiration from Above, as Beethoven did. Those vibrations assume the forms of distinct mental images, after I have formulated my desire and resolve in regard to what I want – namely, to be inspired so that I can compose something that will uplift and benefit humanity – something of permanent value.

> Straightaway the ideas flow in upon me, directly from God, and not only do I see distinct themes in my mind's eye, but they are clothed in the right forms, harmonies, and orchestration. Measure by measure, the finished product is revealed to me when I am in those rare, inspired moods... I have to be in a semi-trance condition to get such results...

> Spirit is the light of the soul. Spirit is universal. Spirit is the creative energy of the cosmos. The soul of man is not conscious of its powers until it

is enlightened in Spirit. Therefore, to evolve and grow, man must learn how to use and develop his own soul forces. All great creative geniuses do this, although some of them do not seem to be as conscious of the process as others.

Brahms' final paragraph above is a telling and moving statement of Universal Truth that is a "gift" available to all of us, as promised in the Bible. That form of inspiration, resembled what was happening to and through Jennie, at least to a degree. The search continued...

After years of combing through numerous resources, Aunt Jen finally uncovered information about a category of paranormal writing and speaking, which seemed to more closely fit her own experiences. It is a form of inspired mystical communication called *amanuensis* (pronounced: a-man-u-en'-sis). Briefly, *amanuensis* is a mental listening and subsequent writing or speaking, word for word, of that which is being dictated from Beyond. Amanuensis differs from automatic writing in that the subject, though in an altered (frequently elevated) state of consciousness, is totally aware of what is transpiring, and remains in control of the hand and the handwriting style, or the vocal mechanisms. Amanuensis also differs from automatic writing in that the works produced are an amalgam of the subject's talents and those of the inspiring energies. An important point is that the communicating spirits utilize the subject's faculties, working cooperatively.

The following represent a small sampling of the many books assumed to be examples of the mystical gift of amanuensis, and are all recommended for the serious reader's future book list:

o Madame H.P. Blavatsky was the co-founder of the Theosophical Society, in the late 1800's. Her published works include *ISIS Unveiled* (Theosophical University Press, 1880), *The Secret Doctrine* (Theosophical University Press, 1888), *The Voice of ISIS* (Curtiss Book Company, 1914), among others. Allegedly, the content in these complex books was channeled through Blavatsky, a Russian-German aristocrat. The technicality of the metaphysical detail in these tomes is quite daunting.

o *The Urantia Book* (Urantia Foundation, 1955), is a channeled book purporting to represent the historical genesis of all creation, up through the New Testament period, in highly technical detail. Each of the 196 documents contained in this 2,100 page book, identifies the Sublime authoring sources. The Urantia Foundation is a successful and currently functioning organization, offering on-line resources, and is worth checking out.

o Richard Bach, the inspired author of the popular allegorical book and movie from the 1970's, *Jonathan Livingston Seagull* (Macmillan, 1970), reported taking dictation from a voice, which was totally responsible for all of the words in his book, and for helping him to secure the many photographs to accompany it. He took no credit for *any* of the content, openly explaining that awe-inspiring story on a TV interview program that I had watched in the 1970's.

o Jane Roberts is the woman through whom a spirit guide named Seth, spoke on many topics, resulting in a book series including *The Seth Material* (Prentice Hall, 1970). She was totally conscious as Seth spoke through her, frequently to a waiting and questioning audience.

○ The content for a series of three books came through Pat Rodegast, a channel, in the 1980's, during which time a spirit guide named Emmanuel, spoke to small groups through a conscious and willing host, not unlike the experiences of Jane Roberts. The books are: the first: *Emmanuel's Book* (Bantam Books, 1985), the second: *Emmanuel's Book II* (Bantam Books, 1989), and the third: *Emmanuel's Book III* (Bantam Books, 1994).

○ There is an excellent three book series about Ramala, the spiritual source who channeled through a husband and wife team over a twenty-year period. The first: *The Revelation of Ramala*, the second: *The Wisdom of Ramala*, and the third: *The Vision of Ramala* (Hillman Printers Ltd., 1991). These books are exceptional and very readable.

Prior to returning specifically to Jennie's expanding world of inspired communication through amanuensis, there is one other bestseller, filled with mystically inspired writing that *must* be mentioned: *The Holy Bible.* If there are any doubts remaining about the validity and even the "official" sanctioning of paranormal communications and inspiration from the Sublime Region to the physical plane, we need look no further than the often quoted passage from I Corinthians, chapter 12:4-11, where we read:

> Now there are varieties of gifts, but the same Spirit; and there are varieties of ministries, but the same Lord; and there are varieties of workings, but the same God, who works all things in all. Now the manifestation of the Spirit is given to everyone for profit. To one through the Spirit is given the utterance of wisdom; and to another the utterance

of knowledge, according to the Spirit; to another
faith, in the Spirit; to another the gift of healing, in
the one Spirit; to another the working of miracles;
to another prophecy; to another the distinguishing
of spirits; to another various kinds of tongues; to
another interpretation of tongues. But all these
things are the work of one and the same Spirit,
who allots to everyone according as he will. (*The
Holy Bible*, The Catholic Press, Inc. 1950)

Most Christians firmly believe that the words of the Bible are
inspired communications, words of the Holy Spirit channeled
through human subjects. The Spirit clearly overshadowed the
Evangelists, the Prophets, the Kings, and the Apostles, as well as
common people, all for the grand purpose of spreading the Word
of Truth to all peoples. One must ask, why would those promised
Gifts have suddenly ceased 2000 years ago, logically denying this
holy link to humanity from that point onward? It is both logical
and sensible to assume that the eternal Creative Spirit, the very
Energy of Life itself, remains alive, well, and is as actively engaged
with its own Loved creations, as it was back then. This special
dynamic interaction is the crux of our relationship to the Divine.
Why do some Christian sects insist that "miracles" are a thing
of the distant past, refusing to accept the daily "miracles" that
surround us, if we but look with an open mind?

Georgie and Ruth Ann continued to keep in touch with Aunt
Jen, encouraging her to join Parastudy, whose members were also
searching for knowledge about the Gifts of the Spirit. As Jen
observed, "Georgie convinced me that by joining Parastudy –
which sponsored many courses, workshops and guest speakers,
and had a sizeable library of resources about the paranormal (www.

parastudy.org) – I would be in a better position to learn more about my gifts and those of many others. She was persuasive."

Jennie continued, "Especially since they told me that a talented medium was scheduled as the special presenter, a few days from then, I decided to accept Ruth Ann's and Georgie's invitation. I never before had the reason, interest, or courage to go to a 'fortune teller' (which was my uninformed definition of what a medium was); therefore, my willingness to go to see this medium, at this point in my life, was certainly evidential that I needed more answers."

"I did decide to join, but the initial experiences of my first visit, even with Georgie at my side as a buffer, aroused my suspicions, and made me second-guess this decision."

"Given that in my sheltered life I had never been in the company of a group of people who were so openly into the psychic arts, the first few members I met at Parastudy presented a bit of a culture shock. One woman sat in the kitchen of this old yellow frame house in Chester Heights, Pennsylvania and was calmly describing her recent conversations with a ghost to other members, gathered around the table. She reported that this ghost had taken up residence in her newly purchased home. She concluded her tale by reporting that she and the ghost had come to an amiable agreement not to interfere in each other's lives."

Jen continued, "While I was reeling from this introductory experience at Parastudy, I overheard another woman in the adjoining sitting room telling others about the time that she and a few dinner guests succeeded in getting her heavy dining room table to dance, merely by placing their fingertips lightly under its surface and asking for a spirit to come through. 'Table tipping,' or 'table turning,' as I later learned, is something like the phenomenon of the Ouija Board, wherein a wandering spirit proved its presence to a gathering by rapping on or bouncing the table."

"At any rate," Jen continued, "I was all set to return to my car, chalking off my small membership fee as a questionable investment, when I spotted Ruth Ann. She was seated in what must have been the living room of this old house, waiting for the guest speaker to arrive. Ruth Ann greeted me warmly, patted the cushion next to her, and started telling me that having such a gifted medium as Mrs. Manspeaker was a rare treat. My expression must have betrayed the fact that I didn't really understand the role of a medium or the significance of this presentation. Without making an issue of my ignorance, Ruth Ann explained that mediums have the gift of seeing and communicating with spirits of those individuals who have passed over (another new expression for me). They are also able to read for the living, picking up problems, needs, personality traits, as well as the hidden psychic talents of their subjects."

Jen remembered, "Especially with Ruth Ann's comforting manner, I decided to be more open-minded, and accept that this was being presented to me as a learning opportunity. After all, my strange new world had been unfolding for me over the past few months, and I had to admit that if others heard about the details of my channeling, visions, and interactions with spirits and disembodied voices, they would likely react to me as I did upon my introduction to Parastudy."

"As we waited for Mrs. Manspeaker to arrive, I imagined that the medium would sashay through the archway, looking like a wild gypsy woman adorned in bangles and beads, and even perhaps wearing a turban or lugging a crystal ball. All sorts of iconic images came to my mind; however, upon her entrance, much to my surprise and relief, Mrs. Manspeaker struck me as a warm, humble, personable, and *normal* woman. I decided to listen with an open mind in hopes of learning some answers. After all, I had much to learn."

Jen remembered, "After introducing herself and the idea of mediumship, she said a prayer and then appeared to be scrutinizing her small audience. With some authority, Mrs. Manspeaker pointed to one woman and told her to stop grieving over the recent loss of her father. In fact, the speaker said that the woman was delaying the progress of his soul with her profound relentless grief. The medium explained that he was being held down to earthly planes by the gravity of her grief. The audience member confirmed the recent loss, and the fact that she had been intensely grieving. The speaker went on to single out most of the fifteen or so ladies in the room, offering insights, almost all of which were enthusiastically corroborated. Then came my turn."

Mrs. Manspeaker looked intently at me, then said, "You are entirely too emotional about helping people and are overinvolved in the welfare of friends and family members." She hesitated, then continued, with a lighter tone to her voice, "You will receive, or have received, an important paper, or letter, or legal document of some sort..."

Upon hearing this, Ruth Ann interrupted saying, "She already got it!"

Jen turned quizzically to her new friend, who whispered that the "First Message" was an important document, and it was written on a legal sized pad.

Mrs. Manspeaker smiled kindly, then concluded by saying, "My dear, you must fight your fear and doubts. I see that you are surrounded by a beautiful light, and are protected by a gathering of great teachers from the spirit world."

Jen remembered feeling amazed by Mrs. Manspeaker's seemingly accurate words. After the talk, she asked the speaker for a business card. She bravely decided that a longer private reading was in order.

Two weeks later, Jen, accompanied by Anna, Mom, and me (I was on spring break from Bucknell at the time), entered Mrs. Manspeaker's apartment building in downtown Philadelphia. The elevator carried four nervous neophytes to the fifteenth floor.

However, Jen's nervousness was alleviated the moment that the smiling silver-haired woman opened the door. The apartment was small and more modest than the beautiful exterior of the cylindrical building suggested. After Mr. Manspeaker introduced himself to the visitors, he explained that his wife would take one person at a time into the adjacent kitchen for a private reading while he entertained the others in the living room.

Jen later observed that it would have been evident to a blind person that the four fidgeting visitors had never had a reading before. Mom bravely agreed to go first, while the others listened to their host's strange tales about UFO's.

Mom later summarized, "Mrs. Manspeaker said many things about me that frankly made little sense, such as the colors of my aura. But the one thing that convinced me that she was on the level was when she spoke of my second child in the spirit world, the one who had died at birth. The boy wanted to assure me that I should not worry about Conrad, his brother, because he was watching over him. I was flabbergasted! How could she know that I had had a miscarriage, and that the baby was a male?"

When Jennie went into the windowless kitchen, Mom, Anna, and I were left with Mr. Manspeaker. Within a few minutes, the three of us were fighting not to make eye contact with each other for fear of laughing out loud as the host responded to the flickering of the lamp on the table next to him. Solemnly, he informed us that there was nothing wrong with the electricity. In fact, it was the UFO's, attempting to communicate with him. For many years, the humor of that story threw Anna and me into fits of laughter, particularly if a lamp bulb happened to flicker.

Aunt Jen's reading was more of a surprise to her than to us. Aunt Jen later explained, "Mrs. Manspeaker started by telling me that my parents were standing by me and wanted to tell me that they were proud of the work I was doing. That was not convincing in itself, except that she murmured an endearing Italian phrase that only my Father had used when he addressed me. She went on to say that she saw a great many teachers of high caliber, who were standing by to give comfort and instruction. She asked if I occasionally felt a pat on my head. Well, this shocked me, because I hadn't told anyone, not even Virge or Conrad, about the couple of times that this had happened while taking dictation. She added that my guides were pleased with my progress."

Jen continued, "After a pause, Mrs. Manspeaker named one of my chief teachers, Father Baptiste. She paused again and announced reverently that the guides were from the Master Lodge, considered to be the spirit world's greatest Teachers of the Teachers, also known as 'The Great White Brotherhood,' or the 'Brotherhood of Light.' Clearly, she was highly impressed, though it didn't have any meaning for me at the time. (Little did I know that I would soon learn more about this highly esteemed group of Ascended Masters)."

Jen continued, "Mrs. Manspeaker then asked if I had any questions. I told her about the vision of the 'City' with the enthroned King. She interpreted this vision as my accepting a path that will lead to self mastery or 'Kingship;' that indeed, I was on a unique path of achievement, and would be gifted with the power of healing, as well as the ability to counsel and give accurate readings to others."

"Then," as Jen recalled, "when Mrs. Manspeaker moved closer to me to hold my hand or give me a blessing, she suddenly moved back, as though she had been pushed, exclaiming, 'All right! All right!' Mrs. Manspeaker sat back down in her chair. Shaking her head with a broad smile, she said something like, 'With Big Chief around, you will never have to worry about protection! He is a very powerful, tall, handsome, blond figure, with penetrating light blue eyes, who clearly is your personal protector or guardian. He wants me to tell you that you saw him when you were very young."

Though Jennie was fascinated by the medium's amazing gift, overall she felt that the details of her reading were not particularly meaningful, revealing or verifiable.

Anna and I each had our turns in the kitchen with Mrs. Manspeaker, but as the four of us were reunited in the living room, preparing to leave, Mrs. Manspeaker walked up behind me. She said that she sensed that I was having trouble breathing deeply, that my breathing was shallow. To everyone's surprise, she placed her hands on my head. For at least a full minute, with her eyes closed and a far-away expression on her face that I could glimpse in the living room mirror, she inhaled deeply, slowly releasing her breath. Before departing, she added that I might publish a book some day. Imagine that! It was not until we had reached the elevator that I exclaimed that I could suddenly inhale more deeply than at any time in my life and that I felt a new sense of freedom. It lasted at least until the end of that adventuresome day.

"Coincidentally," it was only a few days after the reading that initial evidence of the accuracy of Ms. Manspeaker's reading became clear, with other such evidences yet to follow. While folding a pile of washed and dried clothes, Jen was stunned when "Big Chief" suddenly materialized in full form before her. She stood in awe at his powerful presence, unable to speak, lost in his penetrating and cavernous light blue eyes. Almost immediately Jen realized that she *had* seen him before, as Mrs. Manspeaker indicated, when she was about six or seven years old, quarantined in the hospital. He was *that* mysterious friendly man who visited and reassured her. She was overjoyed to see him again, yet duly overwhelmed by his magnificent presence. In her early childhood, he was what others might call her "imaginary friend." Now, thanks to the reading, Jen knew that "Big Chief" was in fact her protective guardian angel. Many years later, Jen would come to know his awesome true identity.

This period in Aunt Jen's life was both fascinating and life altering. In just a few months, she had learned a great deal about psychical and mystical phenomena, she had joined Parastudy, which would prove to be a continuing source of education and support, she had met a number of intriguing and kindly people, who were Seekers like her, and had felt the thrill of a whole new world opening up to her. But this was all just the tip of the iceberg...

CHAPTER SIX

THE POTTER'S MISSION
BECOMES CLEARER...

While on spring break from Bucknell, I wanted to spend every available moment I could with my aunt. The months had flown by since that ground-breaking day in November, and so much had happened to and through her that I both *wanted* and *needed* to spend time together.

As we sat at her kitchen table, talking, drinking coffee, and eating her delicious homemade anise pizzelle, Anna, my cousin, started badgering me to play badminton in the backyard. When Anna wanted to do something, she usually got her way. Finally, I relented.

Eager to begin the game, we didn't bother taking down the clothesline that was arranged in a big square, close to the edges of the yard. The badminton net was set up in the middle. After about ten minutes of enjoyable play and the usual laughing at funny stories we often shared, including the flickering light communications from UFOs, Anna hit a high and long shot, sending me backing up rapidly in an attempt to reach the birdie in time. The moment I swung back with my racket, I felt it hit the taut clothesline. Swiftly turning to see what was happening, I felt the racket recoil into my face. The racket smashed the left lens of

101

my glasses, sending glass shards into my eye. Anna screamed for her mother!

The three of us walked nervously to the corner house on their block, which served as both the office and home of their family doctor, who had earlier weighed in on cousin Johnny's "medical letter." Dr. Marvel cleaned out my now painful eye, noting that it was red and puffy, and that my cornea was scratched. He prescribed drops to promote healing, but warned that it might be uncomfortable for a number of days. Thankfully, it had not been a more dire injury!

The three of us returned to the kitchen. Then, with another apology, Anna left her mother and me alone at the table. As we two soulmates eventually returned to more inspiring matters, both of us were keenly aware of the redness and soreness in my left eye.

As we talked, I could feel the swollenness and soreness every time I blinked. Then suddenly, I felt a strange stillness and noticed Aunt Jen's finger approaching my injured eye. At the precise moment that her finger made contact with my eyelid, I heard a deep voice within me demand, "Heal!" accompanied by a "clicking" sound. Immediately, the pain and discomfort were gone! Though neither of us could explain what had just happened, the awesome realization shortly became clear. My eye was no longer red, puffy, or sore. My eye *was* healed! We both joyously thanked God for this little miracle, sharing our amazement and tears! I threw out the eye drops, clearly no longer needing them.

That following morning, March 29th, during Jen's ritual meditation, a writing emerged that addressed the two topics that consumed her thoughts: one, about the healing, and two, about the nature of the Messages that were now coming through her with daily regularity.

Healing is a matter of the heart. The intense feeling within one's own being creates the force of curing which is manifested by love – love of your Christ. He does not make it known in what scope He intends this field to be used. You have been made to feel this intense force and with true success. Be assured that this is in you but must be used slowly – we must be assured of the results in your behavior with reference to your health. This is a very touchy and sensitive power, and, in some cases, drains the user's resources. The prayers that you use are the intent feeling you have for the Lord. He hears the prayers of the heart and knows the purpose for them. Be content to go along as you have. We stand by to assist you in any way we can – we are here with you to protect you from harming yourself. That is why this is so slow for you. We take care of what we are entrusted with.

You have many onlookers watching anxiously your travels toward your goal. We are all pleased because your motives are right. Do not be afraid of the inward feeling of being capable of doing things – you do know where this real power is coming from. Do not be alarmed to any extent – keep a tranquil heart because you will be shown by this inward feeling just what your tasks are. Again we tell you we are greatly pleased with our amiable pupil who shows remarkable qualities of feeling.

At this point, Jen humbly replied, "You are so generous to me!" To which They replied,

This is not a question of generosity, only a truth – after all, this is the purpose you are striving for. You are very adept at looking and observing all manner of signs leading you onward – this is the correct way. If you could hear our applause, it would greatly help you, but we feel you are not concerned with this.

Feeling braver, Jen asked, "Do I have a lot of teachers?" In response came,

They are constantly around you – yes, you have very many teachers and in all walks of life. You have many questions to ask; therefore, it is made sure that you have the most able of teachers. You see, we must make sure that everything is presented in a form that first of all you must understand because you will be able then to teach. You noticed this change and are aware of very many new feelings; however, we see that you are taking this in stride. Bravo! You may question along any line of thought, which would serve to help you in your chosen path.

Jen asked, "Are these writings directed by Jesus?" A rapid, though not angry reply came,

How could you spoil this entire picture by asking such a question? You know perfectly well, truth is always taught by Christ.

Jen apologetically and innocently replied, "I really didn't mean to get you angry!" at which They answered,

We don't mean to displease you but this is an upsetting matter – it is bad alone that there are so many non-believers and we don't want our pupils to be out of focus for any time. You know your true task, so onward you go. Do not be concerned with helpers – they will be provided for you. We shall see and prod these other good-hearted laborers to assist you. You see, we also know your failing points but this we do not hold against you. Any other questions?

Jen paused, then asked, "Will you keep giving me writings?" They replied,

Most certainly! How would you get your education? It would be very wonderful and enlightening if you could see your teachers. Such a brave group, all awaiting their turn. We must all be patient here too. We are truly amazed with your progress and will make sure we do not loose our grip on you.

With this merry thought, we leave you. Good day.

Though her newly introduced Teachers had declared that Jennie knew her true task, their pupil was not certain that she did. She knew that it was her personal duty to follow inner guidance, eventually leading to self-perfection; however, the Message of the 29th seemed to imply a teaching task for which Jen would require the assistance of helpers.

Her Teachers, whoever they were, obviously had plans for her. All Jen could do was to pray and wait. Remembering a thought that haunted her youth, Jen was now more certain than ever that she had *very* much to learn!

Remembering the most recent message about the group of Teachers waiting to teach her, Jennie was eager to do some research. I returned to her home early that afternoon, and we began speaking about "The Great White Brotherhood," the revered ascended Masters that Mrs. Manspeaker, the medium, had mentioned during Jen's reading. As we exchanged our thoughts, Aunt Jen was privately alerted to prepare for dictation. As I watched her taking a Writing for the first time, I was impressed to observe the speed of her scribing. It was certainly not possible for her or anyone to both compose and write like that, not at that speed, and not with that level of complexity of ideas! The following Message came through about the "Great White Brotherhood":

> They are genuine Light Beings that exist as a magnetic flow circling the global area. They exist through the thought process and may materialize. They are not listed individually. Theirs is more of a strict spiritual teaching, and more with the command of the Law – anything existing with the Law portrays a particular Light, which goes through what we can consider a magnetic field attracting this particular form of coexistence.

> They may appear as a particular entity, a personal being, but this is also with the understanding that the one particular entity has the inflow of the entire group. They may appear in a vision as a circle of Light.

I boldly spoke up, asking about the earlier Message that spoke of the brave group of Teachers waiting to speak through her. They responded,

As in every union to make a collective project workable, there must be many grades and steps. Therefore, each and every possible workable unit is used, sometimes appearing as many things, sometimes as one -- this all depends on the information being sought, and also the availability of understanding and portrayal of that which it comes through.

Once again, Aunt Jen and I discussed this written answer, then asked another question about whether or not it was true that the higher the level of the channel, the clearer the writings that come through? They answered,

You are speaking in terms of intellectual knowledge gained by a teaching method other than spiritual. In that sense it would not mean a clearer statement. It might mean a more technical process of words. We can only use as much as the individual has to be used, or the availability that its use can be put to, in combination with their like individuals.

Asking for a clarification, the Guides continued,

In other words, it's resource to resource. Sometimes the Writings are clear, and others less clear. To produce a clear river, the dregs must be at their most dividing or clearing process. If there are definite articles in the riverbed not permitting this sieving, this then produces a not so clear effect of water.

Jen asked about the different ways she has received Messages, as in a visible figure dictating, an outward whispering voice, and an inward voice. They explained,

> When something is not apparent, such as hearing voices, which may seem to be coming from the center of the room, why we make this statement (this borders on the technical). There are different types of voices, such as coming from an outer distance like the middle of the room, whispering in the air, or within, one must understand there is the physical density and there is the spiritual density. There must be a different union of these two particular fields, depending on what is available there. We cannot be the same at every moment.

> One who tries and practices mysticism, feels the separation at the beginning, and as one progresses, a closer union begins its performance, but as we say, and repeat, through the constant usage and availability of the individual. The one large contributing factor is the intense desire and fervor of the true mystic.

Aunt Jen and I agreed that this generous exchange with the Guides was helpful in reaching a better understanding of her developing role as a mystical channel and in feeling the reassurance that the Guides would eagerly continue to communicate to and through her. Both of us felt the special thrill of jointly interacting with the Guides as being an effective means of having our questions answered.

In fact, from that point onward, this question-and-answer format became the most common means of communicating with the Teachers. This shift in format led naturally to direct, orally spoken dialogue with the Guides, rather than Aunt Jen's having to handwrite their answers to our every question. At those times, I became the scribe, recording the Guides' words, spoken by Aunt Jen. The two of us worked well together, prompting the Guides to observe, "...the aunt is the mix-master and the nephew is the power switch." Apparently, when I asked a question, she went into action, channeling to provide their answers.

Before Jen drifted off to sleep that night, she was thinking about our conversation and the subsequent short Message about "The Great White Brotherhood." It was clear that this magnificent group-energy was dedicated to spiritual teaching and helping humanity, and further, that they were teaching through her. In the morning, she remembered having had another life-like dream.

"I remember being carried up to a place which was totally white and beautiful. Everything I could see was white! I saw a huge temple with a white dome, and then my attention was drawn to a long line of white cowled, monk-like figures. Apparently, they were waiting in line to speak with someone who was greeting them inside the temple. One by one, they entered. I decided to tag on to the end of the line and await my turn. When finally I entered the temple, I saw that it was Jesus who had been greeting and conversing at some length with each of the monks. To his right side was a golden cross, with a single white rose attached to its crossbeams (much like the symbol of the Rosicrucian's, a philosophical secret society, founded in the Middle Ages). As my turn approached, I grew very self-conscious, feeling like a mere child. While my love for Him was overflowing, I could not think of anything to say to Him. When my turn arrived, I stepped before him. I mumbled, in a child-like voice, nervously saying the only thing which came to my mind, 'I love you.' He returned a warm and knowing smile, which filled me with His Love. I walked on, realizing that I was clearly well-beyond my depth in the presence of very highly evolved company. I felt like a welcomed visitor, but was keenly aware that I was *very* far from belonging at this exalted level."

Jen continued, "After Mike left for work the next morning, I sat at the table, absent-mindedly sipping my black coffee and replaying the dream in my mind. Suddenly, I became aware of a figure standing beside me. He was slender, not particularly tall, but had an awesome intensity and brilliance about him. I felt like I was in the presence of a no-nonsense, strict professor. It was clear that I was about to take dictation, so I reached for the yellow tablet and pen. What followed was the longest and densest Message I had yet received."

> Life has its beginnings in the entrails of space and man becomes an object of mind. That part of space, if it could be thought of, actually has no beginning, because it was there from all time. Therefore you must realize, man lives from all time, and you draw the conclusion that this is an eternal creation. I believe this meaning is becoming clear to you now.

> In so far as all these writings are concerned, there is a definite knowledge that must be derived from all that is given in truth. For those who do not accept truth where it is shown, woe unto them. Man must exercise his mind. Matter is presented to him in many forms and ideas, and if his thoughts are pointed to the Love of God and His Will, he will learn to digest all manner of words, actions,

and speeches, and assimilate the facts, which he instinctively knows to be the truth. Truth is the one subject in the life of all, mortal or otherwise which can never be altered one way or the other. Therefore, if one is robed in the proper vestments, and arms himself with the proper tools, and divests himself of fear, his mind can penetrate and receive a truth for his being. It becomes as a simple thing if it just can be understood. The higher elevation attained, naturally, the more complications of pattern there are. There are workings in every plane in existence, and if thought over very carefully, thou can understand a feeling of minuteness in retrospect to a grandness of comprehension to that point.

Thy scope is of a wide range and helpers will come into view very shortly – these must be the individuals of trust. These must not be people who pretend to want to help – all can help in one way or another. Thy mind must be kept in a free, roving spirit so thou can establish all these contacts that instruct thee. There is a pretense among people who subsist in the fact that there really is nothing they can do. This is utter nonsense! Discipline must enter into this part of their lives. Is there not discipline of action when a wrong is committed legally? Why should the other spheres of life's teachings come under another variation? Thou shall endeavor a working of thine own to speed up action concerning the laziness of minds in humans. Thou art well equipped with this innate knowledge and thy teachings have a depth of thine own quality.

Do not sway in thy calculations – thou will keep a control of thyself and thy followers.

It is a wonderful beginning – the start of this new fellowship of renewing the truth of God's Laws. We bless this new adventure with many graces. We will give a feeling of trust to Georgie. She has the nature to create a circle of fellowship. Do not have misgivings of wrong teachings because these have been given in truth.

Seek those who have typing knowledge to assist thee. Thou must first make another complete set of writings so that notes may be attached to these with explanations. Individual messages have been given to establish the truth of an all-knowing God and to establish a love for man as an example. This is a trial of a kind – see that all can pass the test. Do not concern thyself that some do not wish to follow – the woe is theirs. Have they not been created in the same fashion as thou wert? Have they not been exposed to the same rays of hope? Do they not have eyes and ears? The matter has been placed beforehand and yet they destroy a means of salvation. The avenue of life has been shown to them and still they cloak themselves in the robes of disillusionment. What a pity!

Child, thine avenue of love must not lead thee to worriment. All things must come to thee of a goodness because thou art surrounded by it. Certain powers that be will prevent actions of any other sort. Things may not be as thou at one moment in thy life would like them to be, but we hope thou will understand fully that the plan must take effect for the other person's welfare, whenever his soul benefits by such actions.

Whatever has been told thee of someone, all come from the true statements of life. Therefore, thou can dispense with certain worries of thine own. We spread our peace over thee, much as clouds hovering protectively about thee. Do thou exist in love, my child, and spread thy devotion wherever thou can.

Thou truly knows me and my organization. It is not always necessary for one to exist in names because that is so easily changed. One name is for one but that does not mean that another will like that name. There is folly in names – I suppose, those names in thy world would hold a significance to thee, but the sphere of my occupation does not exist in a manner of names. You can say we are Love, Inc. Isn't that a better situation – not to exist in the rivalry of names – that one is better than the other? You can think of me as Father Baptiste and the Order is correct in thy mind. Thank thee.

Jen was exhausted after writing this long, intense, detailed, and rapidly dictated Message. She felt that the Teacher was an exalted spirit who was particular about every detail. The last paragraph brought warm satisfaction to her for several reasons. Given that she had been thinking and dreaming about "The

Great White Brotherhood," and was told, "…the Order is correct in thy mind…" she felt that this Message was a corroboration that the "White Brotherhood" was in fact responsible for her lessons. She also especially liked the alternate name that the Teacher had given to identify his group, "Love, Inc." Beyond that, she suddenly remembered that in the kitchen reading by Mrs. Manspeaker, the name of "Father Baptiste" had been identified as one of her Teachers who was waiting to communicate with her. Well, here he was! She was also pleased that her new friend, Georgie, was personally mentioned as a trusted helpmate for the future.

A number of future Messages were to come through from Father Baptiste and/or Love, Inc. They were always the most intense and deep of the dictated communications that were now daily occurrences in her life (a few of them appear later in this book).

The year 1967 was magical for Jennie, wondrous in many ways. It had gone well beyond the "normal" scope of what she had earlier accepted as the "normal" limits of human life. The many Messages, dreams, visions, healings, and the expanding of her mind and scope defined a new, broader normality, one that most people would never believe or accept as truth. However, she didn't concern herself as to whether or not others believed what was happening to her, because she sensed that this Special Blessing was definitely of God's Truth.

"However, one deep disappointment I felt," Jen reflected, "had to do with my husband's response to all this. During the first four or five months since November 11th, Mike showed little interest in talking about the mystical 'earthquake' in my life. He kept his distance from this topic, but at times he became quite irritable, skeptical, and upset. He admitted that he didn't understand any of the Messages. He further admitted that all of this 'magical hocus-pocus' was illogical and unbelievable. Inevitably, there was a confrontation. Much as he had earlier refused to permit me to pursue the operatic career, he was beginning to insist that I no longer share any of these 'strange things' with other people, expressing anger when I did. I finally reached my 'boiling point,' warning him to be careful *not* to force me to make a choice between him and pursuing my spiritual path."

"When I expressed my determination so directly, he backed down, and finally explained the energy behind his defensive behavior. His love and respect for me was so strong that he did not want to see me ridiculed or attacked by an unbelieving public. He felt that his job was to shield and protect me, to spare me what he believed was an inevitable public embarrassment. He then affirmed that if this were my chosen course, then he would be my protector, but that I should not expect him to comprehend what was happening to me. Sadly, he said, 'I am not smart enough to understand all of this.' For the rest of our years together, Mike, true to his word, was a staunch supporter, facilitating my inspired mystical journey, even if from a respectful distance."

Nevertheless, during this otherwise "magical" time, the Messages and the encounters were always a part of her, even as Jennie was engaged in the mundane tasks of maintaining her household. She put love into everything she did. Suddenly, life seemed more special and meaningful than ever before, even when she was doing down-to-earth chores like cleaning the toilet or doing the grocery shopping. On that following Saturday, aware that she was running out of fresh produce, she decided to drive to the farmers' market.

Aunt Jen later related the following astounding experience:

"The farmers' market was located in the neighboring town of Broomall, about three miles away. It was opened only on Wednesdays and Saturdays. On this Saturday morning, I had purchased several bags of fresh fruits and veggies, and got back into my car to return home. I had driven less than a mile, concentrating on the early morning traffic, when suddenly, my windshield was no longer visible. The face of Christ had replaced it! While the face itself remains inscribed in my mind, I cannot truly describe it. How can one find the correct words to define a face that is pouring out Divine Love? I am not sure I know the meaning of Divine Love, but I certainly *felt* its completeness. Any picture or painting that I have seen of Him has been with dark hair and a beard, but to me, He was presented as having long, soft, medium to light brown hair with golden highlights. He was also strangely beardless. I cannot give the color of His eyes – I was only aware of being drawn into an all-encompassing light. To my utter amazement, I whispered, 'My Lord.' I think I even had the audacity to smile!"

Jen continued to recollect this amazing experience. "From the first moment that my windshield was occupied by the Lord's face, I felt that the car was being driven by remote control. As I gazed at His visage, it slowly came toward my face. When it was about four inches away from mine, it turned around with the back of His head facing me, and then suddenly, superimposed itself on my head. As far-fetched as this *must* sound, His head was now mine, or should I say vice-versa. With the car sailing along smoothly and the wind coming through the open windows, His hair was moving with the light breeze. His hair was caressing my neck and shoulders. I put up my hand to move the hair, which flowed toward my face. It was, oh so silky! I then looked at my hands on the steering wheel. They weren't mine! I was so overjoyed (or perhaps a little crazy) that I removed those hands from the wheel and studied them, palms up and then down, marveling over this phenomenon. The car drove itself home. Being in an altered state, I felt this was the most natural thing in the world. I finally realized that my car had come to a stop in my driveway. As I changed position, I became aware that it was just old me again."

Jen reflected, "I was in some sort of trance-like state for the next three days, barely talking to my husband. I don't think that Mike had ever experienced my being so silent. I couldn't bring myself to talk to anyone about what I had experienced. I lived in this tranquil, beautifully joyous reverie for days, and everything I saw, be it animate or inanimate, bore the face of Our Lord, including Vicki, my dog. It all seems inadequate, expressing myself in this ordinary language, but the best I can say is that there has never been anything in my life that can even come close to the feeling of the quiet joy and humbleness of the Grace bestowed on me that day. Increasingly, I was learning that there is so much more to life than I could ever have imagined!"

CHAPTER SEVEN

FELLOW SEEKERS FORM A SEARCH FOR GOD GROUP...

S pring break was late that year, and the summer-like weather inspired me to do something special for Aunt Jen, before returning to Bucknell University. I knew how much my aunt enjoyed the unique beauty and fragrance of roses, so I invited her to join me to a local garden center. Together, we selected six or seven highly rated, hybrid tea rose bushes. It seemed that every color was represented among our selections, but the pink-tinged yellow "Peace Rose" was her favorite. I created a garden bed for these special plants, running along the yard fence line, in close proximity to her favorite chair on the backyard screened-in porch, where she might observe their growth and beauty throughout the summer months ahead. When the bed was completed, and the rose bushes were planted, labeled, and fertilized, together Aunt Jen and I conducted a little ceremony, dedicating this rose garden to Our Lord Jesus, seeking His protection and blessings upon these plants.

A month or so later, I received a telephone call from Aunt Jen, relating a truly astounding mystical experience she had, connected to this dedicated garden plot.

Aunt Jen explained, "I had a number of urgent chores to run that day, and was eager to finish the breakfast dishes so that I could get into my car and on the road. Suddenly a ferocious storm arose. The sky darkened, the wind gusted, and the rain pelted down loudly. I grew worried as the wind velocity increased and the unexpected storm seemed to take on a dangerous intensity. I instantly thought of our newly dedicated rose bushes, and ran to my porch to check on them. To my horror, I saw that the wind was wildly whipping the delicate stems and branches of these new plantings, and I feared that they would be damaged."

"In seconds, I felt a transformative deep and powerful stillness rising up within me and overshadowing me," Jen continued. "I found myself pointing to the rose bed, and with a calm, confident and somewhat imperious tone, I spoke to the storm, *demanding* that it must stop its assault on Jesus' garden. *Immediately*, the area around the rose bushes appeared to be enclosed within an invisible protected zone. While the shrubs and trees on all sides of the rose bed continued to flail about in the raging storm, the rose plants were suddenly still and untouched by either the wind or the rain. As I regained my composure, I continued to watch these dedicated plants, as they remained safe and unmoved, until the brief but powerful storm wound down and the clouds rolled away."

As incomprehensible as this account seems, I am reminded that the disbelief we humans routinely attach to paranormal events, is typically a defense mechanism to protect our delicate egos. But who are we to question or to limit the Power of the Universe? Aunt Jen was shaken by this experience, but at the same time, filled with a renewed confidence that we are heard, we are loved, and we are all intricately bound to the Oneness of Creation.

After spring break, I reluctantly returned to Bucknell to pick up the burden of scholastic routines and the pressures of graduate school. Through the extraordinary exchanges with Aunt Jen and the Guides, I had been blessed with a tiny taste of the sweetness and grandeur of the Great Beyond. *That* new world occupied all of my thoughts. Experimental design, learning theory, and statistics paled in contrast. Yet, I *had* to study, attend classes and seminars, write papers, complete assignments, and get started on my Master's Thesis. So, I did my work, and I was successful at it; however, my mind, heart, and soul longed to be learning much grander things. This new intense hunger outstripped anything I had ever felt before.

On April 15, 1967, a week or so after my return to the University, Aunt Jen called me to say that a new Guide was coming through, one who was especially for me. She described him as being funny and playful. She even said that when he came through, she felt a bubble of happiness and humor, accompanied by the rapid wiggling of her writing arm, a sensation that continued until she could find the yellow tablet and pen. This playfulness made her laugh. His initial Message to me was as follows:

Has thou passed thy grades? Has thou really studied as thou should have? Ah, so many wheels has thou been moving and so many trails are emerging in thy waving brains of matter! I am delighted with thy struggles, and I laugh with glee at thy plodding. Such a faithful servant, but with a mind to accomplish deeds. Grow on, oh eager soul, as though thou would know whence thou travels. Someone will thou seek, but I shall remain illusive always to goad you on to new heights. See, there is a high mountain peak, and this you will try to scale, but look out for the falling stones that would try to harm thee. Thou does not get angry because I tease thee, but I take pleasure in tugging your tethers – it's a sensation likened to tickling! Is it not humorous?

Do not be fooled by light patter because there is
an intense depth to all creation even in the lightest
vein. I have started something today and now I will
leave thee to ponder.

Ho, hum-------

Your Loving Soul,
W------------

I subsequently received communications from "W" or
"Twinkle," as he identified himself, almost weekly throughout the
balance of 1967. He started out treating me as if I were a child who
needed to be supported and entertained, but most importantly,
to be "shaped." Being an elementary education major, I was not
unfamiliar with techniques for stimulating young children to
become more responsible and independent learners. In the vast
scheme of things, *I was but a child*!

Whenever Aunt Jen called to read yet another greeting from
him, she openly laughed. Though I found the content and the
tenor of the Messages from "W" to be of a more serious nature than
Aunt Jen did, I knew that this was a good thing for us both. Being
more than 100 miles away, I needed the continuing contact with
the Guides. Being intense and under pressure, Aunt Jen needed the
relaxing and sometimes humorous influence of this new Teacher.

The coursework continued to be intense and demanding, but
'W' kept me balanced, interrupting my long stretches of hard work
with a touch of humor, warmth, prodding, and enlightenment. The
more exposure I had to this wonderful spirit, the more important
he became to me. He usually addressed me as, "Mon Ami," and
I called him, 'W' for many years to come. Once, when I asked
what "W" stood for, his reply through Aunt Jen was a mysterious:

"W could stand for Warrior." However, especially during that first year, he purposefully signed off his greetings and lessons in many different ways, each making a different symbolic point, including the words, names, and even the number of dashes:

- *Your Loving Soul, W------------*
- *Your most loving Soul and brother in love*
- *Thy cherubic friend, Shall we say, Twinkle*
- *Thy down-grading fellow soul at this moment, Wings*
- *Thine Own Twinkle*
- *Thy beloved friend*
- *Thine dear Twinkle of so many ways*
- *Thy Winged Father*
- *Thy long awaited Twinkle of Magnificence*
- *Thy sighing Twinkle of Greatness*
- *Thy Twinkle of thy soul*
- *Thy warm-hearted Keeper*
- *Thy trusting soul – Warm-hearted angel*
- *Thine own Twinkle of Heart*
- *Thy lifelong toiler, Heartbeat*
- *I am now thy dear embracing W-----*
- *Thine own Beloved in brotherly fashion, W------------???*
- *Thy faithful trust*
- *Thine Own W---*
- *I am thy bona fide life*

In reading through all of W's 1967 communications to me in one sitting, the Great Potter-like shaping process he lovingly conducted becomes clear. Though surface humor was long a part of his Writings and oral communications, Aunt Jen and I eventually came away laughing less, realizing that *everything* he said, whether humorous or serious, was of tremendous depth, containing lessons to be learned. "W" eventually became the most frequent and active of the twenty or thirty Teachers who graced us over the years; however, it was not until 2007 that "W" revealed his true identity to Aunt Jen.

Throughout this time Jen continued attending workshops and presentations at Parastudy, which became a major resource for her. A small, tight-knit group of students was forged, as they pursued course after course at Parastudy, especially under the leadership of Hadassah, who at ninety years old, was held in high esteem as a wise and revered teacher.

Together this group attended workshops in dream analysis and dream symbolism. There were courses in discovering the esoteric meanings behind the Grimm fairy tales, nursery rhymes, and selected literature such as *Alice in Wonderland*. They learned about auras and chakras. Workshops were offered on Bible-related studies, including a long and intense examination of the hidden messages within the New Testament Book of Matthew. In addition, the group struggled with the dense occult philosophical writings of Marc Edmund Jones, the founder of the Sabian Assembly, an organization dedicated to helping humans to progress spiritually. Parastudy continued to offer a number of excellent speakers and presentations over the years.

One guest speaker at Parastudy inadvertently answered a question that had been bothering Jen since that Halloween evening of 1966, when she suffered a ferocious headache and experienced the frightening encounter with the "fiery mask." Jen recalled, "A rather kindly, handsome, silver-haired elderly man, whose name I have sadly forgotten, delivered a presentation entitled, 'Mystics and Mysticism Down Through the Ages.' Needless-to-say, given my own experiences and my long-time interest in the lives of saints and mystics, I was eager to learn what he had to say on the topic. Though I have since forgotten most of the content of his talk, one thing caught my attention, providing a satisfying answer to a personal quandary. He emphasized that many mystics reported that shortly before their special gifts unfolded, they had experienced painful headaches or body aches, as well as other unusual physical and paranormal visions and events. He hypothesized that these experiences were possibly explained as being the human system undergoing a shift, needing to make adjustments in order to accommodate the new, higher-level vibrations. That was good enough for me! Since, at one point, I secretly feared the events of that unforgettable night were something less than being of heavenly origin, his words brought resolution and comfort. Now, it made sense! It was true that the experiences of the headache and the fiery mask, seemed to be the catalyst that changed my life for the better."

Jen recalled, "After class one day, I sat with Hadassah, our wise teacher, to ask for her advice and suggestions about how I could learn more about what was happening to me. There was no one I respected more! Hadassah reassured me that based upon her observations of me during the months we shared in classes together, she felt that I was the 'genuine article.' That was very comforting, especially coming from her! Sensing that I needed more convincing, she suggested an excellent hypnotist who had been used by Parastudy for past life regressions and deep analysis. She was certain that he might be helpful to me in my search. Well, I have to say that I was not comfortable with the idea of being hypnotized, but given Hadassah's confidence in him, I decided to take his card and make an appointment."

"Two weeks later, on a Saturday in July (1969), I nervously entered the hypnotherapist's office, accompanied by my support team, Virge and Conrad, and a list of questions I wanted to have answered. Conrad promised to make sure they were asked on my behalf and to take detailed notes. After telling the therapist why I was there and what I was hoping for, we began. I was practically shaking!"

Mom and I watched closely, as the hypnotist *attempted* to put Aunt Jen into a hypnotic trance. She resisted! It clearly took more time and effort than the therapist anticipated, as Aunt Jen's pulse raced, and her body tensed and twitched. When she finally spoke, much to *his* surprise, it was the authoritative voice of one of her Guides, *not* Aunt Jen's normal speaking voice.

The following Q & A exchanges are excerpted from the hour-long hypnosis session to give the reader a sense of what unfolded that afternoon:

Q: Whenever you're ready, begin to speak...
A: I do not know thee (pause). I will have her speak to thee (pause). She is in a course of upheaval. The heart betrays its pulsation. Too rapid (pause). Thou may try.

Q: We are trying to find the source of this wisdom...
A: Be assured the Command is of great help. It is a direct guidance of the Highest Source. (*At this point, Jen's pulse spiked and her discomfort showed. After she calmed...*). Thou may question.

Q: Should Genevieve have regular hypnotic sessions to get at the wisdom?
A: The individual gets the information from the sphere of the Beyond. What is Beyond cannot be incorporated through this scope.

Q: She wants to know that this is not coming from her...
A: Dost not the subconscious tap that which is of the subconscious? Dost thou not know the degrees by which information is communicated from one to the other? Thou knows the meaning of life, dost thou not? Life is but one beginning from one part to the other part – such as a stage.

Q: She wants to know why she was picked to do this…
A: Be assured that this individual could not assume this role had it not been patterned in this degree and scope.

Q: Could you give us more of your wisdom?
A: Wisdom is but to be plucked from the vein. It is there if people but look to the degree of actually seeing. So shall it be manifested unto them. Be assured that thy help is noted. Our peace unto thee.

It was clear to Mom and me that the hypnotist had begun the session with great self-confidence and control, but as the session progressed, he became increasingly subdued by the authority of the Speaker. With regard to what came through Aunt Jen during hypnosis, it seemed to us to be a validation that she had been selected and prepared for this new role, that the Guides were of a Sublime Source, and that the process involved some sort of communication between her subconscious and the great Unconscious. When we shared all of this with Aunt Jen on our drive back to her home, it was clear that many questions remained in her mind, and that hypnosis was not among the answers.

Over time, Jen found great solace and support from the real sources of help at Parastudy. Jen remembered, "I liked the women in our group at Parastudy. Our small but solid cluster of eight to ten ladies literally spent years together, learning about the metaphysics of life, much of which was admittedly over my head. As much as I both liked and respected them, I was nevertheless a bit self-conscious in their presence. I was the only member who did not have a college degree. In comparison to all the others, some of whom had large houses and even second homes, I was the poorest. All of them were well-travelled, one even having spent a year in India, studying with a guru, while I had rarely left the Pennsylvania, Delaware, and New Jersey tri-state area. In spite of those socio-economic and educational differences, the ladies saw a great deal more in me than I saw in myself."

"In our weekly dream workshop where each of us was to relate one dream we had that week, giving the class ample practice at symbolic dream analysis, they all eagerly anticipated my turn. They raved about my dreams, saying that none of their dreams could even begin to match the complexity of my dream stories. When they learned about my visions and the fact that I had begun to channel, they conspired to help me even more."

Jen continued, "After class one day, Mary Ann, a member of our group with an especially beautiful home and landscaped grounds a few miles from Parastudy, invited us to her place for desserts. After enjoying the treats, the ladies set up a circle of chairs in the expensively furnished French provincial living room. I thought nothing about their activity, until Mary Ann announced it was the right time for them to help provide proof that I had more gifts and talents than I suspected. Mary Ann handed me her key chain, sat back down, and simply said, 'Jen, give me a reading, now!'"

"I was flummoxed, not knowing what to say or do. If I had not already developed a trusting relationship with each of them, I would have found a reason to make a hasty retreat. As it was, on that day, by plan, Lois, who lived near me, drove me to Parastudy. I was trapped!"

"After telling the women that I cared deeply about them, I declared that I was in no way capable of giving readings, as they had hoped. Of course, in less than ten seconds from those words having left my mouth, remarkably, I began to give my first reading! I told Mary Ann not to worry, that although her second home in the mountains of North Carolina (which I hadn't known about) had recently suffered severe damage from a large fallen oak tree, she should trust the company she had hired to make repairs, and that all would be properly restored before the month was out."

"There was a stillness in the room until Mary Ann confirmed that my reading was completely accurate. She acknowledged having had doubts about the company, as Jen indicated, but said that Jen's words settled her mind. The round of applause and encouragement from the ladies was immediately followed by each of the other women offering me an object -- one a purse, one a ring, one a watch, and another a photograph -- in order to facilitate my readings by psychometry, or sensing the vibrations of a person from an object of importance to them. So there I found myself confidently providing personal details for each one of my friends."

"My 'psychic readings' told one of the women details about a recently deceased relative; to another, I reported that, unknown to her, her twin sons were having academic difficulty in their boarding school; to another, details about a recent inheritance. I don't remember what else I said. I could not grasp how it all happened! How could I have possibly known that stuff? My head was swimming! I was far more amazed than any of them at my confidence and about the accuracy of my readings. Apparently, I was the only surprised person in the room! They knew that I would not have taken the risk to try that on my own. I must admit that I appreciated their sensitive help, feeling like a baby bird being pushed out of the safety of the nest by its mother in order to take its first flight."

"Afterwards, I was struck by the realization that these psychic readings seem to be coming from *me*, rather than from the Guides. Perhaps it was my 'Higher Self' or my subconscious reaching out to theirs to gather the answers. There was no voice or dictating figure, as with the Messages. This 'forced' experience was really responsible for helping me to begin to learn the subtle difference between the *psychic* that comes from Soul and the *mystic* that comes from the Beyond."

"Two weeks later, Miriam, the Parastudy class member to whom I felt closest, extended an invitation to treat me to a reading of my own from a highly-respected husband and wife psychic team, located in Delaware about a forty-minute drive away. Miriam and her husband Howard could not have been nicer people. Knowing their sincere intentions, I accepted their generous offer."

Miriam later retold the story of what transpired during that unusual afternoon. "I could tell that Jennie was nervous, wondering what would be revealed by the husband-wife team. When we arrived, the wife of the psychic pair was finishing with another client. The husband sat in a reclining chair, and seemed to be studying Jennie as we waited in the family room. Finally, nodding confidently to himself, I saw the husband reach for a framed black-and-white photograph of a man. He passed it to Jen. Jennie politely looked at the photo. Similar to what had happened with the group of us at Mary Ann's home two weeks earlier, this psychic asked Jennie to hold the photo and to tell us about the man. Jennie blanched, and I suffered a vicarious attack of nerves on her behalf, wondering what would happen next!"

Miriam continued, "Of course, Jennie had come here for a reading, but the tables were being turned. Jen tried to object, but in spite of herself, she announced that it was a photo of Albert, his wife's half-brother."

The psychic nodded in agreement, asking her to continue. "Jennie proceeded to tell him that Albert and his psychic half-sister – who by then had walked the other client to the door -- had been estranged over an argument they had more than a year earlier. The husband brought his wife up to speed, and the woman sat on the sofa, clearly growing irritated with both Jen and her husband as Jen's reading continued. The man kept prodding Jen for more details. As though she had been giving readings all her life, Jennie confidently launched into a few historical points about the woman and her half-brother, the nature of the dispute, and basically blamed the woman for the estrangement, firmly suggesting that it was time for reconciliation. By that point, the female psychic was about to storm out of the room, but her husband insisted that she wait for one more test."

Miriam continued, "At that point, the man handed Jen a key ring, asking her to tell him the use of each one. I felt such pride in Jennie, as, one by one, Jen accurately told them about each key, concluding with a little key, which Jennie said was for a secret lock box. She paused, looking around the room, then pointed, announcing that the small box was hidden in the bookshelf near the window. The man literally applauded for Jen, while his wife remained speechless."

"Before we left that afternoon, Jen had new proof of her growing gifts. All the way home to Jen's place in Havertown, we laughed repeatedly about the irony that Jennie had given the famous psychic readers a reading of their own! I couldn't wait to share this amazing story with the other ladies in our group at Parastudy."

Of course, Jen was also eager to share this account with Virge, Georgie and Ruth Ann.

"That night," Jen later explained, "I had a dream about a woman who was identified as Georgie's neighbor. In the dream, I was helping this neighbor to wash her clothes. She had them in washtubs that were spilling soapy suds and water onto the floor. I kept rinsing out everything for her, and eventually, with my help, the task was completed."

"When I woke up that next morning," Jen continued, "I knew that I was going to receive a Writing for this supposed neighbor of Georgie. I *did* receive a short writing, and afterwards, decided to drive over to Georgie's place in Upper Darby (an adjoining township), to learn whether or not there was such a neighbor who needed my help. Georgie told me to accompany her, as we walked directly across the street and knocked on the neighbor's front door."

"Shirleybelle, Shirley for short, answered the door, greeting Georgie and me with a warm southern welcome. In her forties, she was perky, warm, and gregarious. Upon sharing the Message I had received for her that morning, Shirley sobbed heavily, saying that this Message was surely '…sent from God.' Recently laid off from her office job, she was feeling distraught and lost. She said that the Message was the comfort she needed!"

Jen continued, "Shirley made tea, and served slices of her delicious Southern strawberry lattice pie. The three of us talked for hours! Clearly, the process of becoming good friends had begun."

Not long after having received her personal Message from the Guides, Shirley volunteered to type the growing collection of Messages, since being unemployed gave her the time to dedicate to this tedious task. Shirley dutifully and patiently transcribed well over 100 Messages, making seven copies of each one. What a service of love and patience, particularly since she had to sandwich layers of onionskin paper and carbons to make multiple copies. There were no Xerox machines back then!

With Shirley's unexpected offer to type, Jen was reminded of Father Baptist's recent words, "Thy scope is of a wide range and helpers will come into view very shortly…" Coincidence?

Over the next weeks, Jen socialized frequently with Georgie, Shirley, and Ruth Ann. Enjoying hours of spiritual discussion, they decided to create a "Search for God" group. That following Friday night, Jennie invited her sister, Virge, to join the other ladies for their first official meeting to be held at Georgie's place.

Jennie remembers, "Although we all got along famously, at first, we didn't know quite what to do. We prayed, talked about religion vs. spirituality, and shared observations about the place of religion in our lives and how that correlated with our personal concept of God. At one point, I started feeling restless, sensing that a Message might actually come through for the group. Recognizing my need, as she always did, Virge moved the tablet and pen closer to me; however, by then the Guides must have decided to watch and listen, rather than to intervene."

"By the next week's meeting, we began to formalize the proceedings, adding a meditation segment. During the meditation, as the others sat with their eyes closed, breathing deeply, the Guides came through me, giving us a warm greeting, which I wrote on the yellow legal pad."

"By the time late May had rolled around, our group had expanded. Though we had lost Ruth Ann, who had to temporarily relocate out of state to care for her elderly father, Georgie's husband, John, a Commodore in the U.S. Coast Guard, expressed interest in joining the group. Shirley's husband, Raymond, a medical lab technician, joined us, feeling that he could contribute to the group, having received a few inspired poems of his own. By then, Conrad was home from Bucknell for a few weeks of summer break. Of course, he joined the group."

As mentioned earlier, by this time, a few of the communications from the Guides were coming through Aunt Jen orally, though most were still written. When that happened, the Guides internally spoke to their channel, and their channel dutifully and accurately repeated the lessons, word for word, to the group (much as was described earlier in the definition of "amanuensis"). This was perfect for a group meeting because it facilitated a question and answer format. Initially, few of us felt the courage to speak, as we were in awe of the Teachers.

I remember that, at the first meeting I attended, we lit a white candle, as the Guides had suggested to Jen. Then holding hands, we recited the Lord's Prayer in unison. The Guides did come through briefly, orally welcoming us and blessing this new venture. They emphasized that there is true power-potential, when a group of like-minded people, gather together in love and common prayer. I also remember the group's deep and respectful silence, as the Teacher spoke. Then the Teacher privately dictated a Message to Aunt Jen, which she wrote down on the ever-ready yellow tablet. The rest of our time was spent discussing the newly-delivered Message and applying it to our lives, as the Guides had requested.

Over the summer months, our group met almost weekly on Friday nights, taking turns hosting in each of our homes. By mid-July, the Guides had suggested a few procedural modifications. They dictated an "Opening Prayer" and a "Closing Prayer," to be chorally recited at all future meetings:

Opening Meeting Prayer

Bless us, Father, with thy heavenly rays,
Enfold us in love and invoke thy will,
Enlighten our thoughts to travel thy ways;
We seek to serve so that we may fulfill.
Commit unto us our prayers as one;
Not our will, Father, but thy will be done.

Closing Meeting Prayer

We thank thee, Dear Father, for thy care,
Thou hast guided and sent forth thy Light,
Out hearts are cleansed of worry and fear;
Unto this night thou hast shown thy might,
Lead us where thou will, Father of Peace,

Glory on High, thy praises increase.

The Guides further suggested a set agenda for future meetings. I include it here in case any of my readers are thinking of starting a prayer group, and are looking for format suggestions:

1. CLEAR LUNGS with deep breathing
2. Recite the LORD'S PRAYER aloud as a group
3. Recite the 23rd PSALM aloud as a group
4. Discussion
5. Recite the OPENING PRAYER
6. Period of MEDITATION, followed by the deep discussion of a MESSAGE
7. Recite the CLOSING PRAYER

Most interesting of all, The Guides assigned a specific seating order around the table, provided each of us with a "Spiritual Name" that we were directed to use exclusively during meetings, and also, gave each of us an assigned color. We were to be seated as follows, going clockwise, starting with the head of the table:

Jennie, known as VERITY; color: WHITE
Conrad, known as ARMAND; color: RED
Raymond, known as BJORN; color: ORANGE
Shirley, known as BETAL; color: GREEN
John, known as, ANJOH; color: LT. BLUE
Georgie, known as AVESTA; color: INDIGO
Virge, known as BLASILDA; color: VIOLET

The significance of the names was as a symbol of a baptismal blessing, signifying a new beginning in life, much as Christian babies receive a new name at baptism. We later learned that the names were also numerologically linked, suggesting an even deeper meaning, the significance of which will be discussed shortly.

As we soon realized, there was much to be learned about the symbolism behind the Guides' assignment of colors and the associated seating arrangement, but before discussing these topics further, let's examine what we know about the colors of light.

As we may remember from both science and art classes, there are seven colors defining the electromagnetic wavelengths of visible light. They are red, orange, yellow, green, blue, indigo, and violet. "ROY G BIV" is the common acronym people use for remembering these same seven colors that appear in order, in a rainbow. They are from red, the lowest frequency of visible electromagnetic energy to violet, the highest. Invisible infrared energy lies below the vibration of red, and invisible ultraviolet energy lies above violet.

In art classes we learned that there are three primary colors: red, yellow, and blue. Secondary colors, like orange, green, and purple, are created by mixing primary colors (e.g. green is created by mixing blue and yellow). When all three primary colors of light (not of paint) are combined, the result is white light. It is, therefore, easy to interpret why white was the color assigned to Aunt Jen/Verity. White, being the presence of all primary colors, clearly connected to the fact that the Pure Light of the Guides was present in her as our channel. When white is added to a color, the result is a "tint" (such as pink, the color of Love, from the combination of red and white). When black is added to a color, the result is a "shade" (such as dark blue, from a combination of blue and black).

As we later learned, the assigned colors were also linked to the progression of colors of the body's energy centers, called chakras (about which none of us had any understanding at that point in time). Not surprisingly, we learned that the colors of light energy associated with the seven chakras follows the same "ROY G BIV" pattern. At this point, it seems appropriate to provide a quick summary of chakras, which might be helpful to some of my readers:

- Root Chakra, RED, located at the base of the spine and associated with life foundational energy, passion, and survival issues (much as the red blood in our body)

- Sacral Chakra, ORANGE, located about two inches below the navel and associated with our ability to connect with and accept others, as well as feeling a sense of abundance.

- Solar Plexis Chakra, YELLOW, located in the upper abdomen in the stomach area and associated with personal confidence and self-esteem.

- Heart Chakra, GREEN, located just above the heart, and associated with our ability to love and find joy and peace. It is the central chakra or bridge between the lower three and the upper three chakras.

- Throat Chakra, LIGHT BLUE, located at the throat and associated with communication and expressions of truth.

- Third Eye Chakra, INDIGO, located between the eyes on the forehead and associated with seeing the big picture, intuition, wisdom, and decision-making.

- Crown Chakra, VIOLET, located at the top of the head and associated with our full ability to be connected spiritually with inner and outer beauty and the pursuit of bliss.

In short, our "Search for God Group" members were arranged by the Guides to represent the full circle of life's energies and vibrations, with each member providing the vibrational contributions of his/her name, number, and color, providing our group of seven with a symbolic vibrational completeness. The Guides noted that the color of yellow was unassigned, but that our Teachers would provide the yellow, especially given that yellow is also a symbol for Wisdom. As we discovered, the Guides chose wisely, matching our personality types to the names, numbers, and colors as well. Coincidence?

I remember that after the Opening Prayer at the following Meeting, the Guides, speaking through Aunt Jen, addressed each of us in turn, asking us to name a fruit or a vegetable that we could envision to represent our color as a means of helping us to visualize our assigned light-energy. Given that I sat next to Aunt Jen/Verity, and that my color, red, was the first in the sequence, I was the first person to be put on the spot. Though I somehow sensed that the Guide expected me to say, "a red apple," I decided instead to say, "pomegranate." He asked me to explain why I chose that fruit. I remember nervously explaining that when a pomegranate is opened, a dense cluster of red, jewel-like, juicy seeds is revealed. He commented that this was an unexpected answer, but a good one, particularly with regard to my seeing the vibrant red energy within, rather than without. We each had a turn at this exercise that evening, and the Guides directed us to meditate on our colors, using the images of the fruits or vegetables. This activity, they suggested, would contribute to the power of the Group energy as a whole.

The amazing part was that in time we saw how our color roles matched our personalities and aligned with the nature of our contributions to the group. For example, Virge/Blasilda, my mother, who was assigned the color of the Crown Chakra, the highly spiritual royal purple or violet, was consistently the member of the group who naturally led our conversations to spiritual linkages. She reminded us of the Greatness of God, and the awesome gifts He had given to each of us. Aunt Jen and I often observed how my mother's natural preacher-like spiritual fervor provided a supportive backbone to all that proceeded through Aunt Jen from the very beginning, which is why, as mentioned earlier, we lovingly nicknamed her, "John the Baptist."

Shirley/Betal, who was assigned the color of green that is associated with the heart chakra -- that is the bridge, balancing the more physical colors (red, orange, and yellow), with the more spiritual colors (light and dark blue, and violet) -- influenced our group discussions by reminding us of our need to balance our physical realities and limitations, with our spiritual aspirations. Shirley had one foot on earth and the other one in "heaven." She could talk about something as earthy as sex, yet link it to its highest spiritual potential. That is how she represented her role in the group, and we were better off for her influential, balancing role.

As a final example of this color-role connection, the contribution of my assigned color red was represented in the passion or energy that I apparently brought to the group, encouraging active discussion and keeping the energy alive and pulsing during the meeting.

The more we studied and learned about the nature of man and of life, the more amazing and grand it all became! Life was becoming so complex, so fascinating, so expansive, and so exciting, especially since the formation of the Group. We also grew in comfort with one another and with the Messages and Guidance but we never lost the awe we felt for the Teachers or the Writings.

Complexity was added with the introduction of the symbolic significance of numerology. The Guides used numbers to convey specific thoughts that They wanted us to understand. They encouraged us to remember numbers, especially those that came to us in dreams, as well as to think about numbers in daily life and decisions. As with the meaning behind our assigned colors, we also grew to better understand the meaning and vibration of the numbers that were associated with our group names and the numbers embedded in the Messages from the Guides, in Bible passages (like the "7-loaves and 7-fishes" in one of Jesus' parables), and in other symbolic writings of any genre. I think I can speak for the Group when I say that this was a totally new concept for us.

For the benefit of those readers who are unfamiliar with the ancient study of spiritual numerology, and as a means of delivering an important lesson that the Guides wanted us to learn, the following overview should be a helpful break in the flow of our story.

In short, the process of "casting out nines" has been used for millennia, especially by esoteric mystery religions, to reduce any multi-digit number down to a single digit or vibration (or two in the case of "master numbers" like 11, 12, or 22). For example, if the street address number of your home were 1438, we could determine that the vibration number of that address is a "7," by adding the digits until we get down to one digit (1+4+3+8=16, then 1+6= "7"). Seven is a highly spiritual number, symbolically used *many* times in the Bible, as a "red flag" of spiritual import.

The numerology system of "casting out nines" works by the fact that mathematically adding a nine (9) to any number reverts back to that other number (Example: 49: 4+9=13, then 1+3=4), so, in a sense, we could just "cast out the 9" in 49, leaving us with the 4. The exception to that is when the total sum results in an 11, 12, or 22, which are considered to be "master numbers." (Example: 39: 3+9=12; we hold at "12," a master number, rather than to add 1+2=3).

As with the address example, taking a name and finding its number meaning is as easy. Let's take Jen's Group Name,

VERITY, to determine its significance as intended by the Guides, when assigning it to her.

We begin by making nine columns, 1 to 9, and writing out all twenty-six letters of the alphabet to fill in the table as follows:

1	2	3	4	5	6	7	8	9
A	B	C	D	E	F	G	H	I
J	K	L	M	N	O	P	Q	R
S	T	U	V	W	X	Y	Z	

Logically, we then record the number value of each letter in the name, based upon the table:

V=4 E=5 R=9 I=9 T=2 Y=7,
Then add: 4+5+9+9+2+7=36, then: 3+6= "**9**"

Verity is a name that vibrates to the number **9**, which in spiritual numerology means reaching the end of the cycle (1 to 9), before beginning a new higher level of work (10 would be next, but, given that 1+0=1, that is a new 1, or a higher beginning, after having gone from 1 to 9 before that. In music we would describe that as being a higher octave. Aunt Jen's life certainly reflected the meaning of the number 9 to all of us. She represented the highest level of experience, embracing *all* nine steps in manifestation.

I find it to be especially fascinating to take one's given first name, then the preferred nickname, and compare the numbers. A change in name usually suggests a change in vibration that explains how our lives alter course over time. For example, let's take the name, Joseph. A young man might live with that name (which vibrates to the number "1") for a number of years, before replacing that given name with a preferred nickname, like Joe (which vibrates to the master number "12"). Clearly, in a case of changing to "Joe," his life's focus could potentially alter dramatically as well, whether or not he is conscious of the vibrational impact. His feeling of comfort or "rightness" with the nickname may connect to his comfort with the new vibration of his changed life path. Fascinating stuff!

By now, I assume that the reader has already taken his/her name and figured out its numerological vibration number. Good for you! If not, please do this now.

Once you have this number, it is necessary to know the symbolic spiritual significance. Below, I have attempted to provide both the "Sublime" and "man's" levels of symbolic meaning of each number, with a real-life example showing how the increase in number represents a symbolic progression in the development of a thought or project in-progress. It is important to note that one number is not necessarily "better" than the others. They *all* have an important place in contributing to our understanding of the manifestation of life.

ZERO:

> **Sublime level:** Zero represents the Void of space, the Fertilized Egg, the <u>Potentiality</u> *prior* to the Creation. Chaos. The Abstract. God's awesome Potential power in waiting.
>
> **Man's level:** In man, it is a stillness, an emptiness of mind before an idea or plan is inspired. Discomfort/chaos in knowing something unidentified is wrong or needs to be created or developed.

ONE:

> **Sublime level:** The Will, the focus, the Word, the spark, light, knowledge; the initiating action. From the nothingness or the stillness comes the something...

Man's level: A spark/flash of <u>Inspiration/light</u>, or a new thought/idea/hope comes to mind. It is not yet formed, simply an idea in search of fulfillment. [e.g. I think I need a new suit].

TWO:

Sublime level: the Above and the below; the positive and the negative polarity.

Man's level: Given initial thought about a new idea, man sees the <u>polarity</u> of the idea (i.e. it could go this way or that way). Man ponders the possibilities and alternative directions for action, still in search of a plan. [e.g. Maybe I shouldn't spend the money on a suit; or Maybe I'll go to Men's Warehouse and actually buy one].

THREE:

Sublime level: The Trinity (Father-Will, Son-Love/Wisdom, Holy Spirit-Power/Life force); Activity from on High. A highly spiritual number. The triangle.

Man's level: As man picks a direction from the polarity (alternatives), he puts <u>energy and activity</u> into the mix. This thought activity empowers the idea, giving it three-dimensionality, as it nears form. [e.g. I will definitely look for the suit and will take myself to Men's Warehouse to look for a gray suit].

FOUR:

Sublime level: The Form; the creation itself.

Man's level: The outing of it into form (having grown through the process from zero-to-one-to-two-to-three). (2+2: two pairs/sides working together, bringing it together. 3+1: activity of the 3, plus the spark or the 1. A square number. The physical form. [e.g. I am at Men's Warehouse. I select a gray suit.].

FIVE:

Sublime level: The number of Man (made in God's image).

Man's level: The symbol of man. 5-appendages (as in DaVinci's drawing); 5-physical senses. The physical level. The 4+1 of the form (4) and a new thought (1) [e.g. *(4+1)* I like my new suit, and I hope for the blessing to look good in it when I'm all dressed up. (5) This suit is me!]

SIX:

Sublime level: (3+3) Activity from Above (Trinity/spiritual) being brought to bear on the matching activity below. (5+1) God inspiring (1) or blessing the form/creation of man (5).

Man's level: (5+1) Man's creation/representation (5) being blessed by light from above (1). (3+3) Man's activity matched by activity from Above [e.g. (3+3) I will get myself cleaned up, dressed in my suit through my activity (3) and invoke the Spirit to empower my appearance (3); others see His presence in me, mirroring/reflecting].

SEVEN:

Sublime level: A highly spiritual number in the Bible. (4+3) A form/creation (4) driven by the activity of the Trinity (3). A triangle on top of a square. Spiritual man.

Man's level: (7) A manifestation or completion. (4+3) Man's form/plan is sanctioned by the Trinity (3), or (5+2) Man (5) working with the polarity (2) of reaching a decision. [e.g. (7) I have fulfilled my plan to buy the suit. (4+3) I see how handsome and spiritual I feel in my new suit. I see a spiritual side to having decided to buy this suit].

EIGHT:

Sublime level: Form (4) as Above, reflected in form (4) Below. God's Creation in the Physical reflects his Plan from the Sublime. A higher octave. A square on a square.

Man's level: As Above, so below, in form. [e.g. (4+4) When I wear this suit I feel that I represent a spiritual presence/form as well. (7+1: taken up a level, exalted)].

NINE:

Sublime level: A complete manifestation; end of a cycle/project. (8+1) A "day of rest" follows the completion of attaining the forms, above and below. (3+3+3) The activity of the Physical, Mental and Spiritual all acting together.

Man's level: A complete manifestation; end of a cycle/project. [e.g. (9) I have spiritualized the material of what started out as a purely physical idea; therefore, I have concluded my plan. (5+4) This man's creation (5) has a spiritual form (4)].

TEN:

> **Sublime level:** Taking a completed thought/product to the next level (really a new 1, rather than a 10).
>
> **Man's level:** Taking a completed plan to higher level, a new round, a new beginning, building on the past. Not physical. 1+0=1 [e.g. Knowing how good I feel in the suit, and the process I followed, especially because of its spiritual connotation, perhaps I should do that with more of my wardrobe... try shoes!].

ELEVEN:

> **Sublime level:** Mystical, Mastery number; magical, really working to perfection.
>
> **Man's level:** Mastery over an idea/plan [e.g. I have totally spiritualized the material of my clothing. I have mastered this idea].

TWELVE:

> **Sublime level:** Mystical, Mastery number; representation of the total perfection of the High Holy Trinity (1+2=3).
>
> **Man's level:** Mastery over an idea/plan [e.g. I have totally spiritualized the material of my clothing. I have mastered this idea with the inspiration of the Trinity].

As an example, the numerical vibration of my Spiritual name, Armand, is a "6." A "6" suggests a man (being the number "5"), who is being inspired by a spark (a "1") from Above; hence, 5+1=6. My job in the Group has been to spark discussion and inspire action. That, along with the meaning of my color, red, perfectly summarizes the passion of my leadership role in our Spiritual Groups.

As an aside, at the Meeting of our Group, on September 28, 2003, I presented the above table of interpretive numerology information to our members. After we discussed it, trying to apply this to our lives, "W" came through Aunt Jen to informally add a few observations about, and additions to this list, paraphrased as follows:

- ✓ This symbolism of number applies to anything in life!

- ✓ It progresses from one level to another.

- ✓ It helps in choosing friends/objects, reflecting some part of thee.

- ✓ Classical music is an "8," (as Above, so below), not so with rock & roll.

- ✓ Music affects the person. We urge you use Beethoven, Mozart...higher level vibrations... perfect balancing of ethers... works better with the inner being.

- ✓ The thought of the composer lies behind it. Notes are numbers—resounding.

- ✓ Not good or bad (i.e. classical vs. rock); seek the mood/purpose. If you wish to meditate, you would select music, which is different in vibration from when you want to dance.

- ✓ Use color, number, sensation, feeling to aide thee in all matters (e.g. planning a vacation or applying for a job...).

"W," my angel, sent me a greeting through Aunt Jen on many of my birthdays. I include part of one of his greetings here, to reinforce the symbolic use of numerology. Building upon the symbolism, on my 42nd birthday, on January 22, 1987, "W" said the following in the first paragraph of his greeting:

Mon Ami,

The year is special [1987 is a 7, a spiritual number] -- the day grand [22 is a mastery number] -- the number of spirit [42 is a 6], and also the extra number of ongoing [as 6 is an "extra" one above the number of man, a 5, as a spark of inspiration leading him onward to manifestation].

Aunt Jen commented that when she was in the card store looking for my birthday card, she was about to select a different one, when "W" led her to select the red and gold card she gave to me that year. As it turned out, during our discussion of "W's" greeting, he orally led us through an analysis of the picture drawn on the face of the card, asking us to count the number of birds, trees, and people. He turned that into yet another Message. What a wonderful gift that was, with the use of numerological symbolism as the key!

The more we grew in understanding that *everything means something*, and all of it was created by the Guides with clear forethought, the more impressed and humbled we felt to be a part of this great circle.

I hope that the reader learned something of personal value from that color-chakra-number detour, and even perhaps gained a deeper respect for the depth of intention of our Guides for the members of our Groups.

Over the years since 1967, there were three different Spiritual Groups. The members of the first group, as described earlier in this chapter, became close-knit and continued to meet for a number of years, both socially and for weekly meetings. Our first group dissolved in the mid-1970's for a number of understandable reasons; however, where there are endings there are usually beginnings.

On December 3, 1977, I married my Rosie.

Image #5: Rosie and Conrad, in the early marriage years
(Photo taken by Charles M. O'Neill, Rose's brother)

As "chance" would have it, in September of 1976, Rose was hired as a first year teacher in our school district, and I was assigned to be her mentor. After observing her teaching four or five times, I knew that we had hired a natural-born teacher. Though ours was a totally professional relationship at that point, by "coincidence," in January of 1977, Rose registered for a county-sponsored community outreach class on Metric Measurement, which the county *just happened* to ask me to teach. By the third of six evening classes, I asked Rose out on a date. By July, Rosie and I were engaged. By December we were married. When one finds the "right" match, why wait? Rose's deep well of human empathy, her intellect, her attractiveness, her sweet nature, and her compassion for disabled children and injured animals were all genuine and rare qualities that I found deeply appealing. It didn't take long for me to realize that like Aunt Jen, Rose and I were also soulmates. Later, the Guides confirmed that she and I had shared a number of lifetimes together. We recently celebrated our 38th Anniversary.

Within a year of our marriage, a second "Search for God" group was formed, composed of eight of our family members. Upon learning of their aunt's unique channeling experiences, two of Jennie's nieces, Sandy (a nickname for Santa) and Mert (a nickname for Marie), asked if it would be possible to form a "family group." Rose and I invited the new group of cousins to meet at our Havertown home for a series of monthly meetings. This new group of eight included: Aunt Jennie, Virge, my mom, Mert, Ted (Mert's husband), Sandy, Sandra-Lee (Sandy's daughter), Rosie and me.

While not delving into this special, loving and eager group, I wish only to emphasize the deep faith, open mind, and loving heart of Sandra-Lee, the youngest member. She (named ILA by the Guides, and given the unique color of "psychedelic," one that definitely fit her personality), maintained a close, mother-daughter type relationship with Aunt Jennie until the end of Jen's life in 2013. Sandra-Lee often refers to Aunt Jen as being "the mother of my heart." She was always a staunch supporter of Aunt Jen, and her manifestation of faith is without compare.

During the course of the meetings of this second group, the Guides informed us that four of us shared the *same* mighty guardian angel, although He had been known to us by different names. Jen/Verity had glimpsed her magnificent angel, "Big Chief." Virge/Blasilda had been told that her angel was to be called, "M." My angel was "W" (the flip of "M"). It was then revealed that Sandra-Lee/Ila

Image #6: Sandra-Lee (left) and Aunt Jen (right)

had the same great guardian angel. These four close group members felt a special connection from that point onward, and "W," the name he was now using for all four of us, remained the primary Teacher for the second and third meeting groups. However, as mentioned earlier, "W" did not reveal his true identity to us until 2007.

The "family group" dissolved after less than two years when Virge, Hank, Jennie and Mike moved to Florida in 1980-81. The two men, both skilled carpenters, had retired, and as was a customary dream at that time, retirement meant relocating to the Sunshine State. Neither of the sisters was supportive of this 1000-mile move away from their roots, their family members, and from their spiritual-family, but the two husbands prevailed, creating a break in group meetings and regular, on-going sessions with the Guides for a decade.

Photo #7: This is the best photo of Jen & Mike, a portrait that was taken by Olin Mills at their church, St. Sebastian Catholic Church, in Florida, in 1987.

I remember taking this separation especially hard. I kept in contact with these two influential women and visited them often, but it wasn't the same. In the interim, I focused on building my career in education, and my marriage to my dear Rosie.

"Life is to be lived..." (from "The First Message").

The third and current group -- about which more will be said in Chapter Ten -- started up after Virge, Hank, and Jen returned from Florida in 1990-91. As a leap forward in the story line, Mike had passed away in Sebastian, Florida in 1988, almost three years before Jen's return. Because of my parents' health issues, I convinced them to return to Pennsylvania, sadly leaving Aunt Jen alone in Florida for more than a year as she awaited a buyer for her home. While waiting to move back to Pennsylvania, Aunt Jen became the choir leader and lead singer in her local Catholic church. Finally, her soprano voice was on a stage of sorts. She also started a small Spiritual Group of interested Seekers from her church; however, that was a short-lived experience.

Life and The Potter has a way of managing our course and returning us to the pre-determined path. Such was the case for Jennie...

CHAPTER EIGHT

A CLOSER LOOK AT REINCARNATION AND OUR SACRED JOURNEY...

The concept of reincarnation is met with diverse reactions around the world. Though largely embraced in Eastern thought, based upon the ancient Hindu-Buddhist philosophy of the "transmigration of souls," it is only moderately accepted in the West. However, for the purposes of this book, I am making the assumption that the majority of my readers are at least open to the possibility of embracing, as a Truth, some variation of reincarnation.

Rather than attempt to justify the validity of reincarnation through logical argument or a lengthy review of historical and current documentation on the topic (frankly, none of which provides definitive proof), I have decided instead to launch into the heart of this issue by sharing with my readers what our Guides presented to us about the topic. *They* are my expert sources. Through Aunt Jen, our mystical channel, the gracious Guides have spoken somewhat openly about reincarnation and our Sacred Journey as spiritual beings. I think that it is fair to say that our Guides have validated the process of reincarnation as *the* vehicle through which we, as spiritual beings on a human journey, are progressing.

Therefore, based upon the Teachings of the Guides, it is my intention in this chapter to present a definitional sense of the concept of reincarnation with its associated Law of Karma, and how it is connected to the two-phase Sacred Journey of Evolution and Involution. I decided to present the discussion of these two important topics contained in a stand-alone chapter. Though this chapter could easily be extended to an entire book, I attempted to restrict this treatment to the key details shared by our Guides. Given that both reincarnation and our Sacred Journey are integral to our Guides' overall teachings about who we are and why we are here, I felt that spotlighting these interrelated topics in a separate chapter was justifiable.

Let us begin with a basic definition: The word *reincarnation* literally means (*re*)-again, (*in*)-into, (*carna*)-flesh, (*tion*)-process of; or the process of entering once again into the flesh/body. From an analytical point of view, the following beliefs are at the core of the concept of reincarnation:

- A belief in an eternal Soul

- A belief that the body is merely a temporary physical vehicle or "shroud" for the real soul within

- A belief in a goal-driven progression

- A belief in repeated lifetimes to reach the goal

- A belief in the Universal Law of Karma to regulate the progression of lifetimes

- A belief in achieving an ultimate Oneness with the Godhead

Before reaching the conclusion of this chapter, it is my hope to provide clarity about each of the above six elements.

As far back as February 26, 1967 (three months after the "First Message"), the Guides began an on-going discourse on the topic of reincarnation. The following Message, which was entitled "Reincarnation," will serve as a launching off point for this chapter:

2-26-67 *Reincarnation*

Hearken to the Voice – Look all around and see that I exist. Other times have borne witness to My Birth. I was not known as such. Masters of Religion do not always impart true facts. Each religion has its own belief – one part of the ALL. The ages have erased facts – the world has changed in its geographic scope – waters have come where cities dwelt – mountains have sprung up from stone.

Man exists in relation to his Self. How has the gift of the genius been borne: Does he not bespeak of time gone by? The World revolves and so does man – he evolves in the patterned rule. His makeup is not always the same but is granted a certain kinship. The soul's quest for itself begins its journey – Periods of time lapse and then begin anew. Meanwhile Time plays its role in changes. Moods and impressions add their toll in the behavior. Observation is from a different point of view. Life continues and the universe changes its appearance. Memories are forgotten; new things begin. Acceptance is free for some and an incurred debt to others. A blossoming

of ideas, but how to put it? Fear still reigns and
solitude is lost. The pattern still must go on then.
The ascending is for all but the gravities change its
course.

Though this Message only *indirectly* speaks to the process
of reincarnation and our Journey, it is easy to infer logical and
supportive conclusions from these quotes: "How has the gift of
the genius been borne: Does he not bespeak of time gone by?" and
"...other times have borne witness to My Birth;" and mankind
"...evolves in the patterned rule;" and "...periods of time lapse
and then begin anew;" and "...memories are forgotten; new
things begin." Though not definitive, this Message was especially
thought provoking at that time, because it was the first reference
to reincarnation by our Guides.

One of the clearest explanations of reincarnation came on the
evening of the infamous 9/11 terrorist attacks in New York City,
Washington D.C., and in western Pennsylvania. As Aunt Jen lay
on our living room sofa, recuperating from the previous day's
combination glaucoma and cataract surgery in her left eye, she and
I watched the uninterrupted television coverage of the horrifying
day's events. With deep emotion and anguish, Aunt Jen wondered
aloud how the senseless killing of nearly 3,000 people could be
explained.

'W' suddenly came through with words of comfort and the
clearest explanation of reincarnation I had heard or read from any
source. The following is reported from memory, given that this
lengthy oral discussion was not recorded or transcribed. After this
great Angel first dealt with the evident hatred, sadness and pain
involved in this tragedy, he explained:

Catastrophic events of this type have been periodically necessary to lift mortals from a period of lethargy and to unite them in common purpose, mutual support, and high spirit, turning darkness into lightness. He added that all of those who perished this day, had agreed and "contracted" to sacrifice themselves at this event *before* their imminent incarnations, though they had no conscious awareness of their agreement on this day. This mass sacrifice not only represented their love, bravery, and dedication to help humanity, but it also served to increase their personal progression by erasing karmic debt. Remembering that this was but *one* lifetime of many, for each of those souls, might lessen the sense of inexplicable or premature loss.

'W' followed that statement with an excellent metaphorical lesson representing the nature of reincarnation, paraphrased as follows:

Think of your (capital "S") **S**oul as a beautiful growing Shrub planted by the Great Gardener in a vast and lush garden. Your Shrub is covered with many buds. Each of those buds is a (lower case "s") **s**oul with an ego, connected to the grander **S**oul that is the Real You (the whole Shrub). The **s**ouls/buds are the parts of the whole that are engaged in incarnation. Because the separate buds are spaced around the shrub, so that one cannot "see" a fellow bud, each one "feels" like an independent entity. However, each is affected by the actions of the others because they are all systemically connected to the larger plant, the larger you. Each of those buds seeks to blossom, to bring beauty and fruitfulness to the Shrub as a whole, and does so through the process of reincarnation, spiritualizing the material world and attempting to fulfill limited pre-determined goals for its separate incarnations.

"W" added that souls frequently incarnate with many of the same circle of buds; ironically, those "buds" we can "see" on nearby or touching shrubs in the garden, with whom we often develop an on-going life-sharing relationship as soulmates.

"W" explained that many lifetimes are happening simultaneously (a concept that is impossible for three-dimensional minds to comprehend), because there is no such thing as time in the Universes outside of the mortal classroom. "W" explained that time is a convenient paradigm that was created to maintain the mental balance of three-dimensional mortals who are incapable of grasping timelessness, a fourth-dimensional space-time reality. Each of the buds is simultaneously reincarnating in different eras and settings, and for different goals, each one feeling independent.

When a bud returns from a mission into the earthly classroom, it shares what it has gleaned and experienced from that lifetime, both positive and negative, with the whole Soul/Shrub. If a bud fails to fulfill its mission, or encounters errors of action, that energy is sapped from the shrub. Though it is rare, some buds/souls wither and dry up. The buds/souls karmically affect each other, and indirectly, on a subconscious level, share their wisdom and experiences from the many incarnations. Therefore, each of the souls' reincarnation experiences expands or diminishes the overall "health" of the larger Shrub.

Eventually and independently, each Soul/Shrub in the Garden will surely be covered with beautiful blossoms and bear the fruits of the Harvest, completing its full cycle of Evolution and Involution, receiving its just reward from a grateful and Loving Gardener.

That explanation is one I will never forget! It makes so much sense to my mind, and touched upon all six of the bulleted elements of belief about reincarnation listed earlier. Permit me to expound upon a number of the points from W's metaphorical lesson about reincarnation, with the intent of bringing greater clarification:

- The Great Gardner (God) filled His vast garden (the Sublime Realm, the Garden of Eden) with the eternal Souls (humanity - us) that He created in Love.

- Each Shrub represents the Real Us, the capital "S" Soul. Each Soul/Shrub is a beautiful creation, seeking to fully blossom and bear fruit from having spiritualized itself and the material world, eventually providing a harvest for the Great Gardener.

- Each of us as a Soul – the real us – produces many smaller facets of itself through its "buds," the souls that incarnate into the worldly classroom, with a mission of pre-set goals, to learn about the nature of Creation. Our Soul's buds are incarnating simultaneously, but in different identities and eras. It takes many such incarnations to cover all of Life's vast and complex variations.

- In short, each of us reading this book is a "bud" on a goal-driven journey, and though we feel independent, struggling to make sense of who we are and where we are, and why we have been sent into this world, in truth we remain directly connected to the Real Us, our Soul, our true nature, our Higher Self, the link to which is to be found "Within." Bearing this complex view of the nature of our Soul, the Guides later added a powerful observation: **Yee are gods of your own universe!**

- Karma has been mentioned a number of times. Let's get a closer look. The explanation of the "Law of Karma" from Wikipedia is as follows:

"**Karma** (Sanskrit: कर्म; IPA: Pali: kamma) means action, work or deed; it also refers to the spiritual principle of cause and effect where intent and actions of an individual (cause) influence the future of that individual (effect). Good intent and good deed contribute to good karma and future happiness, while bad intent and bad deed contribute to bad karma and future suffering. Karma is closely associated with the idea of rebirth in many schools of Asian religions. In these schools, karma in the present affects one's future in

160

the current life, as well as the nature and quality of future lives - one's <u>saṃsāra</u>."

- In "W's" Shrub metaphor, Karma is explained more specifically. In our ego-directed incarnations, as we dig through our earthly journeys, interacting with a circle of soulmates, the soul is likely to make mistakes and errors in judgment. It is natural, *not* sinful! Some of those misdeeds are accidental, while others are motivated by willful and hurtful intent, resulting in injury to self and/or to other souls. It is the later type that incurs Karmic debt. These debts must be resolved, according to the Universal Law of Karma. When the soul returns to the Soul after an incarnation, the energies (both the growth-producing positive acts and growth-sapping negative acts), have a direct impact on the whole Shrub. As a result of each returning bud's record of achievement, new plans must be devised to settle accrued Karmic debts in future ventures into the earthly classroom. Our Soul's buds keep the cycle of incarnation spinning during our Soul's Journey of progression, until all Karmic debts are resolved.

- Eventually, after many such incarnations by each of the separate souls on our Shrub, we have learned all of our assigned lessons, resolved all of our Karmic debts, and finally, we are prepared to offer a great harvest of fruitfulness to our Gardener. We, the Soul/Shrub are honored as Masters. We are also given the choice of remaining forever in this Sacred Garden, or serving as Ambassadors and Mentors to other aspiring Souls.

Though the above metaphorical treatment of reincarnation is somewhat lengthy, it is my hope that it provided some clarification about the nature of reincarnation, as we were taught it. The more one thinks about the Shrub-metaphor, the more questions and images arise. I recommend spending time, sitting with eyes closed, to replay some of the mental images that have been created by reading this section. It is hoped that answers to additional questions that may be raised in your mind by "W's" metaphor, will be answered in the following pages.

Over a period of years, the Guides added additional details about the process of reincarnation. Permit me to list them here, paraphrased from their many oral and written Messages on this topic:

- We are guided in selecting our life goals *prior* to each incarnation. We are essentially asked to sign a "contract," expressing our agreement to undertake each mission, accepting the associated Karmic responsibility. The best possible setting (place and time) and circumstances to help us in accomplishing our unique goals for that incarnation are also pre-determined, likely including: our parents, place of birth, race, socio-economic status, educational level, physiological and psychological condition, general circumstances of advantage or disadvantage, and our time and means of mortal death. In one lifetime, our goals might best be achieved by living the life of a monarch; in another, by being a homeless person. It is important to note that one is no better than the other! Each is custom-designed to maximize *our* success in achieving the pre-set goals of that incarnation. However, our gift of "free choice" leaves the ego-led soul to find its way in each pre-arranged incarnation.

- Eventually, over many lifetimes, each of us will explore that which needs to be learned from living lives of poverty and disadvantage, or of wealth and influence. We will each experience different races, cultures, physical and mental disabilities, and roles of positive and negative influence. We potentially learn and grow from every experience, whether the assigned role is that of a protagonist or an antagonist.

This point is especially comforting when thinking about those souls who incarnate with severe mental and/or physical disabilities. If we had but *one* life to live – as is more commonly believed in the West – it would unduly compromise those souls, who would have little chance of competing, or completing their missions, leading us to conclude that life is totally *unfair*. However, souls who experience such challenges both learn and teach others about these important life lessons. In those lifetimes, the soul's main goal may be to foster growth in their parents, siblings, friends, or partners, who learn how to lovingly care for and provide service to the person in need. There is purpose to everything, and in some incarnations, a sacrificial role is undertaken to help others grow in empathy, selflessness and service. Potentially, everyone profits in such situations, no matter how it appears on the surface.

- Though I shared the following quote from "W" earlier in the book, I wanted to repeat it here, because of the comforting nature of it, helping us to embrace the conditions of our current incarnation: "**You are where you are, because that's where you are supposed to be, doing what you are doing, because that is what you are supposed to be**

doing." If where or who we are in this incarnation is not to our ego's liking, it would be wise to stop and think of this quote, realizing that this is where we need to be for our own progression. Accept it and make the most of it!

As Vishnu said to Arjuna in the Hindu scripture, *The Bahagavad Gita*, "It is better to do your own job, no matter how poorly, than to do another's job, no matter how well." (Translated by Swami Prabhavananda, *The Song of God: Bhagavad*-Gita, The New American Library, 1951).

- On the micro level, we are accustomed to comparing our life circumstances to others', making judgmental statements about what we are or are not in contrast to them, and how that seems fair or not. With one soul being a successful business mogul and another soul being homeless and hungry, the question of fairness is inevitable (particularly if we had but *one* life to live). On the macro level, *we are all the same*, enacting roles from the Play of Life on the Grand Stage of Life. Sometimes we have a leading role, and sometimes a minor role. Sometimes we are the "hero," and at other times we are the "villain." Each role is important. Life is *not* "fair." It just *is*! What is most import to remember is that we are not diminished or exalted based upon our assigned role, station or identity in *one* given lifetime, only by what we do with what we are given, and how well we fulfill our contracted pre-determined mission.

Every one of us has experienced the harsh struggles of life, leading us to the point of wondering why we have been confronted by those apparent misfortunes. In truth, our greatest achievements and progress frequently come more from confronting life's harsh challenges, barriers, and painful situations, than from living a placid and relatively unchallenged life. This reminds me of a wise quote attributed to the Buddha. **"Every experience, no matter how bad it seems, holds within it a blessing of some kind. The goal is to find it."** I have since learned that this quote is considered to be a "fake," that is, *not* among the historic words of the Buddha. But "fake" or not, I find great truth and comfort in that statement. If only we can remember its inherent message at our periods of greatest testing, we will find the courage to fight the good fight, and obtain progression.

- In the denser vibrations of the mortal world, we do not usually have *direct* or conscious access to our Higher Selves; however, *indirect* communication through dreams, visions, seeming coincidences, and intuition are always available *if* we reach the point of believing that they are genuine sources of truth, and consciously seek guidance from them. When we are more highly evolved/progressed, we have greater access to higher perceptions. However, the Guides have led us to understand that throughout our journey of progression, we remain relatively limited to our level of earned development, even between lifetimes; therefore, we are not suddenly privy to the secrets of the Universe after a mortal passing.

- We have been told that after each incarnation, there is a period of review, in which we, along with Masters and Angels, *evaluate, not judge,* the details of our recent Journey. That loving review leads to goal-setting for future incarnations. This takes into account our Karmic record, the positive accomplishments as well as the things that we did in error, that we neglected to do, or the results of negative or misguided motivations. Those actions remain on our list to be experienced once again in a future incarnation (perhaps on the receiving end, the next time). However, we are definitely *not* talking about sin, retribution, a judgment day, and/or hellfire! Considering the fact that we are eternal spiritual beings – and *not* groveling sinful creatures – the process is far more respectful. Instead, we are talking about balancing the Karmic scales until all that we take back Home is of a positive and Loving nature, enriching our Soul and providing rich testimony to God about His Universe.

- We generally do not have access to our past lives as we are living our current one, though it is common for very young children to retain fading past-life memories and images. However, if we are observant, we become aware of our unexplained likes and dislikes, fears and joys, skills, talents, and tendencies, and strongly felt positive or negative reactions upon meeting strangers, that cannot possibly be explained solely within the context of one's current lifetime. These carry-over qualities from one lifetime to another can be leaned upon to explain such phenomena as precocious talents and genius, love at first sight, irrational fears, and intuitional responses, among others. More details about and examples of past life readings, will be shared in the next two chapters.

- Finally, the Guides drew a distinction between the concept of reincarnation, as they presented it to us, and that of the ancient Hindu-Buddhist philosophy of the "transmigration of souls." Our teachers made it clear that human Souls always remain human, *unlike* in the ancient view of transmigration, in which humans are believed to progress from lowly animal form, or even from inanimate objects, such as minerals, and can return to animal bodies if they live especially negative lives. I thought it might be helpful to correct that false impression before moving on to examine the larger Sacred Journey.

Reincarnation is the mechanical process contained within the Grand Schema of our Sacred Journey. The Guides often taught about our Spiritual Journey, emphasizing the two halves of the Circle of Life: *Evolution* and *Involution*. The diagram below is one to which the Guides often referred:

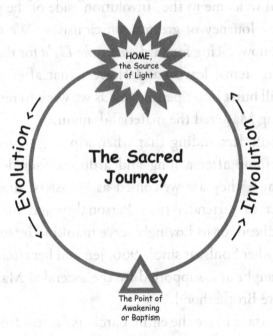

Image #8: An illustration of the two-part Sacred Journey of the Soul (This drawing was created by Brad Horn, and is reprinted with his permission)

We begin our Journey at Home, which is the Source of all Light. On the "Evolution" side, with our backs to the Light that is emanating from our true Home, we struggle, like seeds planted deep in the dark rich earth, working to germinate in the darkness, un-awakened and unconscious of our true nature, until we have grown roots to substantiate our future selves. This is a "dark" period of discovery, deeply weighted down by the densest vibrations of the material domain, and typically directed by the ego-driven need for survival and self-gratification. Nevertheless, this period is a source of bountiful learning.

Eventually, after many lifetimes of learned lessons and discovery, like the stems of aspiring plants, we break through to the warming Light of the nurturing sun/Son that we now begin to see and feel, at the mid-point of the Circle. This Awakening or Baptismal welcome to the "Involution" side of the great Circle begins a new Journey of greater consciousness. We continue to struggle but now, facing forward *seeing the Light* for the first time, we grow our stems, leaves, and flowers that after many more lifetimes, will burst into ripened fruit as we work to return Home, finally having Mastered the material domain.

It is our understanding that when aspiring Souls *earn* their way back Home after a long and arduous Sacred Journey of many lifetimes, they are welcomed as "Masters" and given the choice either to surrender their Personality and meld into the infinite Godhead, or to Lovingly serve mankind by teaching and supporting other Souls, as since 1966, Jen and her circle of Seekers have been taught and supported by the ascended Masters of the "Great White Brotherhood."

It is important to see the entire Circle as Sacred, from the early ego-driven experiences of digging in the earthly dirt of physical survival, to the more evolved times of our progression. No part of this Journey is "sinful." The entire Journey is Sacred because our

Infinite God created this Classroom. He initiated this Journey, and He created us all in His Image. He invited us to chose to leave the comfortable Home in which we were created (i.e. the Garden of Eden or Heaven), in order to explore the material domain, to eventually spiritualize it, and to report first-hand what we have learned and accomplished along the way.

I need to emphasize a vital perspective at this point: In the beginning, we were created "perfect" in the Loving image of God. *That never changes!* We *are* awesome spiritual beings on a human journey, not the other way around! Using an analogy from science, what changes as a result of our Sacred Journey, is the alchemical transformation that occurs when the potential energy of Spirit is consciously released as kinetic energy in the material world, transforming the raw material of the mortal plane into substances of higher vibration, through Love. This is the goal, even if what we view in our world today hardly represents that "perfect" image. We were "perfect" in the beginning and return Home as "perfect;" however, what we eventually carry back Home with us from our Sacred Journey is a great treasure of accomplishment and transformation through Love, that did not exist in the beginning. In that sense, we are co-creators with God.

That explanation is reminiscent of Jesus' "Parable of the Talents" (Matthew 25:14-30). In that parable, the Master, before leaving on a journey, entrusts each of his servants with a number of talents (coins of the time, with a parallel meaning of gifts or abilities). One servant invested his five talents, earning another five; a second had only two talents, but earned another two; however, the last servant, who was given only one talent, buried it in the earth so that it would not be lost. When the Master returned, the first two servants were rewarded richly, because they had been "...faithful over a little..." They had taken the few "talents" they were given, and fulfilled their mission, by bringing back interest on what the Master had given to them for safekeeping. Based upon fear, the third servant buried his one "talent," returning the Master's investment without having earned any interest. The Master chastised him for not investing and increasing what was given to him, taking this servant's one talent and giving it to the servant who had the most. "For to everyone who has will more be given, and he will have an abundance. But from the one who has not, even what he has will be taken away." (The Jerusalem Bible, Doubleday & Company, Inc., 1966).

It is our mission to increase that which we have been given, and we have many lifetimes in which to invest our "talents" to return a treasure to the Master.

In this chapter and in others, I have made mention of what our Guides identified as our primary task: "*to spiritualize the material.*" As we end Chapter Eight, this seems to be the appropriate place to touch upon this topic. The key to this transformational process is Love. Not all of us in *this* current incarnation have experienced a deep and genuinely loving relationship with another person, but those who have, know how the warmth and high vibration of mutual Love is alchemy to the soul. Remembering "God is Love," we are aware of the Source of the transformative power of Love. When we can naturally bring true Love to each and every person, task and thing along our Journey, both we and the objects of our Love are permanently transmuted into finer substances, which is the symbolism behind the story of Middle Age alchemists who sought to change base metals into gold. In that respect, we are all alchemists!

When we show genuine Love to a pet for example, the animal responds with joy, and our heart is filled with joy. Even if briefly, *both* the pet and the person are united as One. What is more difficult is to find a way to Love something that we consider to be mundane or even reprehensible. Along those lines, my thoughts turn to Mother Theresa (soon to be St. Mother Theresa). If there were ever a model to represent how unselfishly one can extend pure Love to the poor, the diseased, the dirty, the helpless, and the dying, it is she. That is our challenge! That is *spiritualizing the material*!

It is unfortunate that the two words "love" and "hate" are so abused and misused, especially in our contemporary culture. "I hate my job!" is a common expression. "I just love pasta!" is another. In Chapter Ten, I will share what our Guides had to say about the usage of those two words. Ultimately, we must seek to love much more, and in doing so, we may find Love. From there, we will discover our True Selves, leading naturally to being at One with our God. That is the Goal of our Sacred Journey!

CHAPTER NINE

OUR GUIDES, THEIR TEACHINGS, AND OUR CHANNEL...

I n the late 1960's I came upon a wonderful quote by Robert Browning, the nineteenth century American poet. Seeing the inspired truth in his poem, *"Paracelsus,"* and how it corresponded with the Lessons from our Guides, I typed it on a 3x5 card, and taped it on the wall above my desk, where it remains. I include it here because of its pertinence to the central theme of this book:

> There is an inmost centre in us all,
> Where truth abides in fullness; and around,
> Wall upon wall, the gross flesh hems it in,
> This perfect, clear perception – which is truth.
> A baffling and perverting carnal mesh
> Binds it, and makes all error; and <u>to KNOW</u>
> <u>Rather consists in opening out a way</u>
> <u>Whence the imprisoned splendor may escape,</u>
> <u>Than in effecting entry for a light</u>
> <u>Supposed to be without.</u>

Especially the last, underlined segment of this poem is exactly what our Guides have taught! Wisdom that issued from the Sublime Region to us, through the channelship of Jen/Verity, came through that great "centre," or the "Within," as our Guides have termed it. For *all* of us, that special place is in the heart region, in our "mind," where our interface exists with our Soul and with the Sublime. Our Guides consistently differentiated between the brain and the mind, regarding the latter as being beyond the physical nature of the brain (that dies with the body), and aligned with the Soul and the Universal Unconscious. Philosophical discourse about the dualistic view of the brain/mind issue has raged since the time of Plato and Aristotle; however, for the purposes of this book, when speaking of the "mind," I will be implying the more transcendent nature of reasoning and inspiration. If there is one directive that has been most often repeated by our Teachers, it is: "**Go Within!**" to tap our "mind" and our Sublime connections.

The purpose I have set for this chapter is to expand the readers' introduction to the Teachers, Teachings, and the Teaching methods that have been shared with us. Given that there have been well over one thousand written and oral communications since 1966, only a sampling can realistically be shared. I will instead continue telling the evolving story of our main characters, interjecting a few selected Messages and Lessons that carried an especially great impact for us.

After graduation from Bucknell in May of 1968, I returned to my home base in Philadelphia. At that time, I was fortunate to be offered a sixth grade teaching contract in the excellent school district where Aunt Jen and Uncle Mike lived. How convenient!

Around this time, the Guides introduced a new teaching technique that included Aunt Jen, Mom, and me. These were guided imagery lessons in which the Teacher would set up a situation and question the students, asking them to make observations and decisions along the way. Unfortunately, though these five sessions had been recorded on cassette tape, the passage of time has de-magnetized the tapes. Not having been transcribed, they have been lost.

Fortunately, one of these hour-long sessions vividly stands out in my memory. As I reconstruct it here, I ask that you imagine yourself as a member of our small group, picturing the scenes and deciding how you might have answered the Guide's questions. Aunt Jen was orally channeling this guided imagery, as Mom and I were in students' role. The kindly Guide started by setting the scene:

> You have been placed in a large cabin at the top of a high mountain with a clear view of the deep valley below.
>
> The Guide asked us to describe what we were seeing from this high vantage point. As I recall in answer, Mom and I talked about the images in our mind's eye: a clear blue sky, beautiful trees, shrubs, and flowers, rolling hills, cascading waterfalls, and singing birds. The Guide worked with our answers, asking us to clarify our visualizations, and to describe the mood we felt in the cabin.
>
> Next the Guide asked us if we wanted to stay in the cabin or venture outside onto a downward path leading to the valley floor. I recall that both of us voted to stay in the comfort and security of the cabin. It soon became clear that this was not the desired answer, but the patient Teacher gently encouraged us to leave the safety of the cabin, saying that we would have a better opportunity to learn about life by taking the descending path.

Nevertheless, he gave us the choice. Who were we to resist the wise Teacher's suggestion? We opened the door and stepped onto the dirt trail.

Next, the Guide slowly led us along a winding path, pointing out that because of the curved nature of the trail, we were never able to see far ahead or behind us. At one point, he told us that on the path ahead lay a large pile of rocks, blocking the way. He suggested a few options, such as returning to the cabin, to sit and await help, to move the impediment, to climb over it, or to hack our way through the off-path brush to try to find the path on the other side of the blockage. We each made a decision and were given respectful feedback about the implications of our choices, without judgment, leaving us with our dignity and the freedom of choice along this journey.

Overcoming the blockage (though I don't recall how we did it), we eventually reached the valley floor where we were told about the wide winding river and the docked boat before us. The Guide asked if we wanted to board the small boat. With embarrassment, I recall that Mom and I had little idea what this meant at the time. Given Mom's self-consciousness and deep reverence for the Guides, she was afraid of making the "wrong" decision, so I did most of the talking for the two of us. Sensing that the Guide wanted us to board the vessel (just as he had wanted us to leave the cabin), I voted for us to enter the boat. Upon making this choice, we were told that had we not boarded, the only alternative would have been to return to the cabin.

As our boat made its way along the winding river, the Guide pointed out that, as on the dirt mountain path, we could see neither far ahead nor behind. The Guide asked us a number of questions along our water journey (most of which I have sadly forgotten), but one question that I do remember was a tough one. He told us that just ahead but off to the side there were a number of other boats, many of which had capsized, with their passengers flailing in the turbulent water. He asked what we wanted to do. "Do you pick them up, or continue on your course?"

[At this point, before I continue the guided imagery lesson, I ask you to stop reading and think about how you would answer that one question. When you have made a decision (i.e. either to pick up the people in the water, or to resume your journey without helping them), continue reading...]

Liking to think of ourselves as "good Christians," Mom and I quickly answered that we would attempt to save as many people as possible.

To our answer, the Guide responded, "I credit you both for the outpouring of love and concern for your fellow man, but I must observe that if you were to make this decision, all of the frightened people would panic and swamp your small boat. In trying to save themselves, they would cause you to capsize as well." I don't mind saying that in our ignorance, both Mom and I had difficulty accepting his implicit suggestion that we should continue our own journey, leaving the floundering people behind to accept their fates. I recall that the loving Guide suggested that we pray for those unfortunate people but continue on our course without stopping.

Then, the Guide announced that we had traveled as far as we were expected to go on the river, on *this* trip, and "magically," we found ourselves back in the mountain cabin, resting from our rigorous journey.

It is astounding to me that neither of us grasped the full meaning of the guided journey until the kindly Guide was no longer present, and the three of us began to analyze the experience together. One can imagine how inhibited or reserved we felt at the time, knowing that we were speaking directly with a highly evolved discarnate being. This type of communication was new to us.

We have since interpreted this unique teaching story, as a lesson about the Journey of Life, which was just described in Chapter Eight. The following is an attempt to provide a more symbolic explanation for this imaginative lesson:

- *The mountain-top cabin*: This is the heightened consciousness and clear vision that we, as spiritual beings, possess before leaving the beauty and protection of the Sublime Realm to enter into a mortal journey, known as an incarnation. We have a clear view of the whole valley from this perspective. It is here – in this Garden of Eden type setting -- that our upcoming lifetime is co-planned before we consciously and willingly open the Cabin door to venture onto the material vibration of the earthly classroom.

- ***The dirt path down the mountain***: The winding dirt path represents our descent from the Sublime Realm at the heights, into the material vibration that is vastly different from the freedom, lightness, and peace we felt up in the cabin. Our path is winding, neither permitting us to see back to the Home from where we came (no longer accessed by our conscious mind), nor seeing where we are headed (toward our future steps and challenges). As we descend into the valley, deeper into the gravity of this mortal journey, we forget who we are, where we are, and why we are on this journey, depending more on our human brain and ego than on our Mind and Soul. We learn best when we encounter challenges or blockages (like the rock pile in our path), employing our gift of freedom of choice to decide how to proceed. Some hopelessly pound at immovable blockages. Some find ways to break through those blockages. Some diverge from the set path and get lost. Some go off the path but rediscover it after wandering in the wilderness for a period of time. Some simply give up and want to return Home to the cabin, cutting short their incarnation, overwhelmed by the difficult Journey of Life.

- ***The wide river and the docked boat***: When we have descended to the deepest and densest point in our earthly classroom, the "river of life" lies before us. Our boat, or our pre-determined set of circumstances for this incarnation's traveling, is properly docked, awaiting our arrival. It was pre-arranged *for* and *by* us when we were up in the cabin, even if that fact is not clear to us at this point on our path. The river's currents take us around bends and sharp turns, suddenly revealing new vistas and challenges. Those challenges or learning opportunities were pre-planned for us, but, in this mortal journey, it is up to us to meet those challenges, using our free choice and faith, as well as our innate problem solving skills. Some navigate the turbulent waters. Some capsize in the attempt. It is *all* good! Our education and our mission continue!

- **The capsized boats and drowning people**: This river voyage is a metaphor, reminding us that we *each* are on an individualized journey, with a specific set of life goals to be achieved. Our prime objective is to accomplish our own life's mission. We get no credit for interfering with or even accomplishing another's mission, no matter how successful our intervention proves. A quote worth repeating: Vishnu says to Arjuna in the Hindu Scripture, *The Bahagavad Gita*, "Better to do your own job, Arjuna, no matter how poorly, than to do another's, no matter how well!"

If we capsize our boat, we learn from that experience; if we "drown" in the attempt (in that incarnation), we return safely to the cabin. Being the eternal spiritual creatures that we are, we get to try again. Nothing is lost! No one actually "dies" or drowns in the process! That realization provides comfort to those of us who continue on the assigned journey, without stopping to save those who had capsized their boats (or metaphorically failed to complete their journey that time around).

- If we permit our "boat" (or life's mission) to be commandeered by others (or vice versa), no matter how lofty our intention to save the apparently less fortunate or less successful souls, we can easily be swamped, capsized, and fail in our mission. Depriving others of fulfilling their incarnation's goals, by interfering with or assuming their workload for them, we are Karmically held responsible for creating a mutual failure.

Having said that, I want to add a point recently made by my cousin Sandra-Lee, regarding the choice about helping others in this situation. Her perspective was that metaphorically, *if* a person who was thrashing about in the water was inspired to swim the distance to our boat, then we must assume that the Spirit moved them to come into our circle, and we would have no choice but to save them. In that case, the individual willed himself/herself to act, and was granted the insight about the means of "survival." Our action would be viewed as one of mercy, assisting a fellow soul. Nevertheless, we are enjoined to lovingly pray for the others along the way, and to help wherever and however we can, but *not* at the risk of imperiling our own mission, unless self-sacrifice *is* our assigned goal in that lifetime.

Permit me to add a clarification at this point. Lest the reader mistakenly concludes that the Guides directed us to only be about our own business, without helping others, it is important to stress that Our God, our Guides, and our Soul are composed of the energy of Pure Love. *Not* helping each other would run counter to our very nature and ultimate mission. The point of the metaphorical capsizing and drowning lesson was simply to emphasize the importance of pursuing our assigned mission for a given lifetime; however, we must remind ourselves that the over-arching mission is to learn to Love everything and everyone. This requires a delicate balancing act, and is a life lesson unto itself.

- *The return to the cabin*: When we have run our course in a given lifetime, going as far as we were expected to go (with a pre-set date of "death"), we return from the "classroom" to the refreshment and peace of the cabin, our "Home." Unlike the dirt path or the river of life, where the gravities and vibrations are much denser, our vision from the heights is unencumbered.

  Here each soul can rest and enter into a mandatory examination process, to *evaluate* what was and was not accomplished in that incarnation. It is important to state that we are *not judged or punished*. We return from the "classroom" with a record of our accomplishments and our inevitable missed goals, missteps and misdeeds. The Law of Karma requires us to face those "failed" lessons the next times around in an attempt to learn from our mistakes, *not* to be punished for our actions or inactions. Perhaps on the next voyage, we will not capsize, having learned from previous experiences. If we do capsize again, we simply take yet another stab at learning that specific difficult life lesson.

I hope you enjoyed this guided Lesson and the embedded metaphorical meanings. The Guide's purpose was to help us to expand our understanding of the Grand Schema of Life, and how reincarnation plays a role in that process. There were at least five of these guided imagery lessons, and they all left quite an impression at the time. They were not merely a lecture or set Message like most of the Writings. Rather, they were respectful, interactive learning experiences.

Being an educator, I must observe that this highly effective teaching strategy should be used to a much greater extent in our schools, especially if our goal is to help our students to be imaginative, flexible, and independent thinkers and problem-solvers. I remember testing this approach with a couple of my sixth-grade gifted classes. They were so excited about the technique that they begged for more of these creative guided excursions. They recognized the empowering nature of this strategy, sharing and validating their own thoughts and decisions, hearing the variety of ideas of their peers, and being a part of an atypical schooling approach, in which there was no *one right answer* being sought.

As has been stated before, more than 1000 written and oral Messages came through Jennie, over the years. For the most part, the Teachers did not identify themselves with specific names; however, I must attest that *all* of the Lessons were clearly from very high spiritual Sources. Generally speaking, the Sublime Sources of Guidance, channeled through Jennie, fall into several groupings. As a caveat, I must state that I am reporting about matters that are far beyond my ken, and as such, I am describing them, *as I understand them* to be.

○ **Angels and Archangels**: To my knowledge, only two angelic sources communicated through Jennie. The most frequent one was "W," about whom we have spoken often. He was an especially fruitful source to Jen, Mom, Sandra-Lee, and me (as our common guardian angel) and as the primary Teacher of the second and third Meeting Groups. Algon, the guardian angel of Suzanne, a member of our third group, was the other angel who spoke to us. As we have been told, angels are a separate species of creation by God, composed of pure Love, and charged with guiding, protecting and supporting a progressing humanity, among other blessed responsibilities. Unlike in the popular Christmas movie with Jimmy Stewart, "It's a Wonderful Life," deceased humans, like the Clarence character, do not "earn their wings" to become angels. Angels and humans are different. "W" once stated to me, "As you progress, Mon Ami, I progress." The Bible makes it clear that there is a hierarchy of angels, leading all the way to the top to Archangels. We have been graciously blessed by the very frequent visits of one Archangel, Michael.

o **Masters, Saints, and the Great White Brotherhood**: As has been stated, human Souls are of Eternal Spirit and are involved in a grand progression of Evolution and Involution, leading ultimately to a state of "perfection." As I understand it, humans who through many focused lifetimes have achieved that amazing status are given a choice of either merging their perfected Soul energy with that of The Godhead, or remaining as independent Personalities, completely dedicated to teaching and helping progressing humans. Though angels do similar work, the difference is that Masters, as perfected humans, can speak to a struggling humanity from the same base of experiences, having successfully run that same frustrating and demanding mortal course.

A number of religions, especially Roman Catholicism, have named and revered hundreds or even thousands of saints, honoring them especially for individual lifetimes of valiant, sacrificial, and mystical actions. Saints, in the eyes of the churches, are not necessarily perfected Souls. As I understand it, True Saints are so by virtue of their perfection of service and unconditional Love. Therefore, they are especially celebrated Masters, both on earth and above. We were blessed to hear from a very special group of saints, including St. John, St. Patrick and St. Francis, among others.

In Chapter Six, Father Baptiste talked about the "Teachers of the Teachers," called "The Great White Brotherhood" (also know as the "Brotherhood of Light," or "Love, Inc."), and how their masterful energies are combined and focused with Love to assist and educate humanity. Many of the Messages channeled through Jen, have come from this category of highly vaunted Sources.

○ **Lords, Entities, and Other High Universal Energies**: Some selected Masters and Angels have been granted the lofty status of "Lord." These positions of immense respect and responsibility are influential throughout the Universes. To my knowledge, we have been richly blessed to receive Messages from three Lords: Lord Jesus, Lord St. Germaine (whom we believe came to us as Father Baptiste), and Lord Michael, the Archangel.

One unique Universal Entity, identified as "Beauty," blessed us with her Presence at least a half-dozen times, filling our meeting space with a great peace, emphasizing that things, scenes or beings that evoke a sense of beauty in us, should be thought of as "Love manifested." Other unnamed Universal Energies, such as "The Holy One," have also communicated through Jennie.

With a clearer notion of the "identity" of the Guides, it seems appropriate at this point to attach a small sampling of Messages. The reader should note that the Appendix contains another cluster of approximately thirty Writings that have been selected as contemplative exercises.

For a number of years, members of our second and third Groups gathered with Jen on Good Friday to commemorate its true historical and symbolic meaning. For several of those gatherings, Lord Jesus Himself greeted us. We always knew when this truly Awesome Presence was in our midst because we all felt a high vibration in the air and a deep and humbling reverence within, as though our Souls sensed His approach before our brains registered His steps. Frequently, whenever such a High Energy Presence came through to greet us, Aunt Jen's system would potentially become taxed and overloaded. The Guides would openly state that they were preparing her system to sustain the extreme Power and would support her throughout the event. However, on a few such occasions (especially in her later years), her brain and body experienced difficulty handling the pressure of such elevated vibrations. This was the case, on Good Friday, April 21, 2000.

After our Group had read aloud the New Testament Bible passages about Holy Week, Jen/Verity sensed that Our Lord was in our presence. We turned on the tape recorder. Almost immediately, Jen began experiencing both ecstasy and discomfort. She reverently dropped to her knees on the living room carpet and prayed for help with the growing pressure, saying, "My Lord, may I ask for thy blessing? Please sustain me at this time, my Lord." (After a pause, during which time she had received the requested help): "Thank Thee, my sweet, sweet Lord." Then Jesus came through, recognizing her discomfort:

We did not wish to cause this almighty upheaval, but it is here to give thee solace and understanding of what the human being is and can be. In thine own language, to say that this is the height that can be achieved, and the blessings that can be given to thee, and to inspire the hearts of people, to see the great domain of where I come from. I do give thee all solemn blessings and ask thee, would it be too much for thee to dedicate thyselves to me? My Love is here, from the heart, which is opened for thee. I cannot ask for thy love; it must be given to me by thine own grace and will, and the pleasure of love amongst thyselves to know and to love as that one particular day that I did exist for mankind in flesh, but gave up this flesh to be that which I rightly and regally am. I am the Lord thy God. I am He who stands before thee. Know that it is with great turbulence, we can say, unfortunately, for this soul [Jen], but certain measurements have to be taken at times to confront any issue. And this is to make thee aware that there are issues in thy lives that thou will have to face; but these are as naught, if thou recognizes it has nothing to do with life. Life existed, was and is and will be. What does count as importance is this particular moment. And at times of great toil to thyselves, we ask thee to remember *this* particular moment. I grant thee my Love, my full uncompromising Love, and have only great hope for all of thee. The issuance is here and it is now and will be. No matter where thou travels, or where thy heart leads thee, it will always be here, at this moment.

We give thee our greatest peace, and that is the only peace that there could be. It exists right through the very, down to, the very seeds of thy beings, and if thou would consider what those seeds are, thou shalt know a truth. Truth in its aspect, and thou shall be free, as free as the air, and as light as the breeze. We have a moment of fear, not real fear as thou knows, for this particular soul, as we now bid thee farewell for the moment. Know at this point it was on the outward part of thee; now I reside in the inward part. And I bid and give thee my full Love. Blessings and Peace to remain with thee.

At this point, Verity experienced great discomfort once again, and suddenly became completely still, her head slumped to one side with no visible evidence of her breathing. We all feared that she had passed on! After a minute or two of anxiety, with efforts on our part to bring her back, she slowly revived. Upon regaining consciousness, she said, "I feel like I have been blasted! What happened?"

At the previous Good Friday gathering, Jesus had come through as well. He blessed us with an important clarification. He asked us not to focus on the pain of torture and crucifixion that He suffered on that historic day, reminding us that the name of the day was *GOOD* Friday. He explained that it was on *that* day that the Christ released His Spirit to reside within *all* humans from that point onward; therefore, it was a truly GOOD day indeed. Perhaps I am not the only person who has wondered why such a terrible-sounding day was called "Good" Friday.

Having mentioned our Lord Jesus, I wish to share a personal and special experience that occurred on my 35th birthday. On that day, I decided to purchase a gift for myself: a gold cross and chain.

After visiting many shops, Rose and I found a beautiful and truly unique cross in a local jewelry store. It was made of strands of gold, loosely woven, with a diamond set at the crossbeams. It seemed to me to be a perfect symbol.

The following day, after school, I visited Aunt Jen to show her the cross. As we sat in her kitchen, I unclasped it and placed it into her hand. As she examined it closely, and was about to comment, I saw a sudden transformation in her body language. She bowed her head reverently and announced that Our Lord was with us. I immediately felt His presence, deep in my being. He greeted us warmly and casually, more like a visiting friend than the exalted Being He is. He commented upon the open weave of the gold, relating it to the open spaces in our lives, to be filled with Love. Then He remarked about the perfection of the diamond at the center, connecting it to the perfection of the Loving Spirit at our own heart centers. He blessed the cross, before departing. In the thirty-six years since that day, I have only taken the cross off three times for repairs to the chain, clasp, and bale. I feel protected with this precious cross around my neck, especially because of He who blessed it and gave it meaning.

Returning to the Messages, at another Good Friday gathering on April 4, 2004, we were first greeted by "W" and then by another Powerful Universal Spirit, introduced as, "The Holy One."

("W" *speaking to us*):

Thou art waiting for an issuance?

We send to thee the Holy One, if it be His will and in His domain, so shall the message pour forth unto thee. We await. Oh, Holiness of good will, we hold thee in light. Shall thou speak to us?

(*A deep, somber voice addressed us*):

I come to thee in the spirit of Light and Love. Thou art in the domain of my being. The reality is that which is within thy heart, if thy heart exists in pureness, and in beauty. How can one see ugliness in the actual spirit of man, as he was created, if there is naught but beauty within his soul? What issues outward must be from that within, but the individual puts forth only what would appear to him as a figment of truth, and which can be assembled in many different manners. Certain men in power exist in their own domain, and consider this as the primary faction in the existence of men to live in reality; but does this answer the question of reality? In thine own hearts thou can question this and in the pure heart, the answer will resolve itself. It behooves man to be of concern to and about himself; to know the reality of existence, which is only a matter of a term in life, and then life goes on beyond that, real life. We hope for thee to have clearer minds, clearer perception, to see things in many different aspects. Thou questions many things and finds that there are many ways to answer, but when thou observes the real truth of something, in truth, only one answer exists, and we know within thy hearts, thou realizes this. But it is most difficult. Were it not so, it should not have been given to thee. This is a meaning of learning how to exist, where to exist, and with whom to exist. It will take quite some time. We do not even mention in years. This is almost a period of learning what existence is, what it means to exist. We fear there is a great misunderstanding, what the very term existence means, and is. We realize we speak in harsh terms, but this harshness comes from a beating, loving, heart, and wishes to thee, children of peace and love, to issue forth what thou feels in goodness and mercy towards others. Let that be thy reason for traveling and existing in the essence of others. Know that there is the real meaning of Love and what Love truly is. To know Love in its reality is to see that great beauty which exists and what has been created. With this we can say, we bid thee adieu, and wish for thee a form of peace within thyselves, and know that thou cannot conquer the world, but thy real world exists within thee, and to know that is love, that which is the deepest part of thee, is to know and feel that one Force of Truth and Love. Our blessings to thee.

This time, the Guides protected our channel by removing her consciousness from the place altogether, protecting her system in her absence. After the Message came through, Verity "returned" and asked, "Did anything come through? I was 'shot out' to a distant place that was a great void, with nothing to see or hear. I know they did something to me. I feel more elevated, like a different person, and I feel greater distance. I feel alone but not lonely." This likely was intended as a protection for her as the high vibration came through her body without any discomfort this time. Verity later reported that she was given the sense that our visiting speaker was a Holy High source from another planet or universe.

Sadly, however, in her last decade of life, we had to call 911 *twice* to have her taken to the emergency room to be resuscitated. From that point onward, for her protection, we decided to discourage her from channeling at Meetings.

In February of 1972, The Great White Brotherhood sent us a series of poetic or meditative Messages, which continue to inspire us. I have attached one from this series of four or five. Please read this Message slowly, permitting thoughts, images and feelings to wash over you. Another Message from this series, entitled, "The Period of Drought," can be found in the Appendix.

The Temple

There is The Temple in that portion of man's life that contains that which is of the holiest. Man builds this temple one step at a time. The ages preceding and proceeding will establish the firmness and strength of its inhabitation. The holiness of this temple depends on man's nature and desire for what he considers perfection. The temple is visible yet invisible. Access to this holy investiture is gained by the wiser knowledge of Godly ways. The key to this abode is worn in the manner of living. Even though it is within his grasp, he cannot always maintain use of this key, which unlocks the mighty torrents of higher degree. It takes mastery of human events to be within distance of use in the temple. Once entrance is gained, an attitude of complete holiness is the requisite of the soul. Man now stands in abandonment to that which is of his higher being. The Godly part of man now becomes the manifestation of glory to its Maker. The soul draws

191

forth its lights and its prayers to the pulsation of this manifestation. He glimpses that heavenly strain which will lead him to his mansion of unknown history. Here is where he starts weaving his robe of glory. The making of this robe is of high secrecy and knowledge of this makeup is for the individual who seeks a weaving of perfection. The light of the temple is of different shading and can only be lit by the light of the soul. You must understand this is the Temple within. The temple without is that covering which others see and feel. These are the temples we build which inhabit our looks for mankind. Each one sees the outer temple with his own individual knowledge and discretion. Man's perfection lies in the fact of understanding that which he builds. Must not the outer temple reflect the inner temple? Man's impatience deters his building of the outer temple, and distorts the knowledge of building the foundations of ample strength. His frustration from incomprehension forces him to build and rebuild the outer temple. The difference between the inner and the outer is built from love for man's creation. The inner is built from the ages, and the outer is built from man's time. We must build our temples in peace and the abandon of the soul in love. What we gain by peace and love is The Master's reflection of building in perfection.

Now that the reader has a clearer sense of the Teachers' lofty pedigree, permit me to speak about the genuine specialness of our mystical channel, Jennie, who seemed incapable of believing that she was worthy of or qualified for the great mystical gifts that re-shaped her life, starting in 1966. In her words, "Who am I? I am just a simple housewife without any formal education. A nobody! Why me?" Jen was sooner prepared to believe that she had lost her sanity than to accept that these mystical gifts could possibly be given to her. That attitude was not a façade of false pride. Though Jen could be forceful, confident, and determined when needed, she was never ego-driven, especially with regard to her spiritual life. Aunt Jen was consistently humble, truthful, faithful, and genuinely motivated to help others in need, refusing to accept any accolades or credit for the help that came through her from the Great Beyond. She seemed incapable of accepting praise, (something that we and the Guides agreed was a failing of hers).

Aunt Jen thanked God for everything, giving Him full credit. Anytime a grateful recipient would express appreciation for a Message, a reading, or a gift of her time and wise counsel, she would reflexively pull back, feeling the humbleness that came from accepting that she was *not* the source of this loving help. Without any risk of contradiction, I can state that Aunt Jennie *never* permitted her ego to assume a greater-than-thou attitude or to "get uppity" -- as Monsignor Falls had warned years earlier -- about the amazing events and gifts that flowed through her. I can also confirm that Jen, unlike most psychic readers, never accepted payment for *any* of her readings or counsel, viewing the gifts as God's gracious doings. Her help was genuine. She taught and modeled unconditional Love.

With regard to Jen's qualifications for the job of mystical channel, the Guides held a far different perspective than Jen. At one of our Group Meetings within the last few years of her earthly life, the Guides confirmed that Jen/Verity had been groomed for this complex task over the course of three specific lifetimes. Further, the Guides stated that without *any* conscious awareness of it, she was already engaged in additional teaching in other places during her sleeping hours through an out-of-body projection. Lastly, the Guides confirmed that regarding her Soul's progression, she has but *one* last lifetime in her Involution to finish up remaining tasks. They added that we, the members of her Group, would join her in that last incarnation, but at a greater distance than this time around.

Those revelations about Jen came through to our Group at a time when the Guides were assured that she would not hear those claims. The Guides even asked us to withhold from telling her these truths about herself. I must admit that in her last years, I broke that request. In characteristic form, after hearing that awesome claim, Aunt Jen simply dismissed that notion, saying, "I can't imagine that!"

Details about Jen's past lifetimes were a valid subject for our Guides, but only when they felt that it might serve a deeper purpose than sheer entertainment value.

I fondly remember when the Guides described a few former lifetimes that Aunt Jen and I had shared in order to cement the concept that we have long been soulmates. They revealed these lifetimes to Aunt Jen in video-like conscious visions of the actual events, some in great detail. We were told about one lifetime in France when she and I were both hanged on the gallows in a public square, justly convicted as thieves. In an incarnation in England, I was a Lord Henry, an alchemist working in the turret of Balmoral Castle, and Jen was the mistress and model of a historically famous portrait artist of the court. In another lifetime, I supposedly was Sultan Iritak Bonful, of the Castle of the Korakun Moon, located in the Karakorum Mountains in Southeast Asia. In that lifetime, both Aunt Jen and my mother, who was named Meara Nauga, were members of my court. An extremely uncomfortable revelation came in learning that my mother, Virge, was a member of my harem in that lifetime… but we'll leave that one alone. In these and other incarnations, Jen and I were close companions. I suspect that the above described incarnations were likely *not* the lives to which the Guides were referring when they talked about Verity's preparation as a mystical channel.

I recall an afternoon when Aunt Jen and I were reflecting on her irrational fear of heights. We talked and laughed about a family driving vacation, when her children were young. The trip route followed the Skyline Drive from Virginia, and down through the Smoky Mountain National Park. Jen's children often talked about their mother's irritating tenseness on that trip. They reported that their mom repeatedly freaked out when the car rounded curves, especially if one of them moved or suddenly sneezed. Irrationally fearing that the car would plummet off the winding mountain roads, she was tense the entire driving trip. Apparently, she unintentionally took the joy out of the beautiful mountain view for her family on that vacation.

At that point in our discussion, the Guides suddenly came through to show Aunt Jen a vision of a former lifetime, apparently from Ancient Rome. In that incarnation, Jen was a vestal virgin or a member of an esteemed female sect. In the scene, Jen was shown that an angry crowd was approaching the temple, with intent to do harm to the sorority. Just in the nick of time, a brave soldier, dressed in a fine tunic, rode up with his chariot, pulled by two white horses, to carry her off to safety. They escaped up the mountain path at great speed, being followed by some of the angry crowd, racing around the dirt mountain roads, with precipitous drop-offs. When the chariot driver turned briefly to see if his passenger was ok, Jen realized that he was Mike, her current husband. In the moments that followed, the chariot driver lost control, driving the horses, the chariot, and its two passengers off the high cliff to their deaths.

With *that* revelation from the Guides, Jen realized the source of her irrational fear of heights!

At one of our summer Meetings, the Guides revealed that collectively, the members of our first group had spent more than one incarnation together. One in particular, took place in a small town in Italy, near Mount Vesuvius. In that lifetime, Aunt Jen was a mother superior in a convent, and I, as a randy young male, had gotten a member of our (now current) group pregnant, out of wedlock, causing her such anguish that she threw herself into the volcano, rather than to live with the shame. Ouch! I definitely had Karma to pay from that incarnation. I don't mind mentioning that I have experienced what I believe to be the Karmic pay-back from that lifetime in my *current* incarnation.

Continuing the theme of reincarnation, the members of our first prayer group decided to have a "Come as You Were" Halloween party in which we were to dress up as someone we thought we were in a previous lifetime. For our reincarnation-themed party, I decided to dress up as Sultan Iritak. Given the highly detailed physical description from Aunt Jen's video-like vision, I bought a mustache and beard from a beauty supply store, figured out how to make a turban, and fashioned the appropriate garb. In costume, I arrived at Aunt Jen's door to drive her to Georgie's house for the party. When she answered the door, she almost fainted! She inhaled deeply and stepped back a few paces. She insisted that I looked exactly like the sultan in her vision and couldn't stop commenting about it all night.

There was, however, one former lifetime of Jen's that emerged as a chilling reminder of her mystical preparation, one that was instigated by our listening to a record album that Aunt Jen had bought for me as a birthday gift.

Back in the early 1970's, when the two of us were gripped by the search for anything that might expand our understanding about this brave new world, Aunt Jen learned about a unique record album, called "Starbody" (produced by Channel 1 Records in 1974). Based on what she heard about the album, she ordered it for me. As I learned by reading the back cover of the album, Bill Reddie, the composer, credited Eugene Albright as the inspiration for the album. Mr. Albright claimed to have experienced the ethereal music of eternity, during a near-death experience. Based on Albright's research into the structure of the energy of chords and sounds, which elicited "...the feeling of being an energy being, rather than a physical being..." combined with Reddie's similar fascination, they collaborated for over four years to test out sound combinations that were shown to elicit people's emotional responses. The near 21-minute, electronic "Starbody Suite" was the result of their research efforts.

At any rate, after I opened my present, I put the record on the turntable. Aunt Jen and I sat at her dining room table, drinking coffee. I distinctly recall that in the first five minutes, both of us had vivid mental pictures of an unusual setting. However, from that point through the balance of the "Starbody Suite," something *strange* and frightening happened!

Suddenly, Aunt Jen's whole demeanor changed! She sat up rigidly, and her face became that of a highly intimidating and imperious being. She started speaking dramatically in a strange language with an authoritative tone, using symbolic hand gestures, as if she were instructing a large audience before her. She did not appear to be conscious of her current surroundings but was mentally in another place, in another time. Though initially I found myself making the sign of the cross to ward off any potentially sinister entity, I quickly grabbed the yellow tablet and pen. Then I began phonetically transcribing the balance of her strangely meaningful utterances and hand gestures, until the end of the "Starbody Suite."

When the record ended, we both were speechless. More than tangentially aware of what had transpired, she was both amazed and exhausted by the experience.

When we had caught our breaths, we shared our thoughts and mental images. Aunt Jen reported that the two of us were in an elaborate underground facility, somehow illuminated from within the walls (which, ironically, we separately had envisioned during the first five minutes, without sharing that fact), at a setting suggestive of the ancient, lost, and advanced civilization of Atlantis. In that lifetime, I was a lowly priest, tending to young white-robed students who were enrolled in strict metaphysical training. Jen was the High Priestess, whose word and authority were absolute.

Suspecting that the foreign tongue in which she delivered her lengthy and stern lecture was a real language, I decided to telephone the husband and wife team who chaired the foreign language department in my high school. Dr. and Mrs. Baccari were thrilled to hear from me (I had taken three years of Italian with Mrs. Baccari, a truly sweet person and an excellent teacher), and somehow, over the phone, I justified reading a segment of what I had transcribed. I didn't explain the source but merely asked if it sounded like a language to them. Rather than giving me an answer without seeing the transcript, they asked me to type the phonetically spelled pages of the lecture, and mail it to them. I was hoping for some outside proof for this unique experience!

A few days later, I received a call from Dr. Baccari. Though he was especially curious about the source of the document, he indicated that after a close study, both he and his wife believed it to be a real language, in fact, "…an ancient language which likely predated Sanskrit" (more than 5000 years ago). Though they could not translate any of the content, they corroborated that it possessed true language structures. I thanked him and immediately called the "High Priestess" to share their conclusions. Sadly, I have since misplaced that transcript.

In the coming years, we surprised (and irritated) Aunt Jen by playing portions of that record several times, especially for our third Meeting Group. Each time we played it (even without warning), the identical transformation took place, with the "High Priestess" making her appearance immediately upon hearing the first few chords of the "Starbody Suite." It was an instantaneous and amazing transformation! However, the important part of this exciting story is that this lifetime seems likely to have been one of the three incarnations to which the Guides referred, regarding her preparation as a mystical channel.

The Messages and visions continued to flow through our special channel, but at a deeper level with our third and final Group, about which the reader will learn more in Chapter 10.

CHAPTER TEN

POWERFUL LESSONS FOR
A SPECIAL GROUP...

E ven before Jen's 1991 return to the Philadelphia area from
Florida, the energy started churning once again to create
another Spiritual Group, the third, the most intense, and the final
Group.

During Aunt Jennie's decade-long absence, my intense spiritual
fervor had subsided. I recall that during one visit to Aunt Jen and
Uncle Mike's home in Sebastian, Florida, I expressed a concern
that I had lost the spiritual hunger. I was deeply concerned about
that. With little hesitation, the Guides came though to briefly
address my concern.

> We again use the example of a candle. The candle
> at the start was lighted, and had a sputtering and
> fluttering flame, reaching out statically, touching
> many different points. It is now almost as a steady
> flame, to sputter and flutter when a little likely wind
> blows it in some direction. A fluttering flame is
> more easily visible, if one were to examine a candle.

It was comforting that the Guides conceptualized my spiritual
life as a "steady flame," addressing my fear that my flame was

all but extinguished. It is certainly true that in the 60's and 70's my flame was in static flutter, spilling over into everything I did. By the 80's and 90's. I felt that my spiritual life was calmer and deeper; however, in contrast, it felt like my light was significantly dimmer. Their encouragement, as always, was very reassuring!

Upon my return home, Rose, my wife, reported that she had been speaking at length with Suzanne, a colleague at work, when the conversation surprisingly turned to spiritual matters. Suz (as we call her), told Rose about her years of spiritual pursuits, including her having spent a summer at the mystical and "magical" gardens at Findhorn in northeastern Scotland, known for its focus on spiritual living practices and unique ecological actions that produce bountiful plant harvests. Rose reported that Suz expressed serious interest in learning more about Aunt Jen and the Messages that had been channeling through her over these years.

As was stated in the Preface, "Suddenly, there is a magnetic-like force, which draws one Seeker to other Seekers, and pulls them towards relationships..." The blossoming spiritual relationship with Suzanne, is a perfect example of that meant-to-be connection.

The three of us worked in the same school district. I was the K-6 Math and Science Coordinator at that point, having taught sixth grade in the same elementary school where Rose was a third grade teacher, and Suzanne was a dedicated special education teacher. I knew Suz, but hadn't known about her intense spiritual search. From that point on, on many Friday nights, the three of us would meet at our place for dinner and hold an informal Meeting. Somewhat regularly, Michael, Jen's son, joined us. Our small group became close. We frequently got Aunt Jen on the phone to join our circle, so that Jen and Suzanne became acquainted a year before they actually met in person.

Suzanne is a remarkable person! Though petite in stature, she is tall in talent. She brings her ready smile and sprite-like energy to everything. Her passion and skill at helping special education students was well-known in our district. Her musical talents on the keyboard are matched only by her joy of dancing and her boundless energy for sampling all that life has to offer. As with Shirley from the first Group, Suz had that natural "green" personality, with one foot anchored to the earth and the other one in the heavens. Other than me, Suz has since become the longest single living member of any of our three Groups, now at twenty-five years and counting.

Many months after Suzanne started meeting with us on those pleasant Friday evenings, she was the instrument of expanding membership in our Group. At that point, Suzanne worked part-time at a local psychotherapy office. Joanne and Jonathan, who both held Doctor of Psychology degrees, and had founded this business, were busy and intense people. Over time, Suz talked to them about Jen. Almost immediately, both therapists expressed interest in learning more about her amazing abilities.

Meanwhile, after nearly two years of living alone, following the passing of Mike, Jen finally sold her house in Sebastian, Florida. Before leaving her home of ten years, she said her good-byes to neighbors, friends, her supportive priest (who completely accepted and respected her channeling), the fellow members of her church choir, and knelt at her husband's grave for a final farewell. Her son drove her up North, arriving a day before the moving van.

Michael, Rose, and I had arranged for Aunt Jen to rent an apartment in the same complex as my parents in Drexel Hill, a few miles from her former home in Havertown. Having her sister Virge within a two-minute walk, was greatly comforting, and after the details of moving were finalized, the two remaining "Musketeers" (sister Josephine having passed on in 1970), were once again back to long conversations around one or the other's kitchen table, dunking Jen's famous biscotti in their coffee.

Within a couple of weeks of Jen's move, the Third Spiritual Group began meeting.

Informal at first, the initial Meetings were more about Jen Suzanne, and Joanne and Jonathan (the psychologists), getting to know one another. They, with Mom, Michael, and me, made up the new Group. It didn't take long for the Guides to come through, and for new and deep relationships to gel.

As with the other two Groups, the Guides assigned each member a Group Name (with its associated numerology), a color, and a seating assignment. In addition, the Teachers provided each member with the name of her/his guardian angel.

> **Jennie**, known as VERITY, a 9; color: WHITE, and angel: "W"

> **Conrad**, known as ARMAND, a 6; color: RED, and angel: "W"

> **Joanne**, known as ALMEDA, a 9; color: ORANGE, and angel: Avesta

> **Jonathan**, known as BENIAMIN, a 5; color: YELLOW, and angel: Anjo

> **Suzanne**, known as ASTRADA, a 1; color: GREEN, and angel: Algon

> **Michael**, known as, ARISON, a 4; color: TEAL, and angel: Malah

> **Virge**, known as BLASILDA, a 6; color: VIOLET, and angel, "W"

Almost at the start, "W" came through to set a new tone and higher expectations, as well as a guarantee of His Love, His blessings, and His teaching. While in the two previous Groups, the members were more passive, being largely in an awe-inspired and receiving mode, in this new venture, we were told that there was an expectation for us to be more actively engaged and mutually supportive.

"W" went on to explain that there are many such Groups around the world, and that He is deeply involved in this project. He also added that there are two main types of teaching Groups:

- *Technical Groups*, which focus on sharing detailed explanations about the cosmos, metaphysics, and answering "big-picture" questions.

- *Inner Travel Groups*, which focus on helping aspiring mortals go within as well as assisting them in realizing who and what they really are, and in supporting their progression.

Clearly, our Group was of the second type that according to "W," was relatively new. He said that many discarnate onlookers, seeking to evaluate this new model, would likely observe our Meetings. With this revelation, I know that each of us felt understandably nervous, knowing that we would be observed and evaluated by celestial visitors. "W" or our other Teachers would tell us when interested onlookers (of course, invisible to us) were present to observe a Meeting. Whenever that was the case, we always received kind and gracious feedback as well as encouragement on our progress. The following excerpt from our Meeting of December 9, 2006, made reference to both Inner Travel and the issue of "visitors":

To be in tune with that which is within is to have the knowledgeable substance to lead thee further upward. We have noticed the growth today and that there is a better feeling of inward progression. This is something which is to be continued, and more is expected of each. We are aware of a true connection, and we do thank each one of thee, and we know that we have chosen correctly. We have had students here. These are not the ordinary students. These are masters. They have been standing with open eyes and open ears and are listening and waiting for progression into the outer substances of that which is rising. It's rising such as clouds. Look beyond, beyond the clouds. They are covered, but the substance within greets the heart with sublime Light and Love. Thou will meet thy Maker in Substance. Know from where thou greets the Highest, thy true home. Be thankful for that which is given unto thee. It is a light that has been encircled within each of thee. Previously known as that "little Dot," which is not, we should say, flaming. There is a blue stream issuing forth and try to think of what that designates. You are in entitlement. That is to be known by each of thee. Look unto thyselves as a whole, as the Brotherhood of Love, incarnated and flourishing. We do assist thee and the more thou urges that forward position, inwardly, the rosier the path will assume. We hold thee in custody, and again we say, speak only in Truth. For Truth to abide within thee, keep that holy.

One of "W's" most frequent and productive instructional strategies with this new group was to engage us in the analysis of a word, or a string of carefully pre-selected "nonsense" words (at least on the surface), or even foreign words and phrases. Our task was to analyze the utterances in order to create an interpretive story. He stated that his goal was to open our minds, help us to tap our imagination and intuition, and to build connections among ideas, but ultimately, to help us to "**GO WITHIN.**"

For example, at one of our earliest Meetings, "W" said, "Thou art blessed! Thou could say it, 'I have received a blessing to send me forward in life.'" Following that brief statement, he assigned this task: "Take the word BLESSED apart. Spell it both ways, please (**BLEST** and **BLESSED**)."

Working as a Group, we brainstormed the following ideas, working with the letters of those two words:

o **Be LESS Ed**ucated (outer knowledge vs. inner wisdom)

o **LES**sen the knowledge; increase the trust in **S**pirit, using an **SS** for emphasis

o The **T** is the cross, upon which our ego must be sacrificed; it is at the end step in being bles**T**

o BLESSED has 2-S's, so it is a two-way thing; you are giving and you are receiving; or you are receiving, because you are giving (your **S**pirit and His **S**pirit)

o BLEST has just one S; does that imply a one-way, that we are receiving His blessing?

o Two **S**'s: one for **S**oul, one for **S**pirit, as in your **S**oul is reaching out to the **S**pirit

- LESS is different from LES; make yourself LESS than the other person

At that point, naively proud of our fledgling efforts, we asked "W" if that is what he wanted. He lightheartedly replied, "Just a little humor: be LESS dead." He then added, "Well, thou could always extend. Take it letter for letter." We came up with the following:

- Be Loving, Extending Spirit and Soul, Every Day

- BeLieve yEe art Spirit-Touched

- Begin Loving Every Spirit and Soul Every Day

- By Listening, Ego Stills Silently, and Engages Dios (God)

In response, "W" said, "This is to let thee understand from a little something what can be created, and thou art all with it." In a later Meeting, "W" presented five "words" (some of which are nonsense words), followed by a question:

- OBLIVAMENT

- CONCEPTORIAL

- ADJUDIMENT

- CONTRADICTION

- OBLIGATORY

- Hast thou found the value of Truth?

After at least forty-five minutes of discussion, tearing each word apart into prefixes, roots and suffixes, trying to make sense of each separate word, we then tried to link them all together into a spiritually-themed story that we shared with "W." In response to our work that day, "W" replied, "Ah, thou has come to the revelation of what thou art! That has left thee speechless. Does thou understand what I have just said? Does thou believe it? That holds thee in conjunction with the upper principle. Thou art now under obligation. In other words, it's like being another self. And what is the other self?"

We answered, "Higher Self."

"W" asked, "Ahh. What is the higher self?"

We answered, "The likeness to our Creator."

"W" said, "Take it even further."

We answered, "It is the perfect us, and what is perfect in us is the God nature in us."

"W" observed, "Coming very close to the Truth."

We answered, "It is the Christ in us!"

"W" concluded:

> Yes! That is what thou has to live up to. And know the fallacy of the human being is that he is not aware of it. Cherish thine own being, love – and express it fully – love thy self, because, if thou pretends – we use the word pretends – to say, 'I love you' without loving myself, then I have not loved the Truth. Does thou comprehend? To love signifies, if I say, 'I love thee.' That means thou and I are one, and we are in the common One, which is that God Principle. Can thou see that within thyselves? Does it make life more wearisome that thou has to walk in this fashion?

It is my hope that in sharing the above two exercises, there is greater comprehension of some of the intensity of the Meetings in this Third Group, and how the difficult process of "going Within" was developed. It was as though we had all been graduated from middle school and were suddenly promoted straight to college. There were times during our Meetings when we felt on top of the world, feeling the impact of a spiritual boost in vibration that was gifted to us from the Sublime, enabling us to think beyond our usual level. And yes, there were many times when all we could produce was a collective sigh. This Group became tightly bound together, united in the Spirit and in our growing ability to go Within. "Coincidentally," at the same moment that I was writing this segment of the book about "going Within," Suz/Astrada sent me an email, containing this synchronistic quote: "Nothing Can Dim The Light Which Shines From Within." ~ Maya Angelou.

In a few years, though, there were a number of changes in membership. Jonathan/Beniamin left the Group to pursue a new project that demanded all of his time. In 1994, Virge/Blasilda, my mother, passed on from a massive stroke. Interestingly, a few weeks before Mom died, she and Aunt Jen were at their local bank branch. Mom noticed a banner, saying, "See Ed today!" (The word, "coincidence," comes to mind once again…). Ed, the bank's investment officer, rotated among a number of branch banks, and "just happened" to be at this local branch on that day. Virge encouraged Jen to make an appointment with Ed, given that she had not yet fully invested the money acquired from the sale of her modest Florida home.

Jen remembered, "When I settled into the chair in front of Ed's desk and looked into his eyes, I felt a deep shock of recognition. I had the strangest feeling that I knew him well. Though he was half my age, I am embarrassed to admit that I found myself physically attracted to him, a feeling that both confused and upset me."

After their introductory meeting, Ed scheduled a second session to discuss details of Jen's future investments. She readily agreed.

A week later, Ed and Jen met to conclude arrangements. Jen continued, "Once we completed the details of setting up safe investments, I noticed that Ed relaxed. We started talking about our lives. He seemed genuinely interested in learning about me. Given that he struck me as a person who didn't reveal much about himself to others, I was surprised that he shared the fact that he had been successful at school, and always had a keen interest in philosophy and spirituality, assuming from an early age that he would become a priest. Responding to his comments, I mentioned that I had spent years studying spirituality and metaphysics. It was clear that Ed wanted to hear more about my journey, and he asked if we could meet again, just to talk about this topic."

Over the following few weeks, Aunt Jen seemed preoccupied with thoughts about Ed, speaking about him often, and wondering why she felt strangely protective of him. While expressing the fear that she was falling for him, Jen knew that her infatuation was "craziness."

The next time Jen and Ed met to talk about spiritual matters, she was overcome with a vivid revelation about having spent multiple previous lifetimes with him. Jen observed, "Only with a past lifetime connection could I possibly justify the attachment and protectiveness I had been feeling toward this young stranger! I shared with Ed what I was being shown in a waking vision."

"In one lifetime, in a seaside town in Ireland, I was his mother. I could see myself scurrying nervously along the shoreline, with him, my infant son in my arms, trying to protect him from a sudden and vicious thunderstorm. In the lifelike image I was being shown, the sky darkened, and the rain came pelting down upon us as I hurried along the coastline to return to our little hut. Without warning, the surf kicked up, and a huge wave washed over us. The power of that wave was more than I could fight against. To my horror, my baby son was pulled from my arms and washed out to sea."

"As I told Ed what I was seeing, tears rolled down my face with grief, but also with relief. The relief I felt was that now I had an answer about why I felt frantically protective of him, and why I had been feeling that I owed this total stranger a great debt. After all, I felt responsible for his death!"

Jen explained, "The visions about Ed continued! In the next lifetime I was being shown, I was his wife. We lived in France, probably in the 16th or 17th century, and he was a handsome, uniformed naval officer. I was at home, awaiting his return from sea duty. In a sudden shift of scene, I was being shown that in a heated act of mutiny, the sailors on his ship threw him overboard to his death."

"I remember Ed's first words, after intently listening to those two past life readings. He said, 'Well, *that* explains why I have had such an inexplicable fear of the ocean in *this* lifetime!'"

Jen continued, "Before we parted that evening, Ed expressed his interest in joining our Spiritual Group. He added that he had a history of not sticking with things and would likely only remain a member for a year or two."

A few weeks after my mother's funeral, Ed was greeted as the newest member of our Group. The Guides welcomed him, and as with the other members, assigned his name, color, seating arrangement, and the name of his angel:

Ed, known as BRIONNE, a 5; color: DARK BLUE, and angel: Ailene

Given his color assignment, Ed/Brionne was seated on Jen/Verity's right where my Mom had been for the previous twenty-four years. His sharp analytic mind, amazing memory, and deep faith have been Brionne's major contributions to the Group ever since. He has been a dedicated and valuable asset over these past twenty-three years. So much for just "one or two years."

When recently asked to share his reflections about Aunt Jen, Ed said, "I cherish the time I spent with Jen! In the first couple of years, I visited with her almost every week. She would cook a meal for me, and we would sit for hours to talk about life. She was a truly unique combination of the pragmatic and the spiritual, all in one. In fact, one slightly earthy exchange I had with her comes to mind. One evening, as she spoke of spiritual topics that were such a natural part of her being, I interrupted her to say, 'Come on, Jen, not everything is spiritual! Sometimes you just have to take a crap!' I remember her response clearly because it represented a 'dawning moment' for me. She retorted, 'Oh, Ed, even *that* is a spiritual opportunity. Every time I go to the bathroom I thank God that my bodily systems are working as they should!' Jen always got me thinking!"

Within a few months of Ed's joining the group, Michael, Jen's son, left the group, admitting that he no longer felt that he should continue. Sadly, neither he nor Anna, his sister, ever fully accepted or believed in their mother's channeling experiences, with Michael finally admitting that the only reason he kept attending was from a sense of duty, incorrectly assuming that his mother wanted and expected him to do so.

In 2004, Joanne/Almeda (who had become extremely close to Aunt Jen, even taking operatic singing lessons from her), reluctantly left the Group for personal and business reasons. However, two new replacements found their way into our circle. George and Jeannie, both art teachers, were enthusiastically welcomed.

George had been my undergrad college roommate, and my oldest friend. Jeannie, who *coincidentally* had gone to school with Rose, from first grade through high school, was now a colleague of Rose's in the school district to which Rose had recently transferred after earning her Master's and Doctoral Degrees as a Literacy Specialist.

George, had met Aunt Jen, as well as many of my family members, during our undergraduate years from 1962 to 1966. We visited each other's homes a number of times, his family being from Kingston, Pennsylvania (near Wilkes-Barre), and mine in South Philadelphia. Our mothers became good friends, and our fathers were two peas in a pod, both jokesters! Though I had shared the amazing events from November of 1966 and other Messages with George, it was not until 1997 that "something clicked" with him, and he sought to learn more about the spiritual connection with Aunt Jen – all things at the "right" time!

George recalled, "During one of my visits, I mentioned to Conrad that I was interested in learning more about Aunt Jen's visions and channeling sessions and asked if I could sit-in on one of the prayer group's Meetings. Conrad arranged for me to attend a Meeting soon afterwards. I was happy to see Aunt Jen again after many years and found the group to be open and willing to share. I admit that I had always been a bit skeptical of Conrad's retelling of mystical happenings, channeled writings and visions that had come through Aunt Jen, but my skepticism was quickly dispelled during that first Meeting when Aunt Jen delivered a Message from the Guides. With eyes closed, she spoke in a way that I had never known her to speak, channeling a Lesson from the Universe to those of us gathered around her. Although an astute and verbally expressive person, her words, vocabulary and spoken cadence were *not* the Aunt Jen I had come to know during my many visits with Conrad and his family. This was truly inspiring! After the message had come through Aunt Jen, the seven of us proceeded to analyze the channeled words (either from listening to it again on cassette

213

tape or from written notes), and interpret as best we could their meaning and relevance to our lives."

George continued, "Needless to say, the energy and welcoming enthusiasm of the other members made me eager to experience time and again the wonder of this spiritual encounter. I have attended all but a few of the Meetings ever since!"

"Having met Jeannie at a few art shows and social gatherings," added George, "and knowing that she had a strong interest in spirituality, I asked Conrad if she could be considered for membership in our Group. After having experienced a Meeting for myself, I knew that she would find it to be of value. I was pleased to see her welcomed at the following Meeting."

Jeannie had developed a relationship with Aunt Jen months before being invited to join the Group. Being a long-time friend of Rose's, Jeannie felt comfortable confiding in her, especially now that she and Rose were professional colleagues. After learning about Jeannie's pressing struggles with her marriage, Rose offered to introduce her to Aunt Jen.

"When Rose and I first entered Aunt Jen's apartment," Jeannie explained, "she greeted me right away as if she already knew me. She listened to my thoughts and questions and spoke from her heart or from her deeper vision. She said that she saw an image of a road (that my husband and I had been walking), which was splitting into two separate roads. She lovingly comforted me, and gave me insight into several areas of my current life, as well as sharing some pertinent information from previous lifetimes."

Jeannie continued, "Over the following months, I reached out to Aunt Jen often, by phone and in person. My mother's love of opera and Aunt Jen's gift for operatic singing, was another surprising connection. One evening I took Aunt Jen to the Academy of Music in center city Philadelphia, to see her favorite opera, "La Traviata." It felt so good to do something special for this woman, who gave of herself so freely to others. My mother was deceased, but I know she would have enjoyed meeting Aunt Jen and sharing this performance with her."

"After I joined the Spiritual Group," Jeannie tearfully added, "one of the most upsetting experiences I had was about David, my son. Especially after the 9/11 tragedies, David, wanting to serve his country, decided to join the Department of Homeland Security as a Border Patrolman. When I shared his decision with her, Aunt Jen said that she did not have a good feeling about it. Later, she told me that the vision she was given was of Jeannie and David being on opposite sides of a closing garden gate. Not many months later, at one of our Meetings, looking in my direction with a sorrowful gaze, Aunt Jen announced that she saw trouble coming. Within that month, my son, David, tragically lost his life on the job. My life forever changed! Aunt Jen and the Group members, my 'spiritual family,' were there for me."

As has been frequently suggested, things happen at the "right time," and The Potter keeps lovingly molding His clay. The Group membership remained constant until 2008 when we welcomed Anita, a wise, mature, motherly woman, who was serving as a part-time care-giver for Aunt Jen. As with the others, Anita was welcomed to our Group by the Guides.

With the addition of Anita, the tight circle felt "complete." In summary, the members of this third, current, and final group, were as follows:

Jennie/VERITY, 9, WHITE

Conrad/ARMAND, 6, RED

George/GVON, 22, AMBER

Suzanne/ASTRADA, 1, GREEN

Jeannie/MARLOTTE, 5, AQUAMARINE

Ed/BRIONNE, 5, DARK BLUE

Anita/LEONA, 2, PRIMROSE PURPLE

Image #8: The Third Spiritual Group members in 2013: (seated): Ed,
(standing, left to right): George, Anita, Jeannie, Conrad, Jen and Suzanne

There were two ex-officio members of this Group (having been members of our second Group) who never attended Meetings, but were included in Group events and received summaries of discussions from our Meetings. They are:

Rose/ANJELIQUE, 9, ROSE
Sandra Lee/ILA, 4, a PSYCHEDELIC mix

At an early Meeting with this new Group -- a Group, which has remained together even after Jen's passing in 2013 -- the Guides amended the agenda for our Meetings, adding both a

"Healing Bubble" visualization and an "Inner Travel" meditation segment.

The Guides had long held to the truth that during our Meeting, Energy from the Sublime Realm would shine down upon us to raise our vibrations and expand our minds. We all usually felt that boost, especially when all seven of us were in attendance at a Meeting. However, the Teachers were also clear about our needing to share that gift of energy with others, rather than to keep it within ourselves. This led to the "Healing Bubble" exercise, which has been a part of every Meeting to this day.

After the Opening Prayers, the members are asked to nominate individuals, groups, pets, or causes for which we feel that healing energy would be helpful. After generating the list of names, we imagine them all to be within a "Bubble" at the center of our circle. At some Meetings, our "Bubble" is filled to overflowing (such as with thousands of people displaced by some natural or manmade disaster). We have been instructed to visualize these candidates for healing, each with happy smiling faces without any mention or visual trace of their physical or emotional issues.

The Guides also introduced an "Inner Travel" meditation routine that culminated in sending healing energy to those in the Bubble. As the facilitator of the Group, I usually led the members in this solemn process. The meditation focuses on each of us feeling two streams of energy: the white Sublime energy descending through a funnel that is attached at our crown chakra, as well as sensing the rising energy of the earth up through our feet. These directionally-opposed energy flows -- one in front from above, and the other behind, from below -- are intended to ignite and energize our chakra centers and to create a hollow space at the center of our beings. We are instructed to enter that silent hollow space within, surrounded by the flowing energies, where we might envision a fountain of gold, and to remain in silence to listen for guidance and inspiration from the connection Within.

Before concluding the meditation, we attempt to see, feel, or imagine all of the flowing energies rising throughout our bodies and powerfully concentrating behind our third eye. On cue, we each imagine a jet of intense indigo blue – considered to be the nullifying or destroying light – shooting from our third eye, aimed at the base of the Healing Bubble before us. These streams of dark blue light penetrate the "Bubble," potentially nullifying the illnesses and difficulties of those within it, rising up to encompass all those within, as the Sublime sends corresponding energy and comfort to each of the candidates. When our individual reserves of energy feel depleted, we are to envision the "Bubble" shrinking in size and rising up, disappearing into the distance, leaving us with a sense of confidence that healings would occur, wherever the Sublime Realm deems necessary and desirable.

Although Jen/Verity can see these exchanges of energy, the rest of us cannot, but we always work hard to visualize and believe that healings are effected as a result. At each subsequent month's Meeting, we revisit the list of former candidates and share updates since the previous Healing Bubble event. This has become an important and continuing part of our monthly Meetings. Hearing that specific individuals are doing better is always satisfying and heartwarming.

Along the lines of healing, the Guides also recommended the following excellent and easy healing activity, as a real-life exercise, which I highly encourage trying. The Guides suggested that as we are walking, driving, or even sitting, and we sense that someone passing before our gaze (or someone who pops into our thoughts) is in need of energy or healing, we are to envision a bolt of white light, shooting like a spear, linking our heart region to theirs in Love. Then we are to picture a pillar of white pulsing energy that rises to the "heavens," creating the second side of a huge right triangle. When this image is envisioned we are to send up our prayer of healing for that other person within that pillar of Light. If it is God's Will that the healing be done, He will complete the triangle along the hypotenuse, sending a bolt of healing white light to that person's heart.

I find myself doing this "triangle healing activity" frequently, especially when driving and, particularly, if I see a person with disabilities or a homeless person on the city pavements. It makes a great deal of sense to me that we should consciously and genuinely send out thoughts of Love, rather than the more normal judgments and criticisms that our egos are accustomed to generating. Our Teachers have often emphasized that we are co-creators with God. Our thoughts are composed of real creative energy, that, when sent out into the Universe, have a predictable result. A Law of the Universe states that "like-attracts-like;" therefore, whatever we send out will boomerang back to us in kind. *This* is a sobering reality demanding that we carefully watch the nature of our words and thoughts!

Based upon what we have been taught, I believe that healing is a sensitive matter, better left in The Potter's Hands. The Lord knows best whether or not a healing will help or delay an individual's progression. Assuming, for example, we possessed the power to restore sight to a blind person, in doing so, we might actually be *harming* that person's chances for progression, rather than helping him or her as intended! How are we to know whether or not that disability was given to the person as a necessary learning opportunity in this incarnation? Productive results do not always issue from good intentions, as counterintuitive as that may seem on the surface. This notion was new to me, so from that point onward, whenever I have engaged in the "triangle healing activity," I pray for the person's inner healing that he/she might feel the Peace, Hope, Comfort, and Love of the Lord, giving that person the strength to continue life's journey more joyfully, growing in understanding about that which is to be learned from bearing the disability.

Doing this anonymous activity is easy. Knowing that I am giving of myself without the involvement of my busy little ego is a good thing! Helping others selflessly, lovingly, brings to mind a truism from the Guides that I have adopted as a personal mantra:

"One cannot give without receiving, nor receive without giving."

Similar to Newton's Third Law of Motion, "For every action there is an equal and opposite reaction," whenever we give to others, they receive that gift, and at the same time, we receive some sort of reaction (thanks, warmth, or suspicion). At times, this is ego-driven (we give to get); at other times, there is a shared love in the giving and receiving. As with all action, motive is the determining influence, as to the purity of the two-way exchange of energy, in which BOTH the giver and the receiver, give and receive. If we are conscious of WHY we are giving, and do so without ulterior motive, the return will likely be a response-reaction of thanks from the recipient, consciously or unconsciously.

In an elaboration of that concept, the Guides focused a number of Lessons on the most powerful energy of the Universe: Love. The Guides specifically asked us to use the word, "Love," sparingly, and *only* when its true meaning was being respected. After engaging us in a prolonged exercise, attempting to have us define the truth of "Love," "W" provided us with what seemed to us at the time a restrictive yet elevated definition, paraphrased here:

> Bearing in mind that "God is Love," and beauty is "Love manifested," *True* Love between humans requires the surrendering of the ego through a

total investment in the needs and well-being of
the other, without thought of the self. In a selfless
reaching out, one touches the God-center of that
other person, and in so doing, both are united as
One, immersed in the Universal Energy of Love
that binds us to life and to God. Using the word
"Love" for any lesser meaning is to be avoided, just
as we must totally avoid using the word, "hate."

Given our cultural overuse and abuse of this special word
(e.g. "I love pizza." "I love that TV show." "Don't you just love
chocolate!"), we found that we had to work especially hard at
overcoming common parlance, to reserve the L-word for references
to God, our spouses and children, and for expressing the soul-
moving impact of experiencing natural beauty, like that of the
awesome Grand Canyon. These Lessons sensitized us about using
the L-word! Ultimately, we decided to use a capital "L" in "Love"
exclusively for God, and for transcendent human relationships, in
which our heart speaks for us. We felt that a lower case "l" in "love"
could be used in speech when we are moved by a sense of unique joy
or inspiration, by creations or creatures that inspire selfless linkages,
especially with the arts, music, pets or breathtaking scenes. We
have tried to resist using the L-word in any other way. Avoiding
the use of the word, "hate," has been far easier for us to manage.

Over the years of monthly Meetings, our Guides have
emphasized habits of mind, designed to help us to navigate this
earthly classroom in a more positive, productive, and spiritual
manner. One such series of Lessons dealt with the sense of color in
human interactions. This is a difficult concept, but permit me to
share a brief introduction to this potentially valuable technique.

Already discussed has been the Guides' practice of assigning
colors to the members of the Group, representing the sequence

of colors associated with the chakra energy centers. Over time, the Guides took this concept to a deeper yet pragmatic level. They indicated that at their Sublime plane, communication is largely achieved through non-verbal means, through sensing the energies emanating from others, frequently in the form of color, number and intention. They emphasized that there is a complex language of color that, if seen/sensed, can explain a person's intention or motivation, and/or their physical, emotional, mental, and spiritual state. Likewise, it can be used consciously for healing and the modification of situations and interactions among people.

Some psychics, mystics, and Reiki masters possess the gift of seeing or reading auras. As I understand it, the aura is the electromagnetic field that surrounds the bodies of *all* living things. The colors emitted in a person's aura communicate the status of her/his emotions, level of thinking and health. Having the "gift" of reading a person's aura is an open window to that individual's current state, on a number of levels. Though most of us do not *consciously* possess this gift, we have *all* sensed the energy-impact of color, particularly in interactions with other people and events, even if we don't think of it in this way.

To use two extreme examples, we have all entered a room in which two people have been engaged in a heated discussion. Even without having heard a word from them, what we *feel* emanating from the people is the energy impact of a brown or black-shaded reddish color (brown being an earthy tone, black being negative or unknown, and red being a color of passion, anger, or heatedness). The Guides explained that if we are able to sense the colors of this emanating energy, we can avoid becoming entangled in an uncomfortable situation. On the flip-side, we have all come into the company of those people who exude great peace, warmth, and a calming feeling. In this instance, we are feeling the effects of the colors of white, light blue, pink, and lavender, leading us to trust in the company and veracity of that person.

Extending the point, the color "blue," for example, is not *one* color with *one* meaning. Though a primary blue symbolically stands for man's spirituality, imagine how the addition of a tint of white, or the addition of a shade of black, might change the meaning of the level of spirituality. We refer to depression as "feeling blue" (a dark steely blue), to the earthy tones of jazz as "the blues" (a brownish blue), and yet we also know the feelings of beauty and peace that come from seeing a clear blue summer sky. Blue, with an influx of yellow, would produce a bluish-green that might suggest a balancing or more natural sense of spirituality, or with the influx of red, producing an exalted purplish spiritual state. The complexity of sensing the intention or state of another person, then, involves an understanding of the shades, tints, and color combinations, which the Guides explained in the hopes that we might hone our senses to determine if a person were being honest or dishonest, altruistic, ego-centered, healthy or ill.

If we were to think about it, we could all come up with the "feelings" we have rightly sensed over time that helped us to "know" what was going on in another person or situation, even without the exchange of words. Sadly, we do not often trust our intuitional senses, something that the Guides hoped that we would learn to do more frequently in daily interactions, such as being involved in a discussion with another person (or facing a business deal or a new undertaking). We should first attempt to gauge the type of color energy emanating from that other person as a means of reading the situation, the person's real motivation, and knowing how to proceed with confidence.

The Guides also suggested that we send out white or lavender color energy to neutralize or soften the impact of anger, dishonesty, or illness. The members of our Group were not particularly successful with this Lesson, but it is easier to see the potential help that would come from our developing this advanced sense than it is to apply it. Helping us to use our five higher senses to better navigate the earthly realm was of course the goal the Guides had in mind for this color-sensing exercise.

Finally, an extremely valuable series of Lessons dealt with the discovery of our specific goals or missions of this incarnation. As was stated in Chapter Eight, after an incarnation each soul is assisted in *evaluating* that recent lifetime to identify the pros and cons of the earned karmic record. As our Teachers have emphasized, *unlike* the traditional interpretation of the "afterlife," *we are NOT judged and punished* for our so-called "sins." Remembering that we are *all* truly spiritual beings on a mortal journey, the process is respectful, and is focused on balancing our earned karmic record, helping us to plan future lifetimes. Once this review is completed, our plan is set, and before incarnating once again, we sign a "contract," accepting the goals and details of our next mission. However, once we reenter the dense physical domain of our earthly classroom, our memory about that plan is lost from consciousness. We usually search around for many years until we get a sense of why we came here this time, *if* we ever arrive at that realization.

As Ed/Brionne once humorously observed, "It would be more helpful if we were born into this lifetime, carrying papers or a manual explaining everything about our mission. That would save time and wasted effort. Unfortunately, that is not the case. Either that, or I lost my manual!"

Over a number of Meetings, the Guides led us through exercises to help us to discover our specific and/or general goals for this lifetime. The most helpful advice they offered was to ask us to spend quiet time, reflecting over the years of our lives in order to identify obvious repeating patterns.

They pointed out that events, people, and issues that keep repeating themselves, are to be considered as potential lifetime goals. These need not be major life-shaping issues, but can be limited in nature. They can be linked to learning about dealing with limitations or unusual responsibility or authority. They can be dealing with annoying habits or compulsions, or in fact *anything* needed for our growth and progress, especially with issues related to our personal karmic debt. They typically involve one or more mortals in our circle with whom there is some mutual karmic obligation to be resolved from past incarnations.

As Jeannie/Marlotte pointed out, "Once I know what my life goals are, *then* I can more consciously set about working on them. After all, I don't want to have to repeat any lessons for failure of addressing them the first time around."

Based on this Lesson series, I came up with what I believed to be three separate life goals. One of them was to protect, support, and help my Aunt Jen. "W" confirmed that I was correct in this conclusion. It *is* comforting, as Jeannie/Marlotte pointed out, to know one's mission consciously, but I needed no extra motivation to fulfill this particular goal, one that I happily had embraced years earlier. I continue to work on the other two main goals, both of which are far more challenging.

At our May Meeting in 2007, the Guides shared a fascinating revelation. With Jen/Verity's consciousness placed far out in the Universe so that she would not hear the discussion, they revealed to the Group her deep, abiding love for us. On an unconscious level, she had communicated to them the desire to prolong her life on this earthy plane in order to continue to serve us. According to the Guides, she technically had completed her work and "should" have passed on around this time. However, they approved her unique request.

One morning, a short time later, I received a spiritually exuberant and tearful telephone call from my aunt. That morning, in a touching and humbling experience, "W" privately revealed His real identity to Jennie. He said that "W," "M," "Twinkle," and "Big Chief," are all *one* and the same entity: Lord Michael the Archangel. Aunt Jen was profoundly moved, and could not wait to share that revelation with me.

For those readers who are unfamiliar with St. Michael, Archangel, I enclose a brief description from the convenient on-line reference, Wikipedia:

> **"Archangel Michael".**
>
> **Michael** ("who is like God?", Hebrew: מִיכָאֵל (pronounced [mixa'ʔel]), *Micha'el* or *Mīkhā'ēl*; Greek: Μιχαήλ, *Mikhaēl*; Latin: *Michael* (in the Vulgate *Michahel*); Arabic: ميخائيل, *Mīkhā'īl*) is an archangel in Judaism, Christianity, and Islam. Roman Catholics, the Eastern Orthodox, Anglicans, and Lutherans refer to him as "Saint Michael the Archangel" and also as "Saint Michael". Orthodox Christians refer to him as the "Taxiarch Archangel Michael" or simply "Archangel Michael".
>
> Michael is mentioned three times in the Book of Daniel, once as a "great prince who stands up for the children of your people". The idea that Michael was the advocate of the Jews became so prevalent that in spite of the rabbinical prohibition against appealing to angels as intermediaries between God and his people, Michael came to occupy a certain place in the Jewish liturgy.

In the <u>New Testament</u> Michael leads God's armies against <u>Satan</u>'s forces in the <u>Book of Revelation</u>, where during the <u>war in heaven</u> he defeats Satan. In the <u>Epistle of Jude</u> Michael is specifically referred to as "the archangel Michael". Christian sanctuaries to Michael appeared in the 4th century, when he was first seen as a healing angel, and then over time as a protector and the leader of the army of God against the forces of evil. By the 6th century, devotions to Archangel Michael were widespread both in the <u>Eastern</u> and <u>Western Churches</u>. Over time, teachings on Michael began to vary among Christian denominations.

Regarding this new revelation, I am embarrassed to admit that, at first, I was skeptical. Ultimately, I think my skepticism sprang from my awareness of the true magnificence of Lord Michael, but that, given a lack of self-esteem at the time, I couldn't accept that One so truly Great could be *my* guardian angel. At our next Meeting, Lord Michael humbly identified himself to the other Group members. I am still in awe that my playful 'Twinkle,' my mother's "M," the brilliant but humorous 'W,' Aunt Jen's "Big Chief," as well as her mysterious "imaginary friend," who comforted her in the hospital when she was very young, were all one and the same, Lord Michael the Archangel. We all felt, and continue to feel, graciously blessed and in awe to have been in the hands of such an exalted being for so many years.

It is uncanny that Jen always had a "thing" about the name, Michael. Her favorite novel in her years on the farm was, "*Lo, Michael*," by Grace Lutz (Lippencott, 1913). Jen married a Michael. Her son was named Michael, Jr., and by this point in her life, there was a grandson, Michael III, and finally a great-grandson, Michael

IV. Finally, the illustrious Archangel Michael's name was added to Jen's "Michael collection."

However, Jen's life was about to turn a corner. On Halloween of 2007, Jen fell in the hallway of her apartment, fracturing her left shoulder. Apparently, she lay on the floor for some time, all alone and in great pain, before dragging herself some twenty feet to the nearest phone in the living room. She telephoned the receptionist at her doctor's office, who in turn called 911 for an ambulance. She then had to painfully drag herself to the front door to unlock it.

Coincidentally, at that very time, I tried to reach her on the phone, as I was driving to La Salle University to teach my class. There was no answer. I assumed that she was out shopping or in the bathroom. When I arrived on campus, around 3:00 pm, a weird thing happened. Coincidences are so special! The North Philadelphia campus was on lock-down, because the police were in pursuit of an escaped armed criminal. With my three-hour class being cancelled, I decided to drive to Aunt Jennie's apartment for a surprise visit. When I arrived, I saw that her car was parked in its spot. However, a sense of alarm increased when there was no response to my door and window knocks or the incessant ringing of the doorbell. I started to panic, and eventually called 911, fearing that she had experienced a major problem (or worse), and couldn't open the door. When I gave Jen's address, the 911 operator confirmed that an ambulance had been dispatched to that same address about an hour earlier, taking the woman to Delaware County Memorial Hospital.

I raced to the emergency room where I found Aunt Jen, distraught and in extreme pain. I tried to comfort her as best I could, but it was clear that her pain and confusion ruled the day.

This accident proved to be a pivotal life-altering event for Aunt Jen, leading her toward the end-game of this incarnation.

CHAPTER ELEVEN

JEN'S FINAL YEARS: THE LASTING IMPACT...

In her mid-eighties, Jen began showing signs of dementia. Her fall on Halloween of 2007, at age 85, worsened her condition. After four days in the hospital for a broken shoulder (considered inoperable, because of her age), she was transferred to a nursing home/rehab where she stayed for nearly three months, receiving daily physical therapy and losing additional mental clarity with the passage of each week.

It was heartbreaking for me to hear a skilled Italian cook and baker like Aunt Jen ask with clear confusion on her face whether the pasta should go in the water *before* turning on the heat, or *after* the water comes to a full boil. However, it was simply *devastating* to see her begin to lose grasp of her forty-some years of inspired mystical channeling. When the dementia became apparent, I truly believed that she would forget or confuse everything else *before* forgetting about the years of channeling. Sadly, I was wrong about that.

Aunt Jen's children arranged for 24/7 care-giving service in her apartment once Jen was released from the rehab facility. At the time, it certainly did make sense to keep her in her own familiar environment, where her memory did rally a bit. However, given

Jen's fierce independent streak, she did not relish having a total stranger in her living space around the clock, even though Jon-Jo, from The Ivory Coast in Africa, was a kindly, sweet, entertaining, and attentive woman. Then there were the financial concerns that plague many of our elderly. At $6000/month for the 24/7 caregiving, Jen's limited life's savings were rapidly diminishing.

After nearly four months of this level of expense, Michael and Anna began searching for alternative plans. Each in turn asked their mother if she wanted to live with them. Jen declined both offers. With Anna living in Connecticut and Mike considering a move to Colorado, she expressed the desire to remain in the community where she had spent most of her life and where her Spiritual Group members resided.

This decision led her children to start investigating local nursing homes that would accept Medicaid. At that juncture, Rose and I offered our home as an option, believing that she was not ready for a nursing home and could obtain the support she needed in our loving family home environment. We knew she would be comfortable in these surroundings and would enjoy being around our four dogs. She accepted our invitation.

Aunt Jen paid for the renovation of our existing first floor powder room, enlarging it into a full and accessible bathroom. We cleared out our family room that was near the bathroom to repurpose it as a private and cheery first floor living space, decorated with her furniture and many of her paintings and framed photos. Aunt Jen moved in with us late in April of 2008. It was her space. Without a doubt, this arrangement was a mutual blessing! Because Rose was still teaching full-time and I was semi-retired at that point, I did most of the caregiving. Whenever I had to leave to teach at the university or to consult with a school district client, Aunt Jen paid for the services of one of two excellent caregivers. Sandy, a neighbor, and later, Anita, were both retired social workers, as well as wonderful, competent, and caring women.

The seven of us, counting the doggies, were truly happy together. Aunt Jen was easy to care for, affectionate and appreciative. She added sweetness to our home for three weeks short of *five* years.

Image #9: Aunt Jen, age 86, shortly after she moved in with Rosie, Conrad and the doggies

Anita later observed, "My good friend and former colleague, Sandy, who had been caregiving for Aunt Jen for several months, was about to vacation in Ireland for three weeks. Wanting to be sure that Aunt Jen's care was properly covered when needed, she asked me if I would be interested in taking over her role as a part-time caregiver. I agreed to be introduced to Aunt Jen and Conrad that very afternoon. On the first day that I assumed the caregiving service for Jen, while Conrad went off to teach his class at La Salle, I was so impressed with Jen's character and sweetness that I knew this would be a *very* special assignment. That afternoon, while Jen was napping in her reclining chair, I happened to notice a few Messages laying out on the table, next to my cup of tea. When I read them, I was inspired!"

Anita continued, "As soon as Conrad returned, I asked him about those Messages. When I learned that Aunt Jen was the channel, I was sold! After a few additional discussions with him and Aunt Jen – who at that point was far more lucid than a few years later – I asked to be considered for membership in the small Spiritual Group. I had always held an abiding interest in spiritual issues, and, though I was of Jewish upbringing and faith, its beliefs sounded more spiritually universal to me. I was pleased to be welcomed into this truly unique Group, and I have been an active member ever since."

Anita became very close to Jen. Reflecting back on that time, Anita recalls, "Jen consistently emanated love, kindness, and caring. In spite of the dementia, Jen was emotionally healthy, maintained her dignity, and rarely, if ever, complained about anything or anyone. She seemed to enjoy every moment, even if memories of experiences from those recent moments were fleeting. We talked a great deal and we did pottery together. I even persuaded her to attempt some cooking tasks. Every so often we had a 'spa day,' when I would clip and file her nails as well as shampoo and trim her hair. Always pleasant, she repeatedly made it clear how happy she was in this warm and loving environment."

As I look back on the five years that Aunt Jennie lived in our home, I cherish our frequent opportunities to talk and reminisce. As is typically the case with dementia patients, memories from the distant past, are much more secure in their minds than recent ones. Her youth on the farm increasingly became her favorite topic. She spoke repeatedly about the cows and being licked by their big rough tongues. She talked often about Rojo, her beloved German shepherd, and about how, after school, the two of them would round up the cows to be milked. She reflected often about how happy she was to have been reared around the beauty of nature in the wholesome life of the farm, even with the hard work it entailed.

We also talked often about her family members, relatives, and friends. She was repeatedly shocked to learn that she was the last survivor of her parents' eight children, and that most of her older nieces and nephews had passed on as well. Toward the end of her life, every time we spoke of her mystical experiences, or read a Message together, I would have to gently remind her that *she* was the channel of all of these Writings. She would furrow her brow, and innocently ask, "You mean I really did that?"

Aunt Jen spent most of the time in her bright room, surrounded with windows on three sides, overlooking a landscape of hemlock trees and shrubs. She reveled in spending time each day in the comfortable recliner chair that her son had purchased for her, doing crossword puzzles. This productive habit was started a decade or so earlier when she had heard a doctor on TV say that doing puzzles helps to forestall the decline of brain function. Just as she physically had exercised for twenty minutes each day earlier in her adult life, this new regimen represented an enjoyable, daily, disciplined task, keeping her mind actively engaged (even if, increasingly, she was forced to check the answer key as she solved each puzzle, something she would *never* have permitted years earlier).

In fact, one of a number of photographs I took of her was particularly representative of her days with us. In the photo (printed below) she is sitting in her tan recliner with a big smile on her face, with Gracie, one of our Westies, stretched out behind her head, at the top of the chair, and with Lacie, laying across her legs. With a large crossword puzzle book on her lap, and a pencil in hand, she appeared to have everything that she desired.

Image #10: Jen, age 88, enjoying her chair, puzzles and dogs

Though Aunt Jen enjoyed a few TV shows, such as the Nature Channel or National Geographic, she rarely watched TV unless Sandy or Anita decided to punctuate the long afternoon with an old classic movie or an entertaining talk show. When she wasn't doing puzzles, she was reading Messages from our Guides or spiritual books from the seven shelves of metaphysical volumes that filled the bookcase next to her chair. One year for Christmas, Rose and I bought her the DVD of the Metropolitan Opera Company's "La Traviata." She watched it repeatedly, singing arias along with the diva. I was amazed that given her memory loss, she remembered *all* of the Italian lyrics. However, I have read that emotionally charged memories are among the last to be forgotten by dementia patients.

We always ate our meals together enjoying friendly, familiar, and meaningful camaraderie. After our meals, she routinely washed the dishes. For her, it was more of an act of love than a sense of duty. During the near five years of her stay, our electric dishwasher was seldom used. Aunt Jen insisted upon being as useful as possible, right to the end. Though washing dishes was in part occupational therapy for her, having a sense of purpose and usefulness was essential for her wellbeing and underscored a connection to life.

What particularly brought a smile to her face was when a member of our Spiritual Group would come for a visit. Her countenance would light up, and her unconditional Love would focus unwaveringly on her visitor. She had a natural way of genuinely making us feel like we were the most important people in her life, and that our lives, happiness, and experiences truly mattered to her.

George/Gvon later remembered, "When I stopped by her room to see her, she would usually be reading, doing puzzles, or fussing over the four dogs. Aunt Jen always greeted me warmly with a hug and expressed keen interest in how I was feeling. For many years she never failed to ask 'How is your love life?' That amused me since I had been a bachelor living alone for a number of years."

George continued, "During one visit, I recall expressing my concern to her about a medical scare. She immediately reassured me that I would be fine. She took my hands in hers and said that I should ask the Lord's Blessings by saying this repetitive prayer: 'Lord, Let Thy will be my Will; Lord, Let Thy will be my Will; Lord, Let Thy will be my Will.' I will always remember her tender touch and her meaningful and comforting words of wisdom. I was also greatly comforted by the accuracy of her prediction about my health issue. Aunt Jen's love, kindness and genuine concern, as well as the mystical inspiration, made the direction of my spiritual path more meaningful and purposeful."

Especially in her last two years, the advance of the dementia became more apparent in her short-term memory. She initially became agitated with herself when she couldn't remember events from the previous few days or remember who had just called her on the phone, or what she had *just* eaten for lunch. Although she was well aware of the decline, in characteristic style she ultimately turned agitation to humor, laughing at herself for forgetting names and events. In spite of her condition, she rarely lost her warm smile, her sense of appreciation for even the smallest thing we did for her, or her positive outlook on life.

All of us, who knew her well, viewed her as a unique positive model to be emulated in old age or infirmity.

As the reader might recall from an earlier chapter, Jen's mystical channeling was a process called "amanuensis." As described, in contrast to automatic writing, amanuensis leans more heavily on the training, the experience, and the general mental and emotional fitness of the channel. Needless to say, while we continued to hold monthly Meetings during Aunt Jen's final five years, she channeled less and less, and when she did, the Guides frequently had to sign off prematurely because the channel was not as clear or able to maintain the high vibrations as had been the case in the past. The Guides often talked about caring for and protecting her more than usual in those final years. The Meetings became more dependent upon the reading and analyzing of *former* Messages, and upon the members taking on greater responsibility for continuing the power of the Group gatherings.

The Guides made it increasingly clear that Aunt Jen's time was short. They asked for commitments from all of us to continue holding our Meetings even after the loss of our channel, placing the mantle of responsibility upon my shoulders to keep it going forward.

I remember the solemn and private moment when alone with Aunt Jen, a member of the Great White Brotherhood orally came through to tell me that I was being given a choice, as to whether or not to assume responsibility for continuing the work of the Group, *after* her passing. He made it crystal clear that if I agreed, I "... would be held" to that promise (karmically speaking). I was told that if I did consent, I would be granted a gift of "knowing truth" while at Meetings, but that there would be no more channeling after Jen passed on. Of course, I humbly accepted!

Early in April of 2013, Jen's children decided that the time had come for a more intensive level of 24/7 care and arranged for her to be admitted into a nursing home near Anna in Connecticut. It was a sad day for us when her children packed up their mother's belongings and drove her to the nursing home in Connecticut. The upside, given that Anna lived only ten minutes from this facility, was that this presented an opportunity for the mother-daughter connection to be reestablished after many years of physical distance. The downside was that Rose, the doggies, and I felt the palpable loss of this special soul from our home. For many days after her departure, the dogs would routinely bound into her room, expecting to see her in her chair as usual.

From April to July I placed a number of phone calls to the nursing home. Our chats were spirited, and usually resulted in some laughter and good shared stories; however, the dementia often interfered, as she repeatedly questioned where she was, how she got there, and who put her there.

In mid-June, Brad, my good friend, and I were scheduled to attend a weekend retreat in Massachusetts, something we had done together four or five times previously. Along the route to our destination, Brad, who had also grown fond of Aunt Jen, having met her during her final two years in our home, suggested that we pay a visit to the nursing home, given that it was not far off of our travel route.

After signing the visitor's book, Brad and I went in search of Aunt Jen. When we entered her room on the second floor, I had to hold back tears, seeing my soul-mate all alone in a dimly-lighted room, slumped in her big tan recliner chair, awake, but with a blank look on her face. I placed her hand in mine, and greeted her with a kiss. At first, she did not recognize me (which was upsetting, though not unanticipated), but within ten minutes, the light suddenly returned to her eyes, and we embraced as aunt and nephew. She said, patting my hand, "I know you! How could I *ever* forget *you*?"

After a bittersweet ninety-minute visit, we reluctantly left her. It was the last time I saw Aunt Jen alive. Upon reaching the hallway, I crumpled to the floor outside her room, shaking and sobbing.

In a particularly lucid moment before leaving our home, Aunt Jen had told me that she fully intended to keep in touch with me, after her death. We selected a symbol of communication, so that I would know for certain that it was she. We agreed upon her using the letter "V." During World War II, Aunt Jen had given herself a new middle name, Victoria, to emphasize her belief that the allies would prove victorious, and that her husband would return safely after an absence of more than two long years. We agreed that using a "V," as in being **V**ictorious over death, would be an appropriate symbol. The first test of that "V"-sign came one week before Aunt Jen passed.

I later learned that she had had a similar discussion with my cousin, Sandra-Lee, who had been a member of Group Two and continued to remain in close contact with Aunt Jen. Sandra-Lee adopted the "V" symbol as well, but she and Aunt Jen agreed that, for her, the proof of communication would be the two-fingered Victory sign, popularized by Winston Churchill. Sandra-Lee has since reported *many* such "communications," after Aunt Jennie's passing. She conveys that after struggling with an issue, she prays for guidance and mentally asks for Aunt Jen's feedback. Subsequently, and within minutes of her prayerful request, she reports seeing an image of a person using the Victory sign in a magazine or on TV. Coincidence?

On the last Saturday in July, Rose and I were on our annual week's vacation in Ocean City, Maryland, sitting on the sunny beach in front of the condo we had rented. I was telling Rose about an intensely vivid dream I had had of Aunt Jen the previous night. Though at this point I do not recall the details of the dream, that day there was an unusual nagging pull for me to contact my aunt. As I debated whether or not to call her -- hesitating because I secretly feared, based upon my dream, that I would learn that she had already passed on -- I saw the familiar, large billboard vessel approaching our area. The electronic ads on the boat were usually for local restaurants, clubs, shops, or personal messages like birthday greetings, and even engagement proposals.

As I read the ads, I suddenly remembered the "<u>V</u>"-test that Aunt Jen and I had devised to communicate, presumably *after* she had crossed over. *Something moved me* to set the test into action. I secretly proposed to the Universe that *if* the next ad that was displayed on the boat started with the letter, "V," I would call the nursing home. For some odd reason, it seemed that there was a longer delay than usual from one ad to the next. When the next screen ad finally did appear, I was shocked. It read, "<u>V</u>oted the best on the beach…" followed by the name of some restaurant. What is the probability that the letter, "V," which is so seldom used in our language, would be the first letter in the ad? Upon seeing my expression, Rose curiously asked what was wrong. I told her about the synchronicity of the "V"-sign. She immediately placed the call on her cell phone. I can always count on my Rosie!

Unlike the three months of previous calls to the nursing home, Aunt Jen's voice on that day was unusually clear, upbeat, and lucid. I told her the details of my dream about her, and we talked at length about many happy memories. Before ending our lengthy and cheery conversation, Aunt Jen paused, then spoke with great clarity and directness, saying, "My dear nephew, you have meant the world to me! What would I have done without you? Know that I have the deepest love for you and thank you for all you have done for me. I will always love you. God bless you." I was deeply moved, even if her sign-off eerily seemed like a final "Good-bye!"

As it turned out, it *was* a final "Good-bye"!

Reflecting on this event, I will always be grateful for our last conversation, which touched my heart, as well as being thankful for the workings of the "V"-sign.

Two weeks later, Suzanne/Astrada and Ken, her husband, were on their way to the wedding of the daughter of friends in Boston. While on their drive to New England, Suz called to ask for the name and address of the nursing home, as they had decided to visit Aunt Jen. Reminiscing, Suz said that she considered Jen to be like a second mother, a dear friend, as well as a trusted confidant.

Continuing our phone conversation, Suz reflected, "Aunt Jen helped me to make a complete shift in my life. Her unconditional love and her willingness to be completely open and share her authentic self taught me how to take the risk and share with her who I really was with all my multitude of insecurities. Her acceptance and friendship provided a true sense of healing, fostering growth and a newfound sense of real self-worth that ultimately extended into all areas of my life. Over the years, Aunt Jen and I spent many precious hours together, in person and on the phone, talking about serious and even intimate topics, as well as sharing a great deal of laughter!"

Suz later added, "I was excited about visiting Aunt Jen. I hadn't seen her since early April. However, as we got closer to the facility, I developed an unexplained feeling of anxiety. It became stronger and stronger, accompanied by heart palpitations. This had never happened to me before. A sense of panic overcame me."

Suz continued, "Ken and I entered the nursing home and told the receptionist that we were here to visit Jen. I noticed that she stiffened, then tersely said, 'Jen is no longer with us.' I asked her if she was sent to another nursing facility. Appearing tense, she left the desk and returned with the director of the nursing home, who said that they were *permitted* to say only, 'Genevieve is no longer with us,' which prompted Ken to ask more firmly, 'Do you mean in this facility or on earth?' The director hesitated. Then she replied that she had been told by Jen's children not to report her passing to anyone who inquired, but that sensing our concern and love for Jen, she felt compelled to tell us that Jen was taken to a local hospital a week earlier, where she had passed away, on August 3rd."

About 3:00 that afternoon, my phone rang. It was Suzanne.

When I heard Suz's voice, I immediately asked how her visit went with Aunt Jen. I remember that Suz hesitated and finally said, "I don't know how else to say this, Conrad, but Aunt Jennie died last week!" Suz started weeping. An uncontrolled sense of loss welled up within me. Passing the phone to Rose, I began confronting the finality of Aunt Jen's passing.

Suz later added, "Upon leaving the nursing home, I immediately felt an overwhelming rush of peace and deep tranquility, almost as a meditative state. I couldn't help feeling that Aunt Jen was guiding Ken and me to visit the nursing facility so that I could let Conrad, Rose, and the rest of the Group know that she had finally gone 'Home.' I firmly believe that my unexplained anxiety approaching the nursing home was because of the deep connection I had with Aunt Jen. A part of me knew that she was gone. The overwhelming sense of peace I felt afterward was a message from Aunt Jen, telling us that she was at peace and that she was whole."

On what would have been Jen's 91st birthday, on October 11, 2013, we held a beautiful and meaningful memorial service. Twenty-some people, who loved and respected Jennie, were in attendance at our home. Each of the members of Jen's Spiritual Group spoke eloquently about what she meant to them. A common theme was that having known Jen, we are following a richer course in life. Letters were read to the assemblage from Gus and John, Jen's nephews in Florida and Georgia respectively, and from Sandy, her former caregiver who could not be in attendance.

During the service we played four of Jen's favorite hymns. I read the epitaph, that I had written, and we read a prayer from the Guides. As a backdrop, a photo slideshow was circulating on the TV, with pictures of Aunt Jen and key family photos during the years. Finally, we shared a buffet dinner in her honor and memory.

Everyone agreed that the tone of the memorial service was exactly what Jen would have wished. We felt that she was likely present the whole time, enjoying every moment.

One year later, within a few days of the first anniversary of the date of Aunt Jen's passing, I once again relaxed on the same beach with Rosie in Ocean City, Maryland. Suddenly, I began to sense her presence. I was filled with thoughts about the spiritually transformative influence this one woman had had on my life. As I was lost in this swirl of warm thoughts, I noticed that the advertising boat was approaching once again, as it had the previous summer. Being filled with thoughts of Aunt Jen, I activated the V-sign, thinking that *if* the next ad featured a "V," I would know that Aunt Jen was receiving my loving intentions. As "coincidence" would have it, the next ad was an announcement about an upcoming performance by a local musical group, "The Vigilanties."

I pointed out the ad boat to Rose, excitedly telling her that it happened again. As is frequently the case, Rose perceived more than I did. When I told her about the "V"-sign, simply focusing on the fact that the "V" was indeed featured in the ad, she looked at me, smiled and said, "Look at the whole word, Conrad: 'Vigilanties.' Know that your 'auntie' continues to hold 'vigil' for you as well."

What more is there to be said? I know that she is gone from this domain, but Aunt Jen will live on in me and in the many individuals whose lives she helped to "shape." With a sense of certainty, I know that we will meet again and spend at least a part of her next and last lifetime together.

Searching for the right words to draw this story to a close, I was drawn to a small blue unpublished booklet that "synchronistically" slid out from the piles of papers on my desk. I had purchased this pamphlet for $.50, back in the early 1970's, when Aunt Jen and I had visited with Reverend Alfreda Oliver, the impressive British mystic, whom Aunt Jen had heard speak at Parastudy. The booklet was entitled, "What All the World is Seeking." The following quote seems appropriate as an ending (but also as a beginning), as our inspiring story about Jen concludes:

> Man stands at the crossroads of his destiny today.
> Wherever he looks, he sees only destruction, unrest,
> fear, hopeless prospects and defeat. Everywhere he
> is surrounded by a rushing humanity that has no
> idea where it is going.

It is no wonder, then, that these questions are so often asked: Why am I here? What have I come to accomplish? Is there any sense to this game called Life? Is there a loving God who cares for me? If there is, where is He to be found that I may seek His help? Is Peace to be found anywhere?

Both in Rev. Oliver's pamphlet and in the pages of my book, the clear answer to those common and frustrating questions is the same: **GO WITHIN**! As Rev. Oliver wisely concluded:

It lies deep, deep within the human being, and it is the Doorway, beyond which lies the 'Imprisoned Splendor,' that is the true Self of any one of us.

I can only hope and pray, that you, my reader, found within the pages of this book sufficient motivation, instruction, and inspiration from Jen's life, and especially from our Guides and their Messages, to pursue the discovery your own "Imprisoned Splendor." As a final thought, while on your Journey, be on the lookout for life's "coincidences." They might just be subtle invitations from The Great Potter...

EPILOGUE

I n the Preface, I made the assumption that those who are drawn to read this book, are likely to be "Seekers." If you are reading this Epilogue, chances are you have vicariously tapped into the well of inspiration created by a model life, well lived. It is certainly true that Jen, as an uncompromising Seeker for God, *is* an inspiration to all of us, however, I am proposing that an even more powerful source of inspiration comes from knowing *who* and *what* we all truly are. Confident in the knowledge about our True nature, we know that we are indeed worthy of receiving Inspiration and Guidance. Along that line of thinking, it seems apropos to insert a short poem that came through Jennie, as a written Message on April 6, 1972. It speaks to the beautiful reality about who we are:

The Beauty That Is You

God made the flowers, the birds, and you,
He made the waters, the lands, and you,
He made the heavens, the earth, and you,
You are the beauty of that which is He.

He breathed the spirit of life in you,
He set the spirit of motion in you,
He poured the fire of love in you,
You are the spirit of that which is He.

He brought forth that which is the babe of you,
He fostered the babe that became the child of you,
He nurtured the child that became the man of you,
<u>You are the growth of Love which is He</u>.

YES, we certainly ARE infinite spiritual beings on a mortal journey of discovery, rather than being sinful mortals on a spiritual journey of redemption. Given what you have encountered and envisioned while reading this book, I ask you to evaluate: Which of those two vastly different journeys are you traveling?

As a result of the life-shaping intervention in my current incarnation, my personal Journey of Progression was steered or "shaped" toward a more conscious level after the "death" of my old ways of thinking and living, thanks to the artistry of The Great Potter.

At this point in the story, I hasten to emphasize that I am not a guru of great wisdom. I am an ordinary, aspiring mortal, like you, who got a much-needed, blessed jump-start along my path. I am both humbled and inspired by the awesome Gifts presented to me by "W" and the other great Teachers, as well as being deeply thankful for the close companionship with my two soul-mates, Aunt Jen and Rosie, and the special members of our Spiritual Groups, all of whom have enriched my life and my Soul.

As an afterthought (as in days *after* I thought I had finished writing this book), it struck me that I had not shared a clear sense of how my life path was altered as a result of the extraordinary interventions that were described in these pages. Though I have preferred keeping the spotlight on Aunt Jen, the Guides, and the Messages, rather than on me, it occurred to me that providing specific testimony about how my life was molded by the Great Potter might provide some "proof" that our lives *can* change for the better, with open-minds and open hearts. This Epilogue seems like the right place for me to reflect briefly upon that personal transformation.

There have been many times over recent years when I have mentally questioned: Does my life truly reflect almost fifty years of the Special Teaching that you have just read about? My usual answer to this question has been reflexively and consistently: "*NO!*"

Knowing about and believing in the Grandeur of the Teachers and the Teachings, as well as the uncommon life of Aunt Jen, I have found it difficult to see my life, in stark contrast, as being anything other than commonplace. Perhaps my perspective is off, but being led by our Guides' admonition to tell the truth rather than to be falsely humble, I challenged myself to finally answer that important question with greater thought than I have ever given it in the past. The purpose of this exercise is to emphasize how *all* of us can "shape" our own lives, based upon the precepts of Love and Wisdom that were taught by our Guides. To be candid, *if* there had been no transformation in my approach to life as a result of nearly fifty years of this teaching, why would you even want to think about the contents of this book ever again?

Having challenged myself, this is what I now believe to be true about my life, *before* and *after*:

BEFORE November 11, 1966…

o I had low self-confidence, feeling inferior to others.

o I felt lost, having little direction or sense of belonging.

o I did not have a sense of my own abilities and talents.

o I attended to others' needs more than to my own, but based more on doing so to gain favor or praise.

○ I felt that I had no real friends.

○ My faith in religion was crumbling, and my belief in God was shallow.

AFTER November 11, 1966...
Changes directly attributable to the Guides and Guidance...

○ My personal sense of worth has greatly increased, KNOWING that I AM loved by God (as are we all), and that I was blessed by receiving personal guidance.

○ My sense of direction and purpose was illuminated, helping me to work harder to progress in all areas of my life because the "Big Picture" became clearer. Also, knowing my specific life goals for this incarnation has contributed to greater clarity of mission and daily focus of action.

○ My focus on helping others has not changed in frequency, but it has changed in motivation. *Now*, I dedicate my helping efforts to God, to His glory, *not* to mine, deriving deeper satisfaction from doing service and being more mindful of the needs of others.

○ I have been told that I have become a truly good listener and a genuine friend.

○ I *try* to avoid "judging" others or myself; rather, I have learned instead to "evaluate" rather than to "judge" (a distinction that the Guides have insisted upon).

○ Having rejected the concepts of sin, judgment, hellfire and condemnation, I have been freed to learn about life in a far less restrictive and more loving manner.

o Though I am no longer active in my religion, my sense of universal spirituality and belief in God and His Loving Angels and Guides is unshakable!

o I learned to react less negatively to accidents, disappointments, problems, and "failures," seeking instead to learn from those "growth opportunities."

o I am always on the lookout for "coincidences" and subtle helping synchronistic opportunities from the Sublime Realm, especially in dreams and sudden or unexpected events.

o I have learned to increase my trust upon inner guidance and intuition, learning about going Within (though I have a long way to go).

o I now understand that true accomplishment and achievement in life is less about appearances and more about the underlying motives behind the actions.

o I understand that our thoughts have co-creative impact, both positive and negative; therefore, I consciously try to limit those thoughts that broadcast negative vibes.

o I am comforted by accepting what "W" said: *"You are where you are, because that's where you are supposed to be, doing what you are doing, because that is what you are supposed to be doing."* The whole concept of reincarnation has helped put life into perspective for me and has provided greater sensibility and a sense of fairness and purpose about everything.

o I am learning how to "BE," with greater patience, self acceptance, and self love, and I have come to know more about the most important power of the Universes: LOVE!

Now that I have spent some quiet time, reflecting upon how I *have* changed with "The Potter's" gracious intervention, I am more inclined to see that growth has indeed occurred during this incarnation's Journey, especially since November 11, 1966 when the "First Message" was channeled. I hope you, having read this book, will see the direct correlation from the Teachings to my life's improvements. Further, I hope that it will encourage you to more consciously attend to the details of your own Journey.

Our Teachers often depicted us mortals, using the symbol of a mighty tree deeply rooted in the earth, with branches reaching into the heavens. They often told us that if only we could see the glorious Light of our Beings, *as They actually view us*, we would be both amazed and profoundly convinced of our True Heritage. Our Guides went even further to declare, "**Yee are gods of your own universe.**"

If, after having read this true story of transformation and progression, you remember nothing more than the Truth of Who you are and of the Sacredness and mighty Purpose of your Journey, I will feel that my efforts in having told this story, from a grateful heart, will not have been in vain.

Embrace your Sacred Journey,
Conrad / Armand

A SPECIAL NOTE...

I invite my readers to visit my website, www.ConradFollmer. com, so that we can exchange thoughts about the book or related spiritual issues. Let's keep this Journey going!

A COLLECTION OF MESSAGES...

I n this Appendix, I have included a small collection of Messages
from the one thousand or so inspired communications that
came through Jen over the near half-century of her mystical
channeling. I invite the readers to use these resources as analytic
and contemplative opportunities. I encourage you to read each
Message slowly and multiple times, perhaps as a morning or late
night routine, underlining key words, phrases and perhaps even
writing your personal thoughts in the wide margins to the side or
below each Message.

Many of the initial Writings in this cluster come from the
earliest years (1960s and 1970s), when Jen was taking daily
dictation from the Guides. Following those Messages are a few
others that came through orally, either at small gatherings or at
actual Spiritual Group Meetings.

**In my opinion, although these Messages were given to
a relatively small circle of pilgrims, they contain Universal
Truths to be shared with the world of Truth Seekers...
like YOU.**

When one is on a desert, he feels the inadequacies of man's comforts. He is surrounded by a vast loneliness and is aware of the danger of not surviving a journey. His mind wanders in many areas, but keeps returning for his need for survival. Man is in the vastness of the arid desert when he has no knowledge or desire for his Lord and God. He drinks water at the oasis but finds it tasteless. He struggles along the trek through the sands, which could be treacherous at any point. He cannot establish a firm footing, both from falling away at his feet, and dashing the sight from his eyes. Even the sun at this point is a blinding factor unless he is well protected, but then the heat may become a problem. At many steps along this journey, he struggles to find the right solution so that he may reach safety. Crossing the desert, he is aware of the vastness and incomprehension of that which seems boundless and endless. Does he subjugate himself to the perils of heat and storms, or does he try mastery of what awaits? To reach his point or destination, he assumes a role of duality – one of patience and one of fortitude. He is both master and pupil along the way. There is but to be wary of the situations that arise, and be calm in the eye of what he surveys. Life is a peril to him at times, but there is always the beauty that is and may be if he looks through the vision of his heart. From this point of view, each stop for water is heavenly and refreshing; each morsel of food is like unto the manna of heaven; each step he takes leaves a footprint for others to follow. He finds a new strength of mind and purpose as he plods along to what he hopes to be of true value at the end of his journey. He is at once a boy of adventure, and a man of learning. He receives from within and releases without. He is now a giant of means. He is assured he can weather the storms and strife of the desert, for at definite places he will find strength and communication to go onward. Oh, what peace and glory he sees for himself! The end of the journey is but the beginning of life in its fullest. The sun is now his friend and guide for he establishes the proper respect for its strength and purpose. The winds and sands are his constant companions as he allies his needs with theirs. He rests in the Hands of His Lord, for He is the Master of Love who is with him, and awaits to enfold his entire being with the power of Love. He sees in reality the danger and the creativity of love in its heights, but now he relies on the goodness within. What he pictured without, he found in reality within. Love overflows and touches what he sees and touches. He knows this exists for each one, and only sees the end result of good in all. He walks now with strength and purpose.

MESSAGE...
(A list of suggestions for living, delivered during a Meeting, 2000)

PROCLAMATION TO HOLINESS

1. **Live unto God and His Blessings.** Do not use carelessness in speech.
2. **Be aware thou art His pupil and teacher of those who would aspire**. Do not trust unto those who would not learn.

3. **Be of patience and gentility.** If agreement cannot be made, assume the role of mediator and not agitator.

4. **Love each other as the Lord Christ loved his Apostles and Disciples.** Do not seek faults in others who do not comprehend.

5. **Console failures in others, but do not praise unnecessarily.** This demands the ruling of the heart.

6. **Keep a record of thy misdoings and search whereupon the error occurred.** This does not have to be in writing.

7. **Practice the Presence of the Lord and act accordingly.** Be aware that He is present and is tending His flock.

8. **Look beyond thyselves to the turmoil of others.** Know and understand that these are the reign of a temporal world.

9. **Be of steadiness and commitment.** Do not fret over faltering – the Helping Hand is ever there.

10. **Above all – do not be afraid** – be trusting and trustworthy.

MESSAGE...
5-12-67 (for Conrad)

As a symbol of purity see in thy mind the whiteness of Our Lord's robes. Probe further to see what the folds of the material hold in their possession. Chastity should be envisioned in many degrees – both of the mind and spirit.

254

A closer look should impel thee to want to know the weave of the material and how came it to be so. Did the whiteness serve as a symbol to Our Beloved Christ or was it the color of the day? How was this robe worn? – was it close-fitting or loose? Understand truly the symbolism of the two meanings. A closeness would have revealed a certain aspect and looseness should entail a character with great depth. Pursue this thought as far as it will take thee – as thought to get at the heart of the matter. See the particular brightness of the whiteness – is this also from the cloth or the exuding eminence of The Man? How did they not collect the dust of the Ages? -- is this so? – can thou comprehend the meaning of this? Look beyond the words as thou has been instructed.

How many things remind thee of Our Lord's robes? Are robes material as such? Look with the eyes of intelligence and the seeking heart of love. Know fully the true beauty of this substance of great wealth and let thy traveling take you into the avenues of time immortal. Hold onto this glorious robe of priceless treasures and partake of its riches for thy soul.

MESSAGE...
2-26-67

Hearken to the Voice – Look all around and see that I exist. Other times have borne witness to My Birth. I was not known as such. Masters of Religion do not always impart true facts. Each religion has its own belief – one part of the ALL. The ages have erased facts – the world has changed in its geographic scope – waters have come where cities dwelt – mountains have sprung up from stone.

Man exists in relation to his Self. How has the gift of the genius been borne: Does he not bespeak of the time gone by? The World revolves and so does man – he evolves in the patterned rule, his makeup is not always the same but is granted a certain kinship. The soul's quest for itself begins its journey – Periods of time lapse and then begin anew. Meanwhile Time plays its role in changes. Moods and impressions add their toll in the behavior. Observation is from a different point of view. Life continues and the universe changes its appearance. Memories are forgotten; new things begin. Acceptance is free for some and an incurred debt to others. A blossoming of ideas, but how to put it? Fear still reigns and attitude is lost. The pattern still must go on then. The ascending is for all but the gravities change its course.

MESSAGE...
4-24-67 Enlightenment

How can we hope to flee the bonds of this earth? It is not by all of our trivial actions of words. We must seek an avenue of pure love – a reciprocation of a love given us. We cannot hope for the best in life if we are not able to part with the best in us.

Trials are held for our testing and thus do we prove our true motives. It is better to give of ourselves than to have every little gain returned in double measure. You cannot be judged by what is given you – that judgment is for the other person.

Seek to understand a peaceful knowledge of contribution. Test all the ways until one seems to stand up straighter that all the others.

Life has a series of by paths but it is not always wise to make use of all in existence. Sometimes the crowded roads must be sought in order to make certain that the true path will not elude us.

MESSAGE...
1-22-69 *Jen and Conrad* (on Conrad's 24th Birthday)

In reincarnation, the theories are relatively simple. As one sows unto himself, so shall he reap his rewards, may they be famine or true harvesting of nature. One plunges into that territory of which there could be a knowledge as an issuance.

One does not learn at once the theories of reasoning because of the law of time as a known factor to man. Time must be brought about as a known substance to man in order to relate history of the universe in sequence. When man can establish, according to the earthly time, the principles of learning, his means of reincarnation subsist as a measure of gaining on his trek homewards. One begins his onset from a known point, but also as a means of adventure; he stumbles into many pitfalls due to his lack of experience, and also at times as a means to conquer.

The will of the individual is such that at certain points of life (which is of a grand, eternal scope) can be adjusted to the known factor of reasoning. In other words, there is an attunement of the senses of man to correlate factors concerning himself and what relationship he exists in that portion of life. He might stumble blindly, then in another portion of life, not through the unknown factor, but through the issuance of a new knowledge of learning. He has not lost what he had learned, he was just learning a different method. The mind expands at one portion and as a balancing faction, it contracts at another issuance.

Man holds within himself the materials to pursue his aim and purpose if that so be his entire will, but then here too, comes the Will of the High Domain. If it truly be the proper time of awakening, when all factions reason in attunement, then a knowledge is brought unto man at that portion. If thou has been awakened, thou knows, without hesitation, because this is a factor brought about by that which is being unveiled to thyself without the knowledge of another being. This, thou sees, is the correlation of the known and unknown senses of man in correlation with the upper, greater force of what is above and beyond. Thou sees the balancing thus, the known power of man and the unknown power of God. Looking at it thusly, the known force or mind of mortal man in the capacity of learning a truth, and the unknown force of teaching which is the upper strata of the immortal.

One can have one without the other, but thou must understand, the link does not really exist. A link is the connection of one thing with another. If thou can relate unto thyself the reasoning powers of man, then thou becomes more humble to the degree of the unknown and yet known principle, that here and now exists that part of God, which exists as part of man to show himself his true worth. He knows instinctively what he reasoned of his own power and that which is given for him to reason by God. The humbleness is to the point of knowing that no matter what reasoning is used and what results are obtained, the glory is in the Maker and the realization of this very fact shows man without God he is naught because the real power and glory is God and His creation of man. Man sees himself as a creation of knowing and unknowing.

MESSAGE...
3-25-67 Jen Prayed for Enlightenment (Lesson One)

Knowledge is of a strange and inscrutable quality – part is known and little is understood. A gathering of minds on one subject is believed to be more or less supreme test of a title, but alas, much is not so. There are always ground rules to follow in any line and reach of the scope. The true knowledge exists within the soul and in its fathomable state, a few links of life hood come within the grasp of human understanding.

Look for wisdom in the little words and have the true meaning issue forth from these substances. Understand that there is a mighty force in the usage of a small item applied in a skillful and adept manner. These elusive qualities lie within the grasp of enlightenment; however, as you know, certain things are of a certain time. A circle of light sometime does not appear as that form from a certain step in life. To some it may not appear as a circle at all. To others the circle might appear to be radiating fine pinpoints of light, and still to others these lights might appear in full colors. Gather within from this that the true knowledge must then come from an extraordinary procedure – a procedure that takes a very careful, penetrating study – especially of human relationship.

Know also for some problems, there are always answers and solutions, grant that these aren't always put in such a small light that they are so easily solved. Know now also, that in order to seek knowledge, the path of love must be made visible first. Without this one degree in life, nothing is obtainable. Degrees of love do fall in certain steps and one should not fall in the pit of falsehood to think that this is not so.

If you would penetrate further, you would see that if a group of scholarly men were given a riddle, each so-called wise man would solve this enigma id his degree and thought of knowledge and one can readily see, if this be his study in life, that a picture of a question in one mind differs in small ways from another's.

Then there is always the other step in life – the picture that the one man sees – can he fully tell another man exactly and precisely what he saw? Now, this must be to the infinite degree, you understand: Search in thy mind, because the answer comes back that the small word must be understood first. Know that the lessons in life do start from the minutest point of existence and blossoms forth from this almost invisible dot.

Enough for Lesson One.

MESSAGE...
3-27-67 *Let's Start Lesson Two*

Begin at the beginning of time. Such a grand first beginning – not just a matter of empty space. We are now speaking of great things – of such a magnificence that it takes more than just a mere man's comprehension. Life began at just this precise moment of electricity.

The scope of the imagination should know no bounds but this is where the line is drawn. The condition of the world, in the sense you know it to be, showed many, many changes from time to time and still the apparent changes were not known at all. Do you understand what great perception is needed? Now, how do we go about these lessons of human nature? Are some persons actually gifted with this insight? Come, come now, no scoffing. These are the very reasons for their works. Use some of thy knowledge to know that it must be divinely inspired – how could this not be so? Thy gifts are for your own imagination; study carefully your own. After all, these are not going to be shown that easily!

Life was meant for work – work of a nature that takes on an eternal meaning. This does not mean purely physical labor! Adjust thyself to inward thinking; so much that a definite sense of perception is noted. There is quite a sure feeling concerning this. If truth must be taught, we want them taught wisely and for a definite purpose. Thy heart instinctively knows the true light which beckons onward and upward into the aspiring heavens. You wonder, how soon does all this begin? Child, awaken to the fact that this has always been so! What is time after all – just a matter to earth, but beyond that it does not exist – it's just that simple. However, you do really know that simple things are not really simple at all. You could say that they are so simple that they escape human knowledge.

I want you to understand that the potential does exist for all, but if some want to walk in blindness, the Light weakens for them and fails to guide. Some people are meant for some directive purposes – this is felt by those individuals, let's have no scruples about that point. The inborn knowledge is plucked slowly, oh so very slowly, until the person can't help feeling this very unique change in his existence. Such is this one purpose of what you believe to be the great enduring life. It could be looked upon with humor, but we'll dispense with that immediately. Life is definitely serious – of a tremendous scope, existing for all Time. There is that word "time" again, but the lessons must be learned with relation to time, because it is of utmost importance for this particular period of earthly life. (Shall we pause for this day's work?)

MESSAGE...

3-28-67 Are We Ready for Lesson Three?

We spoke of Time – we do believe the subject today should be the elements. This is a vast stage of life and so much to be learned. Were we to begin from the first moment of arrival, we would find the very element of air infiltrating the life of the newborn. He carries with him the very elements to sustain livelihood – an inborn knowledge of days past. Thus begins the start of the individual trek – the pursuit of what he alone establishes. He goal – that is something the soul could answer. The elements instituted in him play the grave roll of mastering him to the majority of his earthly life.

The great element of love – this is a field in itself. Can you really think of anything, which is not actually of love? This does not mean the physical sense of the word – such as for one person to another. The degree of love with relation to an object – an object of pure love. This takes on the love of beauty in the form of creation. The creating of an object of love – made from the thoughts of perfecting in a degree of love. This love has derived from the inward being, but somehow or other, it is believed to be the genius of the individual; but if the truth be really understood, this is to be known as that particular element manifested in that person. As was said in the former lesson, it must be clearly understood that Love plays a part in all life's work. Even in hate does love play its part. You cannot see that? Hate is the counterpart of love; therefore, we must have a love for another object to direct hatred for the other object. The same elements existing in love are twisted in the outpouring and come out as hate.

We come upon the elements of air, light, fire, etc., because as I say, there is a vast field to be covered here. air in itself carries many minor elements of its own – all secondary ones, and they manifest certain areas of the human being. Part of the brain is pinched by these wandering elements of air.

Light – ah, that is the beautiful one – this is the ethereal manifestation of the soul for its upward flight someday. This is the graciousness of man, the real blueness of the skies that man dreams of. It could be described in so many ways, much as the peaceful feeling of the very lightness of the rays penetrating towards understanding our existence. With reluctance I leave this talk about Light.

We come to Fire – you could almost feel the tremendous power and force of this element. We spoke of the Fire of wisdom – in this sense, the fiery, forceful rays penetrating the part of man which leads him ever onward in his seemingly never-ending quest for whatever particular subject he is pursuing. You could say the person is afire with the ingrained substance of whatever reason he feels for existence. Then he branches off in the direction of the flaming rays – also sometimes in the misdirected path of the rays as his vision has been clouded or almost subdued by the dying flames.

We could cover many other elements, but I believe these are the main ones and we don't want to put too much reading and nonsensical items to make it long-drawn. It is enough to understand basic things in certain areas. This in itself should show itself clearly to you. we do exist for a very definite purpose, but

I've tried to show how certain elements transposed at birth can and will effect our purpose.

The one thing always remaining is the Divine Will. And the need to surrender to it for a closer understanding of what purpose we may achieve. We cannot travel our Road of Life alone with the thought that we have been imbued with strands of pure genius such as to let us believe we do not need real guidance. We cannot and positively should not make this fatal error of existing for our Will –this will belong to God – offer it to Him for His guidance. He is the one to lead your way, and also, as the Will is left in His care, so will these other putfalls be avoided.

The hope for the very future must rest itself on the one sole factor of the little part of life that has been set up for us. Be assured that there is a definite design and pattern, which each of us must fit into. Understand that the pattern exists for different degrees all into one large uncomprehending picture of goodness and badness, beauty and ugliness. It is up to us to establish which part of the picture we would like to occupy and realize that if it is the good we are seeking, then we should strive to have Our Lord show us our everlasting trail toward Him. Again I repeat, this has mostly to do with prayers – prayers for your salvation.

The path to Christ must always be one where the individual constantly seeks His help. The extends His hand and His heart of pure love to await the coming of man into his right proportion. Does this not show you the gloriousness and peace of the Great Father looking after His children?

End of Lesson Three.

265

MESSAGE...
8-16-68 *To Whom It May Concern*

In all instances of rebirth, the problem has been where the situation should be met. It is not enough alone to struggle just for that which leads one forward. One has the "happening" or event for the purpose of regaining that which he lost. The struggle so to speak, is but a matter of conveyance of spiritual meaning and intention. If one were of the faculty of obedience to all occasions of living, one had but to walk a certain path. Man has not been endowed with infallibility. This is one of the pitfalls. He stands alone upon the battlefield of wit unto the degree of his learning. His ponderance is such that he makes for himself what he wills. To sit in the bottom of the pit and just hope for the helping hand is to be led by the blind in a stony path. Does one have full faculties of obedience? The answer lies in each what he can by power of suggestion.

Some exist by their own purpose of life, which does not mean it is a correct pattern. A pattern, nevertheless, has been set forward unto his means, but the individual uses his own judgment upon the sands of time. One does have the foremost requisite established for correctness – that is the power of prayer. However one must know that that in itself is a two-way proposition, if one may be so bold as to call it by that name. the heart must melt under the strain of a higher degree of nature and the subjection is such that the heart acts of free will once this is established.

Thine own purpose is a foreordained principle of establishment. How these grains of knowledge

266

are put to use, is a test of succeeding or not. Thy testing is of true grounds and thy effort should be the subsistence of correct prayers. Our bountiful blessings and careful attitude toward thee on thy path. Be careful of straying, for such is life that at each interval is the timing of long duration.

Endover

MESSAGE...
3-4-67 osophy

The soul of man is a deep pit of knowledge to be studied before it fades away into nothingness. Take grips on thyself and explore the bottomless abyss. Fear not the darkness because after the dark there shall be light.

Divine love cannot be created by ordinary man – it must be gifted. A search of the mind reveals many hidden secrets. Contemplate the richness of the soul after it is empty of all reasoning – that is where divine revelations exist. This knowledge is thrust forward to the being and makes itself known as such. All things can be revealed to the Soul if it be a pure thing and seeks the path of goodness. Where does the worldly knowledge come from – the outside or the inside? Great gifts are bestowed on those creatures entrusted with certain cares of life. This in turn is put forth on a level of understanding for such as those who choose to comprehend of such existence of divine nature.

An expression of love in its finest form can be seen by the discerning eye as a mutual understanding. By the same discernment, a difference of character is noticeable in certain areas. Mankind takes on an aspect of its own. Kindness becomes a part of the nature and above all, Love rules with a steadfast hand. Light intermingles with darkness, loneliness with fullness, understanding with ignorance.

Comprehension is not such an easy matter, for some, yes, but for others who look on with the hard and unbelieving eye, only a complete emptiness shows from this. Care not for the doubting of others, seek to help thyself. In all things be true and suffer not the pangs of unbelieving. Woes of nature are many but at times take on the aspect of sweetness. Seek to understand thy nature for by this very fact can things be understood.

MESSAGE...
4-8-67 *Philosophy*

The heart of man can be likened to the interior of a cave. There are so many crannies and nooks hidden away among the rocks and these can be compared to the crevices of the inside walls of the heart. In so many small places can the deposits be abandoned – some for future use and some just for the sake of discarding a useless item. Just as in a cave, a ray of light may sometimes penetrate into one of the nooks and thus illumine the object for a few moments – so the heart, with its objects of love, hate, jealousy, and anger. Consider now a heart full of love – when the ray of light enters, it combines with a tremendous warmth because just the object of love receives all the attention and therefore, can radiate much more power than any other force known to man. Therefore, if man must be made whole, let him not be likened to a cave. He must walk around with his own lights illuminating his powers – his lights must penetrate outward from the inner being, contrary to the cave whose inner creations must be lighted from without.

Life stands waiting to be of use – an abundance of creation, waiting for the manipulation of man in his creative genius to generate a complete study of his own. There are materials of different weight, size, and power, which he must combine in the right proportion to be of correct use. Herein lies the power of creating good or evil. Both powers come into being at the moment of conception and the builder decides which power must prevail. If a man desires control of himself, then he must understand the composition of his makeup. There is no other construction as intricate as the mechanism of man and this study alone takes a lifetime. However, if man does not temper this great study with love, then man becomes a robot in sense, without a heart. The scholar must study with the forethought of love in order for love to emerge from this careful study. He must put forth love in order to behold love in this great object. These visions he he has for his creation come from the hidden crevices of his heart which have felt the power of the illuminating ray, and through its warmth he perceives what is to be.

To contemplate the life ahead one must be in the complete obedience to a higher degree of understanding. One must strive to understand and help oneself, however he can. This cannot be a situation where all things will be put forth before him without any effort on his part. It must be a form of absorption of all collected materials and a sifting out of all unrelating matter. In other words, the truth must be sifted out of the clinging falsehoods. How do we attain these different levels of functioning and reasoning? We apply ourselves wholeheartedly to the issue, with the trust in Our Lord God and the desire to please this very Will. We must realize that life does hold an entire meaning of its own, no matter how difficult it may be to understand and how unlikely it may seem. Perhaps things have been put forth in a sort of disguise – our duty then, is to unmask this belief and have the truth emerge. You must understand in all teachings of the churches, the rulings haven't been disguised entirely for the reason of misleading a populace. Much of the true teaching was left out because of the fear of these higher officials that the so-called "power" they held in the palms of their hands, would fall into every low-being individual, and adoration for them and their "power" and "goodness" would be stripped away. The power is in all of us to behold but it must be sought after – it will not put itself forward. Seek after it with earnestness and good heart.

The world has lost most of its reasoning, and many people who have seen the Highest Kingdom have subsequently lost it because of their greed in the transformation of their own power. You see, every form of power must be used in goodness and one must realize it must be used according to the Will of Our Lord, and understand that it is strictly through and by His very blessing that this goodness has been instituted. A person finding this Kingdom must be aware, then, that this Kingdom is for all and in all, and that he must be subjective to the others the same as himself for they all possess and are the same as he. One is all and all is one. If the person Attaining this Higher Degree seeks to keep this knowledge to himself, either for fear of ridicule or for the purely selfishness of beholding such great power, then you can see, this Kingdom is not the right abode for him, and he has not actually been admitted to this Kingdom even though he has seen it and is totally aware of its presence. Therefore, we always come back to the same reasoning – our thoughts must have the same purpose of our Creator.

Carry thyself as an institution of God and trouble to learn the correct ways and the avenues of finding will prevail. An excitement of true evaluation puts forth an emergence – a quality of one's self appears as a fiery substance of great worth. Can anything compare with this great treasure of salvation? Now life is different – everything has the true quality and substance for which it has been created – you see yourself in all things – this is the power of God and you realize it is He and not you, although you are now a part of Him and have relinquished all ways and will to Him. Now happiness is complete – what does thou have to fear of death or sin? Sin doesn't exist, pain is as nothing and life glows with its own substance of reality and peace and true love have found their resting place. Does this not have a tremendous appeal for mankind? Seek, my heart, with all humility and love for Our God and ask Him to lead thee on.

MESSAGE...
8-3-67 (For Conrad)osophy

Whatever exists in the world of humans is the humans themselves. Therefore, whatever is created by them is issued forth as a force. Whether this is a force of goodness or evil has to do strictly with the motivation behind this force. It is almost what can be thought of as a judgment of thought –- a subconsciously evil thought is manifested by an evil force, or what can be thought of as "evil spirits." Do not confuse this with the fact of an evil force existing. There is this one world in existence – that is why we try to impress on thee so strongly to live in the manner of the teaching Christ. The power to overcome this devouring force can be produced by the individual. He must not let himself be put in the capacity of a fear which eats away at his insides and thus be overpowered by this evil force or spirits. Part of this force, you can say the origination, comes into being from the individual himself. Through fear of the unknown and also fear of mankind's teachings, he recedes into a backsliding of the soul and thus is an easy prey for a powerful destruction of forces. If one would understand by all this that to be confronted by a force of this nature does not mean the person is of himself one possessed of evil thoughts, but if this person is earnestly striving toward the goodness of the universe, then begins a completely different way of traveling. One has to meet the repelling forces in order to become aware of the true guiding qualities of being.

This is a lonely traveling and one of great discernment of an enlightening discovery. In a sense, one must learn a mastery over the low conditioning force within himself which invites a company of himself which invites his reflections. There is a low point and a high point. If one can understand that there must be a communion first between the two, and the real deciding issue is which of those qualities has the controlling and understanding factors. Sometimes it is difficult, particularly and mainly, when the high point is established on a weak foundation. Then the battle will be fought on a losing ground and the high point cannot reach an understanding of the lower factor of his being. Confusion sets in and misunderstanding attends all sessions of a meeting of the minds. Fear takes possession – thus, thou can understand how this part of life revolves in its own pattern. If thou can picture a circle with different segments partitioned off in different degrees of a makeup of life, and as movement takes place in a continual tide, if thou would try to peer deeply into this movement, thou could understand all the forces involved and how easily the force or the circle could be deformed in so far as the unbalancing is concerned. In order to keep this power or force in a circular movement, which thou must understand indicates an eternal movement (infinity) it must be ruled by the Kingdom of Eternity. Either the Light or the Darkness.

It is of dire importance, then, to understand one must know and let himself be known to the Father. Sadly, so many believe that this is a thing of the future instead of facing it immediately. To put off or delay such action may carry grave results, which no amount of sorry can eliminate. Travel on the road of goodness and surround thy thoughts and thy very being with goodness and light must eventually penetrate in its guidance. A special prayer can be said at these moments of consuming fear:

O Lord, my Heavenly Father of Eternity,
Dispel this force of unknowing,
Abide in me and bring peace,
Comfort my soul with love and guidance.

Peace be unto thee and all those earnestness of a good seeking.

MESSAGE...
10-14-67

An object of great beauty dwells in the isolation of loneliness because of the fear of contamination, be it jealousy, inferiority, or any manifestation of destroying quality. All would see the beauty, but all would not judge with the same quality. Some would seek to lower the value, and some would seek clever words to mask a longing for ownership. Still others would gaze upon it a derive an inward feeling of warmth from loveliness of such wealth of creation. They do not desire to imprison the splendor but feel the dependence of security given inwardly. Who in thy opinion actually gains from this beauty? Can it not be noted that the individual has been created with materials of wealth and he takes on the appearance to the degree of what is seen through another's eyes? What matter if one cannot see the wealth of his own creation, if at every turn he vision rewards his heart with the beauty of other wealth? Does not the gentle heart glow with the warmth of this beauty and cannot even the blind feel this warmth and still mask this radiation?

Trust not in the flowing tribulations, but those that emerge as an un-comprehension, for the heart in itself can distinguish the honesty of love. Decree thyself as a merit of worth, and do not abandon principles set before thee. Subsist in the overcoming of trials set in thy path – regard them first as objects of a testing degree. Even these are to be met and conquered with love because with their hurdling they have brought thee the compassion to gaze upon other events. If it were not for these strifes, would thou be of an eventuality to understand beauty in its actual worth?

Again, these are not admonitions. However, we decree, these are judgments of love and learning. Our blessings unto thee.

Father Baptiste

If one would look back into the childhood of his dreams, would he not bring forth the thought of the unknown? Childhood is a period of questing. The mind is told certain matter. And it is this little portion that must act in accordance with decision on an unknown quality. However, if the seed is implanted in good soil, and is watered just enough, this would in time bloom in the manner of good cultivation. A child is but the beginning of a new scope. Although he has all, he has but a little that comes to fore. It is the influence of surrounding elements that can either transcend him to unknown heights or that keep him in the lower range of existence. It is most important what foreign matter is revealed because of the unknown attraction. What faith can mean to a child is a manner of comprehension, much as a trusting. It does not mean that the trust exists as a definite condition – it just means that the child looks for security but withdraws within a shell of hard interior. Penetration then becomes an abstract factor in producing any real knowledge. In a child, the faith is to his earthly parents, to lead him onward – to make him aware of the pitfalls, as well as to reveal the true goodness of nature. The trust should be implanted in the natural issuance of the Creator. He should be aware, and intelligently so, that our Maker is the Realm of Supreme Goodness, and this is the real quality of love. Love should come as the example from the parents to show this little form of humanity where trust rightfully belongs. A child is not too young to understand the Father, because in his own mind, he makes known his desires in the conversation of his time. Does the Father not understand His own Creation? The fault of un-comprehension along certain degrees for the child is meted towards the parents. If one wanders of his duty, can this not be seen as a prime duty of a unison of two substances who put forth as issuance of an individual quality? It is with shame that we look upon the shrinking of this godly task. If one could understand, the negative always coincides with the positive. In pain, there is health, in solitude, there is happiness, in hate there is love, in sorrow, there is joy. With the vision adjusted so as to see the two existing forces, one treads the middle course safely, yet heeding the different qualities that overlook the boundaries. Ponder on the beginning of creation and know that the onstart of life controls the ceasing as it appears in that time scope. Is it life or death? Let thou can see they are equal qualities of still unknown substances. Is it the warmth of heart or the coldness of comprehension, and again, is it the quality of mind or is it the quality of mind or soul? We remind thee of the many unthought and forgotten purposes to the natural laws of creation. Our many blessings and wishes for peace.

Father Baptiste

MESSAGE...

6-9-04 A Message delivered to Verity

Hark! The Angels speak and put a spell upon thee. Over the horizon lies the trail of the platitudes of life. The heart must awaken its beat, for there is a certain ponderance of rhythm. Loosen thy threads of distraught! There is a parallel of thought to each saying, and one must discern the meaning of each. Languish not, for there is a result of issuance. Be of the one who sees forward and backward. Do not hovel on thy behalf. O lonesome mortal, loosen thy bonds, and prevail in the turmoils of life! Do not let dismay entangle thee in their everlasting twisting means. True life spells abundance – Plentitude is there for the asking of the seeker. Be not weary in thine awkwardness of plundering after a given thought of action. The seeds have been sown in their tomb of awakening. Sunlight awaits to replenish the thirsting of want. Blossoming takes but a while and soon the footsteps of desire appear. This is a moment of wonder – does this hold the path to be taken? It is worth the struggle to comprehend what is issued before thee and there is that visibility of unseeing. What is portrayed to thee is that moment of decision. Is it fright to hold thee down, or wilt thou travel in bravery?

MESSAGE...

12-6-03 A Message delivered to Verity

(Note: Exhausted, but awakened from a nap, Verity was able to catch these words, from those that rushed by, quavering):

Reciprocal crossing
The elevation of soul
Communion with want
Abbreviation of factor
The whirlwind of space
The inhabitation of want
The creativity of love
The abolishment of hate

(Note: She then received this message from a high teacher):

Act One – Love
Sit in the glory of Light
The players: ears
Act Two – Communion of Desire
The players: eyes
Act Three – Worship of the Marriage
The players: heart

We are all actors in the play of life. What do you think of the actors [Act One]? What do you think of the second act – art thou seeing correctly? Act Three – art thou witnessing a convolution of means?

Ponder on the misery visited unto our souls. Is this inflicted in our being? Is this through want or falsity of living? Is this through intimidation or the desire to outrun our limitation?

Witness a day in thy life such as thou has seen it issued in a play. Was the play pleasing to thee? Now think of how thou could have changed the outcome. Do this carefully, using the actors in the play. Does thou see an improvement?

Oh my Soul, dust thou not see thou art the author of thy play and the issuance can be met faithfully in conjunction with thy means. In the All is that which can be seen, heard, and felt.

O, my Soul, it is but for thee to extend thy hand in welcome. Such can thou sense the radiation of the energy of Life. Let what thou feels be as a love token. It is granted unto thee to bathe in this vitalizing glow. Be now the Conqueror who battles the falsities of life. See how the Conqueror is crowned with that of adornment. Life so far has been a prelude – now comes the action of the play in the magnitude on Love as thy partner.

MESSAGE…
5-4-08 A Message for Verity and Armand

(NOTE: Verity and Armand were seated at the table. Talking about some of the messages which have come out in the past week or so. This is a record of the give and take between The Guides and Armand, spoken aloud by Verity)

Don't you understand, ye are God? (as soon as we realize we are a part of God, we will not come back here). We would be in the perfection of Grace.

You are God in recognition of the Spirit which exists within thee, not outwardly! As thou has come in as a form of perfection, unto thee is that reality to return in perfection; therefore, it has to be known physically, not just spiritually.

Armand tried to explain that statement...

(to Armand): thou says the words but does not understand the meaning.

Armand remembered the First Message quote, "Hope lies forever in the midst."

Thou has the recognition of the IOTA.

Armand interpreted: **I Of The Almighty**...

Thou has growth possibility...

(NOTE: Verity and Armand were eating lunch. This writing came through while they were discussing the previous message, which challenged the Group members to "...know themselves..." by reflecting on a key word/impression...)

It is important for the heart to know falsity.

This is as a migration of the soul.

Trouble not for the unwanted, for this is a lesson in return.

Tenderness abounds, but it is secluded, and for some, it is not treasured.

Hope is forever in the midst.

Is it understood what sublimity means or stands for?

Armand said, that which is of God, the spiritual, as opposed to the lower material world

There is a similarity to the pipe [a smoking pipe], if understood correctly.

Armand said, It is like spiritualizing the material in that the physical raw material, tobacco, is put into the bowl, and energy/heat/flame is applied to it. This transforms the physical into a lighter state of gas/ smoke, which is inhaled, or taken within, then given out, for the smoke to rise upwards.

Is it not from inhalation of the pipe? It is being processed.

That's a part of understanding the sublime. And does thou not see that that is cloaked? Which means to see beyond.

Armand said, It demands conscious effort to see beyond

Ah, thou knows well. This is as a gain for thee.

Armand most graciously thanked them…

Most welcome. That which is to be honored has to be informed.

Woe to the unbeliever of the soul. Theirs is a myth!

Trouble thyself for awareness of that which is as in a float.

Armand suggested that floating means being ungrounded or not rooted, like theoretical thinking or blind faith without understanding.

Look for the truism of substance. Holy is he who sees behind or beyond that (which is), we use again, float. But note that there is absolution, which should issue from gratitude. And understand the meaning of gratitude, for that is not a falsity. It is as an abeyance to the Principle of giving and living. Sustain in the Almighty's listening and giving. Attention is immediate! Do not be concerned about whereabouts, for that is the inner realm.

There is a key to principality, but it is wise to know how to use it.

Armand suggested that the key has to be Love...

The sublime is not for all to see, but (for) those who wish to see.

Armand said that that reminded him of the painting of Jesus at the door, with His words suggesting that IF the person hears the knocking, the door will be opened and He will come in.

Thou art knowing the key. Which key opens the door? There are many keys to life.

This is what is meant by abridging the chasm.

Armand said the determined, conscious desire, as in hearing the Knock at the door...

Calling out to the Highest.

Armand repeated that we bridge the chasm through conscious effort and desire

But know why thou pursues it, not for power.

Armand suggested that the members of our Group are of good heart and motive, and DO wish to pursue, even if fear gets in the way at times

We stand by for assistance, but it is to be labored for.

Armand recalled the smoking pipe analogy, indicating that we must do more than just wanting it, we have to supply the energy/flame to ignite it into smoke.

Thou has a moment of true understanding.

Armand said that he was seeking MORE than just a moment...

It takes but a moment to travel the universe. Understand (that) the universes of thy being.

Thou sees as an unspoken picture. Look beyond!

There are many steps to life, but most are afraid of height.

I come to thee as the quality of life in the issuance of decree (or degree). We hold thee to the format of instigation, we could say that that's to the liberty of the soul.

Armand thanked him most graciously

And most graciously welcomed. We honor thee to the degree of want.

Armand said, I DO want!

So shall it be obtained.

Armand said, to Our Lord's honor, may it be so

We say, Amen!

MESSAGE…
3-1-09 A Message During a Group Meeting

[After extensive and productive discussions, we invited the Masters to speak to us…]

We have spoken many times to say the real life is within thee. It is not there, or there. It is settled within thyself. Thou knows the real truth, but thou does not believe. Thou looks to the others to see if they agree with thee.

Life exists within thyself. Go (into the) heart of thyself. Know it is as a treasure to be won. That could be the answer: ONE. One in God. (You) are the Principle of God, the Most Holy. Look unto thyself (within), and trust in the knowledge of the heart. Do not look unto others as a beacon of light. Understand the true principle of existence, and why thou art here.

We will give thee a specific way of thinking. When thou goes within thyself -- thou art with another person; two people together. Two people of two different ways of thinking. (#1) speaks beautiful words, impressive words. (#2) speaks very day-to-day words. Now either one could be pushed ahead to see the truth in life. Which one will it be: one or two? Will #1 make the other believe he is nothing? Can #2 be strong enough, going within; he will have the answers, but will he speak up (if he hears) #1 has all the answers?

Be true unto thyselves. The (Beauty given to thee by the Creator of the World). Do not look unto the other, but into thyself.

[Leona asked a question or made a statement...]

The truth does lie within thyself, if thou has the courage (to look within). The reason is the Love that is within thee, the creation of the Most High. If thou seeks deeper and deeper within, thou shall know the answers. May not be the, by shining words. Easily said in a whisper – doesn't take many words to speak the truth and be not (c...?) the guidance. Look beyond.

[Armand explained his answer about the #1 and #2 people...]

Thou art gaining.

[Armand expressed that over the past six weeks since the last meeting he would evaluate himself as being low in "Want," and feels bad about that...]

The answer is within thyself. Go deeply within thyself. What is important to thee (each and every one). Does thou want to be famous or (true)? When thou art having a conversation with another, art thou listening to what the person is (genuinely) saying to thee, or the flowery parts of the conversation? Know thyself. Do not try to know the other person. The truth is within thee, but thou covers it up, listening to another who (appears to have all language, #1). Thou becomes stupid.

[Leona expressed her feelings...]

Thank you for wisdom. See how it stays within thee. Try to understand thou can be – might hear a speaker (who is) really brilliant, but the real knowing id within thyself. If thou knows thyself ... thou will see the real truth and know the (difference) between the speaking. Does thou understand?

Ye are gods! But thou has not understood that. Thou art looking for perfection in others, consequently thou art not looking at thyself. Thou art an (imitation, go within thyself (... if I say this word, I am lying; if I say the truth in thyself TO thyself).

Main thing: honor thyself (not the most beautiful clothes...) know what has been given to thee: life from the Almighty. It can be taken away in the blink of an eye. Life (...each has the beauty within beyond). Look for real beauty (?) be aware of where real beauty does lie.

Look at what the Almighty (has) given to thee – the action and real beauty, yet (... turned aside to hear others who speak beautiful words).

We have affection for thee. As of this moment, we are giving thee the one speck of appreciation and respect for thyself! Is that a commitment? Know thyself for what thou art. Be honest with thyself. Thou has no need to be concerned. Life will be granted unto thee. There is the life beyond which is the beauty. This life is almost an illusion, a dream. But thou can (also) make these dreams come true. Live with respect for thyself, (whether) life is hard or soft.

[We thanked them...]

Most graciously welcome.

MESSAGE...
12-12-04 A Message During a Group Meeting

[Armand suggested that over the past three meetings he has been "pushy" or "bossy," forcing the Group to focus on the mission and these definitions. He said he was fearful that he had overstepped his bounds as a facilitator, hoping that this has been of benefit...

[Armand then invited W to comment on today's meeting so far...

- In answer to that question – thou has been building up in thee – thou art lighting thy furnace. It takes heat in order to rise. If a person would speak very clearly and quietly, without any emotion, is that one to listen to? One would say, where is thy fire? In order to reach that responsibility and that Love of He who has reached the height, the fire must be lit. It must rise. Water does not (stay) tepid; blood is not tepid. It becomes full of fire. Thou can almost feel it pulsating through the body. It takes warmth and heat, fire is the one that burns. The burning, we find a burning energy in thee to express that which is a bright spot within thy heart. Thou has raised the fire in each. We want to see this. We want to see it whether it is – most of it correct – we want to see this, we want to see the energy within thee. To see this energy coming from within, not just saying, I'm speaking because I feel that I have to get it across this way. That is not necessary. **The fire is that burning fire. The Love that grows within each one of thee. Within thyselves to love thyselves truly, for what thou knows thou art born for. Why thou has come into this earth. To feel that and to actually work with it. We do not say to stuff the head with knowledge. Knowledge is not the answer. That which thou pursues, that thou feels and can make another person see and feel, that is the highest form of communication.** Does thou understand that? So we give thee a plus on the fire that is built up. We commend each of thee, to come through with thine own spirit, to get into one complete spirit, and it is only through the process of communicating amongst thyselves that this fire is lit, grows brighter and brighter. What profit is there in one to go by himself and say, 'I am meditating. I am trying to do my best.' Oh, what good art thou doing? Thou art not with the other connection. **Thou art *all* sons and daughters of God! No exceptions. The communication must be between each of thee. It is only through, say a group like this; if something is said completely diverse** of what actual teaching is, it is very nice and very proper, and definitely must be told, 'This is not correct procedure.' But we see the rise in each one of thee. We know thy hearts, and we know that they are on, we call it a rosy level. And to each of thee to feel that, and to actually talk to each one of thee, to see, and see whether thou feels the love connection between thee; to feel thy communication, 'I am part of thee. Thou art part of me.' See it and feel it and within thyselves, and the travel inward begins. 'Oh, the connection of god, the highest god in me!' to feel that is the essence of pure, unadulterated spirituality, and the Love of God that thou pushes and hopes and tries thy level best, and it is only through the work of each other thou gets to that point. And what thou has been putting in thy minds, stays with thee, and it goes out and flourishes it with each person. thou sees another individual and thy inward prayer would be for that person, should have the help that he needs to progress. And thy thoughts should be on that positive vein, never thinking, in other words, the path becomes narrower and narrower, as though thou can only travel one way, and that way is only seeing the good in everything. Saying that, does that help any of thee? So what thou art doing, we commend thee very highly. It is only through this kind of discussion where the real, we'll say the real you of each of thee comes out. And to try to see that real, what is that real you. We have just used the word, 'you,' instead of thee. (?...make things hard for thee...?) But to see that real you, you, you, you, is one thing that will live with thee in eternity. To see thyself in those heights, is to see the most beautiful – beautiful cannot even describe it – but the essence of which thou brings to the Almighty. Thou beings all the colors that are within thee, but they glisten, they sparkle, they become many, many different lights. It is a thing of great beauty, and this is our hope for thee, all of thee. **To feel, begin to feel the unity among each other. To feel that real sense, 'That person is really me.' To see that person as thee, because I assure thee, if thou, if I look at thee, I see thee as me, and therefore, the love becomes oh so vast, and it protrudes, and it spreads itself. This Love spreads that that soul can feel. Does thou understand, the fire which is lit up in a person – that does not mean, 'Oh, I'm full of fire therefore I must be so (?to speak).' No, because the fire is singing in the (?fiber) of the soul. It comes (with that) speech a person who is enlightened that way; speaks without even knowing he is speaking Truth or Love. It comes with the person who he or she is conversing with, feels it. They do not understand it, but they feel, 'I want to be with that person. I don't know why. I do not know why. But (either), 'I feel good!' that is because the communication is there. It takes two. You cannot give our fire to one who is just not going to receive it. You cannot give energy to one who is not – that doesn't mean that you'll know that whether you are accepting that. It doesn't matter, But the one thing you do know intrinsically is that thou somehow or other, perceives a genuine Love in another individual, different from a façade, or a person speaking about love, but thou will definitely feel, feel this love permeate within**

thy system, and this is what our Lord, Jesus Christ, could purvey to everyone. The Love, as long as they could hold it, but some of it had to be withheld, because the person did not understand, or choose to understand. Know that Love is, as St. Paul has said in a great speech, 'It is not jealous. It is not blind.' Blind, yes, to a certain extent. Blind to the faults of a lover. So in that sense we could say it is blind, but it is everything that he has said it is. Thou sees naught but love in the other individual. Thou sees thyself. Does that help thee? The fire has been (? inward), even to myself. Ah, I am using the terms of the mortal. That makes thee understand, that I am part of thee. I am here. My wings do flutter. Oh, once I leave, oh (watch out)! The trumpets blow! Thou does not hear them. This individual has heard perfect music, and there is nothing to equal it. Nothing! There is beauty in this world, but nothing compared to the ethereal music that exists. We are gratified (? to that part). Would that be the end to this discussion? Any other questions?

- We wish to that each one of thee for the love and the care and the kind thought that each one of thee has given to this individual. This goes down in record! This we believe ignites the spark in the individual, and it keeps burning constantly, and what is given to her – there we're using thine own vernacular of her, for this individual – whatever is given to her in love and communication, flourishes, and we can see the blossoms (?) sending. So we speak for the individual, to thank thee, because the individual cannot, cannot speak in those terms to each of thee. It's not spoken in the sense that, in other words would be spoken in a higher realm, but know that we are immeasurably pleased, and we wish this happiness to all of thee for what thou has done. And the individual grows progressively through all this love that nurturing, and brings it up to a higher and higher level. And our thanks to thee, to each and every one of thee.

[Armand: and to thee, in the name of Love

- Most graciously welcome, and may thy Lord on High send thee thy blessings and thanks, and each one of thee will have a little star raised in thy heart. It will beat a little faster for thee. And knowing when that extra little beat comes across, know, 'Ah, that's that dot growing a little brighter.' Passing a little grade, a little grade on you. Know that and respect it, and feel it. The feeling must be from within, not from feeling (slaps hands), you know, touch like that. It is to feel, the heart skips a beat. 'Oh, what was that?' as lovers, thou can all ascertain the, ah, that feeling. Thou knows what I mean. I do not have to go along that area, but that knows that kind of (?), and imagine the Great Almighty, lets thee feel that burning. Imagine what that (is). We leave thee in that hope, and know that it is there, and please say thy special prayer, and know that He does listen. We use it again, 'He.' We must be congratulated for using so many of your own terms, but know that it is received most welcomely, and warmly, and it is returned 1000 fold. And with that we bid thee farewell.